PRO/CON VOLUME 9

CRIMINAL LAW AND THE PENAL SYSTEM

Published 2003 by Grolier,
a division of Scholastic Library Publishing
90 Sherman Turnpike
Danbury, Connecticut 06816

© 2003 The Brown Reference Group plc

Library of Congress Cataloging-in-Publication Data
Pro/con
  p. cm
  Includes bibliographical references and index.
  Contents: v. 7. The Constitution – v. 8. U.S. Foreign Policy – v. 9. Criminal Law and
the Penal System – v.10. Health – v. 11. Family and Society – v. 12. Arts and Culture.
  ISBN 0-7172-5753-3 (set : alk. paper) – ISBN 0-7172-5754-1 (vol. 7 : alk. paper) –
ISBN 0-7172-5755-X (vol. 8 : alk. paper) – ISBN 0-7172-5756-8 (vol. 9 : alk. paper) –
ISBN 0-7172-5757-6 (vol. 10 : alk. paper) – ISBN 0-7172-5758-4 (vol. 11 : alk. paper)
ISBN 0-7172-5759-2 (vol. 12 : alk. paper)
  1. Social problems. I. Scholastic Publishing Ltd Grolier (Firm)

HN17.5 P756 2002
361.1–dc21

                                                                          2001053234

Printed and bound in Singapore

SET ISBN 0-7172-5753-3
VOLUME ISBN 0-7172-5756-8

For The Brown Reference Group plc
Project Editor: Aruna Vasudevan
Editors: Sally McFall, Karen Frazer, Chris Marshall, Phil Robins,
Andrew Campbell, Lesley Henderson
Consultant Editor: Matthew Lippman, Head of Department of Criminal
Justice, University of Illinois at Chicago
Designer: Sarah Williams
Picture Researchers: Clare Newman, Susy Forbes
Set Index: Kay Ollerenshaw

Managing Editor: Tim Cooke
Design Manager: Lynne Ross
Production Manager: Alastair Gourlay

GENERAL PREFACE

"All that is necessary for evil to triumph is for good men to do nothing."
—Edmund Burke, 18th-century English political philosopher

Decisions

Life is full of choices and decisions. Some are more important than others. Some affect only your daily life—the route you take to school, for example, or what you prefer to eat for supper—while others are more abstract and concern questions of right and wrong rather than practicality. That does not mean that your choice of presidential candidate or your views on abortion are necessarily more important than your answers to purely personal questions. But it is likely that those wider questions are more complex and subtle and that you therefore will need to know more information about the subject before you can try to answer them. They are also likely to be questions where you might have to justify your views to other people. In order to do that you need to be able to make informed decisions, be able to analyze every fact at your disposal, and evaluate them in an unbiased manner.

What is *Pro/Con*?

Pro/Con is a collection of debates that presents conflicting views on some of the more complex and general issues facing Americans today. By bringing together extracts from a wide range of sources—mainstream newspapers and magazines, books, famous speeches, legal judgments, religious tracts, government surveys—the set reflects current informed attitudes toward dilemmas that range from the best way to feed the world's growing population to gay rights, from the connection between political freedom and capitalism to the fate of Napster.

The people whose arguments make up the set are for the most part acknowledged experts in their fields, making the vast difference in their points of view even more remarkable. The arguments are presented in the form of debates for and against various propositions, such as "Is Pornography Art?" or "Is U.S. Foreign Policy Too Interventionist?" This question format reflects the way in which ideas often occur in daily life: in the classroom, on TV shows, in business meetings, or even in state or federal politics.

The contents

The subjects of the six volumes of *Pro/Con 2—The Constitution, U.S. Foreign Policy, Criminal Law and the Penal System, Health, Family and Society*, and *Arts and Culture—* are issues on which it is preferable that people's opinions are based on information rather than personal bias.

Special boxes throughout *Pro/Con* comment on the debates as you are reading them, pointing out facts, explaining terms, or analyzing arguments to help you think about what is being said.

Introductions and summaries also provide background information that might help you reach your own conclusions. There are also comments and tips about how to structure an argument that you can apply on an everyday basis to any debate or conversation, learning how to present your point of view as effectively and persuasively as possible.

VOLUME PREFACE
Criminal Law and the Penal System

The Russian novelist Aleksandr Solzhenitsyn (1918–) wrote that "Justice is conscience, not a personal conscience but the conscience of the whole of humanity." Most societies hold that justice motivates them to pass laws declaring what its members may or may not do. If someone breaks a criminal law and is caught, society— represented by the justice system (law courts)—has the right to punish that person. If the offense is serious enough, the job of punishment will pass to the penal system (prisons).

The U.S. system
The United States is a democratic society that guarantees its citizens certain rights and safeguards under its Constitution. The Constitution also separates government into different branches, at the state and federal level, to prevent any one branch from enacting, enforcing, or ruling on unjust laws. The constitutional framers intended to make their new nation as free and fair as possible, but more than two centuries later, many people believe that justice in the United States is not working well.

Critics argue that crime rates and prison populations have been rising steadily for years. While supporters of the system propose that such rises demonstrate successful crime detection and punishment, critics counter that they indicate the futility of current prison methods: If prison is meant to protect the public from criminals and act as a deterrent to others, how is it that more crimes are being committed and more people are going to jail?

Furthermore, many people feel that the exercise of justice in the United States is racist. They argue that laws such as California's "Three Strikes and You're Out" legislation and policing methods such as racial profiling discriminate against people from ethnic minorities, as does the fact that most police forces and juries are predominantly white. Other commentators reject the charge of racism and maintain that ensuring equal ethnic representation on juries—as in the murder trial of O. J. Simpson—can work against justice being served.

Striking a balance
The dilemma facing politicians, judges, and the police is to effectively punish criminals and deter others from criminal acts, while at the same time safeguarding individuals' rights, such as equal treatment under the law. However, equal treatment is anything but straightforward. Should soldiers be prosecuted for murder committed during war, or does this situation warrant special dispensation? Should juvenile offenders be punished as adults, or should the emphasis be more on rehabilitation because of their youth?

A further dilemma for government is allowing individuals the freedom to challenge laws they feel are unjust— such as the law banning the medical use of the drug marijuana—while protecting the welfare of everyone in society. *Criminal Law and the Penal System* explores these and other dilemmas, allowing you to develop a broad understanding about the nature of justice in the 21st century.

HOW TO USE THIS BOOK

Each volume of *Pro/Con* is divided into sections, each of which has an introduction that examines its theme. Within each section are a series of debates that present arguments for and against a proposition, such as whether or not the death penalty should be abolished. An introduction to each debate puts it into its wider context, and a summary and key map (see below) highlight the main points of the debate clearly and concisely. Each debate has marginal boxes that focus on particular points, give tips on how to present an argument, or help question the writer's case. The summary page to the debates contains supplementary material to help you do further research.

Boxes and other materials provide additional background information. There are also special spreads on how to improve your debating and writing skills. At the end of each book is a glossary and an index. The glossary provides explanations of key words in the volume. The index covers all twelve books, so it will help you trace topics throughout this set and the previous one.

marginal boxes
Margin boxes highlight key points of the argument, give extra information, or help you question the author's meaning.

summary boxes
Summary boxes are useful reminders of both sides of the argument.

further information
Further Reading lists for each debate direct you to related books, articles, and websites so you can do your own research.

other articles in the *Pro/Con* series
This box lists related debates throughout the *Pro/Con* series.

background information
Frequent text boxes provide background information on important concepts and key individuals or events.

key map
Key maps provide a graphic representation of the central points of the debate.

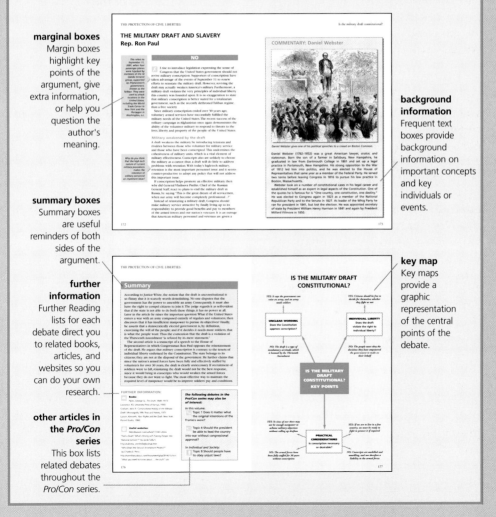

CONTENTS

PART 1
CRIMINAL LAW IN THE UNITED STATES

INTRODUCTION

According to a report published in the July 2001 issue of the *Monthly Review*, the Justice Department budget has increased by 900 percent in the previous 20 years, around 6.5 million people were either in prisons, on parole, or on probation, and around 60 percent of all prisoners had been jailed for nonviolent drug crimes. The National Crime Victimization Survey (NCVS) found that in 2000 people over the age of 12 experienced 25.9 million crimes, 75 percent of which were property related, and the rest crimes featuring violence. It also reported that African Americans were represented disproportionately both as victims and as perpetrators of homicide in the period between 1976 and 1999, and that men, irrespective of race, represented 75 percent of homicide victims and 90 percent of offenders.

Some people believe that apparently increasing crime rates, a growing prison population, and racial imbalance show that the criminal justice system is not working. Others argue that the system is dealing admirably with a rising tide of crime. This section looks at four topics in this area.

Racism

One of the main criticisms of the criminal justice system is the way in which the law is applied to those accused of crime. Among the main focuses of discussion is race and how nonwhites are treated by law-enforcement officials and departments. There are daily news stories that suggest the system is racist. People who come from minority groups in the United States are more likely to be arrested, tried, and convicted of felonies irrespective of their constitutional right to equal treatment. But is this argument valid?

Topic 1 in this section examines how racist the criminal justice system really is. In the first article Barbara Smith looks at several cases of criminal injustice, including the controversial story of Abner Louima, a Haitian immigrant who was arrested by white police officers outside a club in New York. Louima was beaten and tortured by some of the policemen. Smith argues that every individual has a duty to create a more egalitarian and less racist society. Heather Macdonald, on the other hand, considers the Cincinnati riots sparked by the police shooting of Timothy Thomas, the fifteenth black person to be shot by that department since 1995. Macdonald argues that it is a myth that the police are racist and that most of the 15 people shot were wanted for crimes they had committed. She claims that a policeman is "27 times" more likely to die at the hands of a black person than the other way around.

Juries

Many people claim that minority groups are statistically more likely to be arrested for crimes. What happens when they come to trial? Are they treated fairly? Is there equal representation of all races on juries? Does that make a difference anyway? Or do high-profile cases such as the Rodney King and O.J. Simpson trials

Three strikes

Some people argue that the introduction of "Three Strikes and You're Out" laws in a couple of dozen states makes issues of equality and law enforcement even more crucial. This policy allows criminal justice agencies to imprison for life people convicted of three "serious or violent" crimes. Supporters, such as Edward J. Erler and Brian P. Janiskee, in the first article of Topic 4, believe that Three Strikes acts as a deterrent to further crime;

"Justice, though due to the accused, is due to the accuser also.
The concept of fairness must not be strained till it is too
narrowed to be a filament.
We are to keep the balance true."
—SUPREME COURT JUSTICE BENJAMIN N. CARDOZA

---

show that interfering with the racial makeup of juries can work against justice being served?

In the "yes" article of Topic 2 journalist Arianna Huffington reports on a group of residents of Tulia, Texas, who were convicted of drug-related offenses. Huffington notes that most of the people convicted were black; and although most had no prior offenses, they were given extreme sentences by all-white juries.

However, in the "no" argument Sherry F. Colb claims that race-conscious jury selection is a problematic issue. Citing the Fourteenth Amendment, she argues that many court cases support the fact that it is illegal to strike people from juries on the basis of race and that interfering with juries often leads to difficulties.

opponents, however, such as Mike Males and Dan Macallair in the "no" article, argue that this is not the case and that any decline in crime rates stems from other factors.

War crimes

Topic 4 examines whether soldiers should be prosecuted for war crimes. Looking at the My Lai killings in Vietnam, Captain Aubrey Daniel, in an open letter to President Nixon, argues in favor of prosecuting war criminals and says that justice must be served.

George Latimer, on the contrary, argues against the prosecution of war crimes. He states that the My Lai killings were not premeditated and that Lieutenant Calley, the soldier on trial, should not be penalized for following the orders of his commanding officer.

Topic 1
IS THE CRIMINAL JUSTICE SYSTEM RACIST?

YES
FROM "NOTHING PERSONAL"
RADCLIFFE QUARTERLY, FALL/WINTER 1997
BARBARA SMITH

NO
FROM "LESSONS FROM CINCINNATI: A VIVID GUIDE IN HOW NOT TO HANDLE RIOTS"
DAILY NEWS, JULY 22, 2001
HEATHER MACDONALD

INTRODUCTION

Two recurring and contentious themes invariably surface in any discussion about racism in the criminal justice system. They are first the treatment of minority individuals during arrest and in custody, and second the investigative techniques used by the police. Opinion is divided as to whether the data on these subjects presents evidence of discrimination, and arguments on both sides of the debate have far-reaching implications for civil liberties and law-enforcement policy.

In 1999 the human rights organization Amnesty International criticized the United States for its poor record on police brutality. Recent years have seen a number of high-profile acts of aggression by the police against people belonging to ethnic minorities. The 1991 on-camera beating of Rodney King in Los Angeles and the assault on Abner Louima in New York in 1997 were both incidents that led to the hospitalization of the victims and received considerable media attention. The former case led to the setting up of the Christopher Commission, which reported evidence of racism within the Los Angeles Police Department.

Civil rights activists draw attention to the number of fatal police shootings of black men as further evidence of a disproportionate level of police violence toward minority communities. For example, in Cincinnati 14 black men had been killed by the police between 1995 and April 2001, when unarmed black teenager Timothy Thomas was shot dead, making the number 15 and sparking a race riot. Yet was race "the controlling element" in all 15 cases? Many in Cincinnati seemed to believe it was, but in the second of the following articles Heather MacDonald of the Manhattan Institute contends it was not, arguing that the judgment of officers and the level of force used could be seriously called into question in only four of the cases.

Among the police techniques that attract the condemnation of civil liberties activists is the discretionary practice of the "stop and frisk," in which individuals may be stopped and searched. Critics point to statistics that indicate that the stop-and-search rates are disproportionately higher for minorities than for white people. For instance, although black people form only 25 percent of New York City's population, they are subject to 50 percent of the stop and frisks conducted by the New York Police Department.

> "The problem of excessive force is aggravated by racism and bias within the LAPD."
> —REPORT OF THE CHRISTOPHER COMMISSION ON THE LOS ANGELES POLICE DEPARTMENT, 1991

Civil libertarians cite such figures as evidence that the police are carrying out "racial profiling." In other words, they are pulling people over on account of their race and a perception that minorities are more likely to be carrying drugs or weapons, for example. The opposing view holds that there is evidence that minorities are more active in certain areas of crime, such as drugs. Even so, the argument runs, once a vehicle has been pulled over, the decision to search is based not on racial factors but on behavioral clues such as whether the suspect looks nervous or on the presence of inconsistencies in his or her story.

The issue of racial profiling raises complex questions in relation to anti-terrorist investigations. In 1996 Vice President Al Gore chaired a commission on aviation security. One of the strategies under discussion was a profiling system that would take into account, among other details, an airline passenger's national origin and ethnicity. The American Civil Liberties Union argued that such profiles would stereotype people as terrorists on the basis of race, religion, and national origin. The plan was changed so that the system omitted these criteria.

However, since the terrorist attacks on the World Trade Center and the Pentagon on September 11, 2001, some people argue that it is reasonable to focus investigations on Middle Eastern Muslims because the perpetrators of the attacks were Islamists of Middle Eastern origin. After September 11 the numbers of Middle Eastern immigrants to the United States who have been detained rose to 1,000, and Attorney General John Ashcroft revealed plans to interview 5,000 young males who had arrived in the United States from the Middle East. Civil rights activists claim that this approach set an unsettling precedent in a country that prides itself on its principles of freedom and democracy.

The following articles explore the relationship between race and policing. Barbara Smith argues that the criminal justice system is institutionally racist, and that collective action is the only effective way to facilitate changes in policy and the law. Heather MacDonald does not accept the racism accusation in the case of Cincinnati, claiming instead that the city's "racial arsonists" were guilty of whipping up race hatred against the police.

NOTHING PERSONAL
Barbara Smith

YES

On Friday, August 8, 1997, Abner Louima, a Brooklyn resident and Haitian immigrant, went to a Haitian night club after a long week at work to hear one of his favorite bands. Although Louima has a degree in electrical engineering, he works as a licensed security guard. As the club was closing, a fight began among other patrons, and Louima intervened to stop it. When the white police officers arrived, he was arrested.

What then happened to Abner Louima, a person whom I have never met, has affected me quite personally. On the way to the precinct, the police beat him repeatedly. When they arrived at the station, the police made him strip from the waist down in full public view. Then they took him into a bathroom and proceeded to eviscerate him, using the wooden handle of a bathroom plunger rammed up his rectum. Next they forced the filthy handle of the plunger into his mouth, breaking two of his teeth. His bladder and colon were torn up. They put him in a cell. After observing that Abner Louima was hemorrhaging, another prisoner persuaded the police to get him medical help. Several more hours passed before the ambulance left the jail, though, because the officers refused to accompany Abner Louima to the hospital, a required procedure for anyone held in custody.

Strictly speaking, to "eviscerate" means to to take out a person's internal organs.

Handcuffed to his bed

For the first four days that he was in the hospital in critical condition following extensive surgery, Abner Louima was handcuffed to his bed and members of his family, including his wife, were not permitted to see him. Eventually all charges against him were dropped. It is apparent that the police did everything they could to cover up their sadistic and criminal actions. Two months later, Abner Louima is still hospitalized and has undergone surgery several times. [Editor's note: Louima was released from the hospital in mid-October.]

It was difficult for me to sleep during the nights after I heard what had been done to Abner Louima. Every time I awoke, I thought about him and felt the horror once again. Day or night, I was near tears whenever I focused on what he and his family were suffering.

Four police officers were subsequently found guilty of various charges associated with the case, although the convictions against three of them were overturned. One officer is serving 30 years for the assault, and another is facing a retrial. Abner Louima accepted an $8.7 million settlement from New York City and the Policeman's Benevolent Association. For a timeline of the case see pages 86–87.

COMMENTARY: The Rodney King incident

In the early hours of March 3, 1991, Rodney Glen King finally pulled over after leading police officers on a 7.8-mile (12.5-km) high-speed car chase through the San Fernando Valley, northwest of downtown Los Angeles. A female California Highway Patrol (CHP) officer approached King, gun in hand, and requested him to move away from his vehicle. At this point Sergeant Stacey Koon of the Los Angeles Police Department (LAPD) intervened and took over the situation.

The camera rolls

As the drama continued to unfold, George Holliday, a member of the public awoken and drawn to his balcony by the police helicopter and sirens, began shooting with his video camcorder. His film recorded the beating that the police gave King, which amounted to more than 50 strokes with a baton as well as stomps and kicks. Holliday passed his tape to the Los Angeles TV station KTLA, the police reportedly having been uninterested in what he had witnessed.

The spectacle of white police officers beating a black motorist caused outrage when it was broadcast, and the four officers directly involved, including Koon, were indicted on various assault charges. The trial was held in Simi Valley, a conservative suburb of Los Angeles, and the jury contained no black people. The officers' subsequent acquittal sparked riots in Los Angeles that left 54 people dead and 2,383 injured and saw 13,212 arrests. The four officers were then arraigned on federal criminal civil rights charges, and in April 1993 two of them, including Koon, were convicted and sentenced to 30 months in prison. Rodney King received $3.8 million in damages from the city of Los Angeles.

Not what it seemed?

The broadcast video suggested an unprovoked racial attack, yet without trying to justify the savagery of the assault, some people have raised doubts about this verdict. They point to those traveling with King remaining unharmed. They also cite events that occurred before Mr. Holliday switched on his camcorder. Seemingly, Sergeant Koon, on taking control, ordered his men to overwhelm King, who shrugged them off. Suspecting that King was under the influence of drugs (he had probably been drinking), the police then hit him with a 50,000-volt shot from a Taser stun gun. When this failed to quiet him, they tried again. This time King got up and reportedly lunged at one of the arresting officers, and the beating began. The first few seconds of the tape showed possible evidence of this lunge, but for the sake of picture quality the TV station reportedly edited out this section. Could it be that this was not a racist attack, but that the officers tried their best to detain King without hurting him before matters got out of hand?

My despair and fury were quite familiar. As a black American, I have had to live through this kind of nightmare repeatedly since childhood. Although I was too young to know what it meant at the time, I learned the name of fourteen-year-old Emmett Till in 1955 when he was lynched in Mississippi for whistling at a white woman.

Emmett Till was beaten and then shot through the head near Money, Mississippi. Two white men were tried and acquitted of his murder. To find out more, go to www. archipelago.org/ vol6-1/hicks.htm.

What happened to Abner Louima and Emmett Till and all of those black people before and since who have given their lives in order to fulfill whites' sadistic hatred of my people is not exceptional. A few days after the events in Brooklyn, two white men in Virginia burned alive a black man, Garnett Paul Johnson, and then beheaded him. The history and present reality of racist violence affects me quite personally because whenever it occurs I am unequivocally reminded of how thoroughly I am hated here for being born black instead of white.

Run off the road

As long as I am alive in the United States of America, I cannot assume that a similar act of terrorism will not happen to me. I have had my car run off the road in Watertown, Massachusetts, by a white male driver who repeatedly rammed my car from behind and who I am sure would have been delighted if I had crashed into the utility pole a few inches away from where I managed to stop. When I drove to the police station in Cambridge and, still shaking, reported the incident, the white police officers' attitude was one of barely disguised amusement. They told me that there was nothing they could do. Eight years ago in Philadelphia, as I left a memorial service for one of my dearest friends, two white male strangers on the street slammed their bodies full force into mine, simply because I was there and black.

According to the National Vital Statistics Report, Vol. 50, No. 6, dated March 21, 2002, the life expectancy for a white female in 1999 was 79.9 years; for a black female it was 74.7.

Like every black person who lives in this nation's racist cauldron, I know I am lucky still to be alive. I take it personally that from the moment of my birth my life has been consistently viewed as less valuable than a white life. Even if I am fortunate enough to escape an act of direct physical violence, my "natural" life expectancy is years fewer than that of a white woman simply because I am black. I also take it personally that most of the "decent" white people in this country have never lifted a finger to make absolutely sure that what happened to Abner Louima will never happen again and will never happen to me. The fact that more than forty years and thousands of black deaths have occurred between Emmett Till's lynching, Abner Louima's attempted lynching, and Garnett Paul Johnson's actual lynching proves how few whites have ever taken racism not just personally, but as their personal responsibility to eradicate.

But racism is not merely a "personal" problem. Celebrating "diversity" and attending multicultural events will do nothing to insure that racial violence ceases. Racism and white supremacy are institutionalized in every facet of this nation's political, economic, and social life. The only activity that has ever altered the racial status quo is collective political organizing. Legal remedies and policy changes are the result of such organizing, not the cause. So there is something that each individual can do "personally" to create a racially just society, and that is to commit oneself to working with others engaged in antiracist struggle, to commit oneself to movements working for sweeping political and social change. If all those with white skin privilege who benefit from white supremacy would make the decision to end racist oppression, the quality of my "personal" life and that of every other person of color in the United States would be a thousand times better. In other words, if you are white, my life would become much more like yours.

From the late 1950s the civil rights movement under the leadership of Dr. Martin Luther King Jr. campaigned for racial equality. The movement helped bring about the passage of the Civil Rights Act of 1964. For a timeline go to www.infoplease. com/spot/civilrights timeline1.html.

LESSONS FROM CINCINNATI: A VIVID GUIDE IN HOW NOT TO HANDLE RIOTS
Heather MacDonald

NO

In April, when riots erupted in Cincinnati, most of the national media let out a glad cry: Black rage, the hottest of political commodities, was back!

"Riot ideology"—historian Fred Siegel's caustic phrase for the belief that black rioting is a justified answer to white racism—proved itself alive and well in Cincinnati. New York should pay close attention to what has transpired in Cincinnati, however, for the riots and their aftermath offer a peerless example of all that is wrong with the conventional approach to race—especially in police matters.

A fatal police shooting of an unarmed black teenager, Timothy Thomas, triggered the riots, but the violence hardly constituted a spontaneous outcry against injustice. A demagogic campaign against the police, of the kind New York is now quite familiar with, already had heated black residents to the boiling point.

Thomas, wanted on 14 misdemeanor warrants, was shot in an alley in the Over-the-Rhine district of Cincinnati in the early hours of April 7, 2001. For more detail visit cincinnati.com/ unrest.

Rallying cry

"Thirteen black men!"—a tally of the suspects killed by the Cincinnati police since 1995—was the rallying cry of protesters in the City Council chambers there last fall. Thomas' shooting (added to a January shootout death) brought the total to 15, and black politicians and activists—led by the Rev. Damon Lynch, Cincinnati's version of the Rev. Al Sharpton, duly updated their cry to "Fifteen black men."

By, in effect, charging that Cincinnati's cops were indiscriminately mowing down black citizens, Lynch and his fellow racial arsonists stirred up race hatred for the police and set the stage for the riots.

In fact, the list of the 15 police victims shows the depraved nature not of Cincinnati's cops, but of its criminals. Harvey Price, who heads the roster, axed his girlfriend's 15-year-old daughter to death in 1995, then held a SWAT team at bay for four hours with a steak knife, despite being maced and hit with a stun gun. When he lunged at an officer with the knife, the cop shot him. To call such a lowlife a martyr to police brutality is a stretch.

Born in Brooklyn, New York, Alfred (Al) Sharpton Jr. is a Pentecostal minister and civil rights activist. He has run for the U.S. Senate and contested the Democrat nomination for mayor of New York City.

Besides the Thomas shooting, only three of the other 14 cases raise serious questions about officer misjudgment and excessive force. The notion that race was the controlling element in all 15 deaths is absurd, nor is there evidence to support the allegaton that Cincinnati police officers are racist or out of control.

Cincinnati's officers in 1999 had fewer fatal shootings per officer than the San Diego Police Department, constantly lauded as progressive by the liberal press. And a Cincinnati cop is 27 times more likely to die at the hands of a black man than a black man is to die at the hands of the Cincinnati police.

Critics have accused Cincinnati cops of racial profiling, but a *Cincinnati Enquirer* study found no racial pattern in force incidents and that black and white drivers were ticketed proportionately to their representation in the city's population.

This hasn't stopped local leaders from scrambling to pander to black anger in the riot's wake.

Rise of CAN

The city's main response was to form Community Action Now [CAN], a three-man panel—one of whose co-chairs is Lynch—dedicated to "racial reconciliation" through what undoubtedly will be a massive increase in social service spending.

CAN's premise is that Cincinnati systematically discriminates against young black males—an absurd proposition in this well-meaning town whose corporations have long practiced affirmative action.

A tour of the city's poorest neighborhoods gives a better explanation of black unemployment: Young high-school dropouts and truants mill listlessly on nearly every corner, bereft of literacy or basic life skills, often peddling drugs. It is ludicrous to blame their joblessness on corporate racism rather than on their own unemployability, but Lynch and other newly anointed black "leaders" are calling for an international boycott against Cincinnati's "economic apartheid."

New York should take note: Surrendering to the riot ideology in Cincinnati has had its usual effect. Violent crime of all kinds has rocketed upward. Arrests for quality-of-life offenses, disorderly conduct and drug possession—the firewall against more serious crimes—have plummeted since the riots, as the police keep their heads down. None of this is surprising. Not only did the riot ideologists romanticize assaults and looting as a long-overdue blow for justice, but they demonized the police as hard-core racists.

In March 2001 a federal lawsuit was filed accusing the Cincinnati police of 30 years of racial profiling. In April 2002 a settlement of the suit was announced along with changes in Cincinnati's policing. For the background go to http://enquirer.com/editions/2002/04/09/loc_settlement_background.html.

In December 2001 Damon Lynch III, Baptist pastor and leader of Cincinnati Black United Front, was dismissed from CAN after writing a controversial letter. For further detail go to http://enquirer.com/editions/2001/12/04/loc_mayor_boots_rev.html.

"Quality-of-life offenses" can be generally defined as low-level nonviolent crimes such as graffiti, petty theft, and vandalism that eat away at the public's feelings of comfort and security.

Mourners salute as they pray during the funeral service for Timothy Thomas, who was shot by police on April 7, 2001, in Cincinnati, Ohio. His death triggered the subsequent riots.

There is an obvious lesson: The next time an urban riot hits, the best response is to do nothing. Compensate the property owners, then shut up. Scurrying around with anti-racism task forces and aid packages tells young kids that rioting is the way to get the world to notice you, that destruction is power—not staying in school, studying and accomplishing something lawful.

Even better, of course, would be to prevent the next riot before it happens by sending in police in force at the first sign of trouble. Most important, political and business leaders who have not already sold out to the civil rights monopolists should try to break their cartel. They should find black citizens who, unlike the Lynches and Sharptons of the world, are willing to speak about values and personal responsibility and who embody them in their own lives. They should appear with these citizens at public meetings and put them on task forces, if task forces they must have.

If they do it enough, the press will have to pay attention. And when the voice of hardworking black America becomes familiar, the riot ideology may finally lose its death grip on American politics.

In commercial terms a "cartel" is a closed group of producers or suppliers that is able to fix prices at the level it desires. In political terms it is an alliance of groups formed to promote a common cause.

Summary

In her article "Nothing Personal" Barbara Smith describes the effect the 1997 Abner Louima assault had on her as a black American. She cites other cases as evidence that African Americans have a long history of abuse at the hands of the criminal justice system and uses personal examples to assert that racism is as evident today as it was 40 or 50 years ago. She describes two incidents of racial harassment she experienced, one of which she reported to the police, only to find that they would not take action on her behalf. She argues that black Americans are acutely vulnerable, and that the only way to bring about change is for those Americans who perceive the system to be unfair to engage in antiracist struggle and to work toward social change.

Heather MacDonald claims that there are black activists who subscribe to a "riot ideology," the notion that black rioting is a legitimate response to white racism. She argues that in the case of Cincinnati, for instance, black community representatives distorted the evidence regarding fatal police shootings of black men and were responsible for compounding racial tensions. She does not believe that there is evidence to support allegations of police racism in Cincinnati and neither does she accept that antiracism task forces and aid packages are the answers to rioting. She contends that such initiatives send the wrong message by seeming to reward violence. The author argues that Cincinnati's political and business leaders "should find black citizens who … are willing to speak about values and personal responsibility and who embody them in their own lives."

FURTHER INFORMATION:

Books:

Dray, Philip, *At the Hands of Persons Unknown: The Lynching of Black America*. New York: Random House, 2002.

King, Joyce, *Hate Crime: The Story of a Dragging in Jasper, Texas*. New York: Pantheon Books, 2002.

Russell, Katheryn K., *The Color of Crime: Racial Hoaxes, White Fear, Black Protectionism, Police Harassment, and Other Macroaggressions*. New York: New York University Press, 1999.

Useful websites:

www.aclu.org/profiling/index.html
American Civil Liberties Union page on racial profiling.
http://afroamhistory.about.com/mbody.htm
About.com's African American history page.
www.courttv.com/casefiles/rodneyking
Court TV page looking back at the Rodney King case.

The following debates in the Pro/Con series may also be of interest:

In this volume:
Topic 2 Should juries have mandatory representation of people of all races?

Topic 10 Is racial profiling wrong?

In *Individual and Society*:
Topic 2 Is it possible to live in a nonracist society?

Topic 10 Is violent protest ever justified?

IS THE CRIMINAL JUSTICE SYSTEM RACIST?

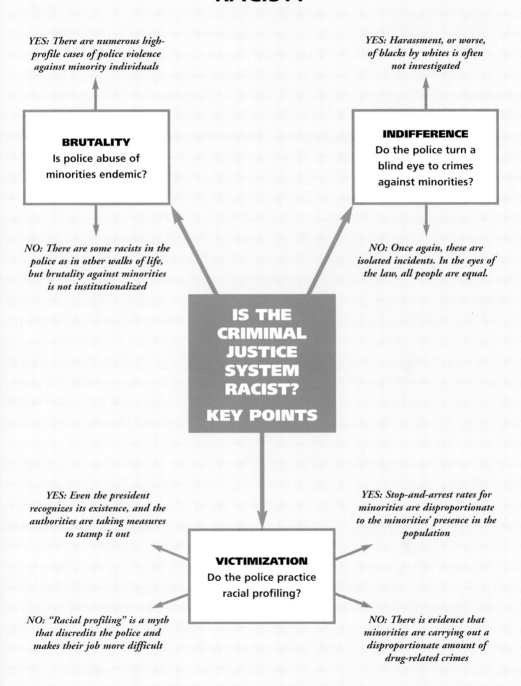

YES: There are numerous high-profile cases of police violence against minority individuals

BRUTALITY
Is police abuse of minorities endemic?

NO: There are some racists in the police as in other walks of life, but brutality against minorities is not institutionalized

YES: Harassment, or worse, of blacks by whites is often not investigated

INDIFFERENCE
Do the police turn a blind eye to crimes against minorities?

NO: Once again, these are isolated incidents. In the eyes of the law, all people are equal.

IS THE CRIMINAL JUSTICE SYSTEM RACIST?
KEY POINTS

YES: Even the president recognizes its existence, and the authorities are taking measures to stamp it out

YES: Stop-and-arrest rates for minorities are disproportionate to the minorities' presence in the population

VICTIMIZATION
Do the police practice racial profiling?

NO: "Racial profiling" is a myth that discredits the police and makes their job more difficult

NO: There is evidence that minorities are carrying out a disproportionate amount of drug-related crimes

Topic 2
SHOULD JURIES HAVE MANDATORY REPRESENTATION OF PEOPLE OF ALL RACES?

YES
"TULIA'S WITCH TRIALS"
SALON.COM, OCTOBER 11, 2000
ARIANNA HUFFINGTON

NO
FROM "THE SECOND CIRCUIT'S RECENT REVERSAL OF TWO GUILTY VERDICTS IN THE YANKEL
ROSENBAUM KILLING, AND THE DIFFICULT ISSUE OF RACE-CONSCIOUS JURY SELECTION"
FINDLAW.COM, JANUARY 16, 2002
SHERRY F. COLB

INTRODUCTION

The 1868 Equal Protection clause of the Fourteenth Amendment forbids the deliberate manipulation of jury composition on the basis of race and religion. The clause effectively bars discrimination during jury selection— a ruling that advocates interpret as a progressive measure, particularly in the light of the United States' long history of selecting all-white, all-male, Christian juries. However, a number of seminal cases have highlighted just how complex an issue jury selection is, prompting legal experts and policy-makers to consider the implications of the ruling for the operations of the judicial system.

In 1996 the Dole-Canady Bill set out to differentiate between "preferential" and "nonpreferential" affirmative action programs. It made a distinction between nonpreferential strategies such as outreach, recruiting, and marketing to attract minorities, and preferential strategies—which it defined as "an advantage of any kind that includes a quota, set-aside, numerical goal, timetable, or other numerical objective." In essence, the bill sought to accentuate race neutrality or a "color-blind" principle in federal law by prohibiting the federal government from granting a preference to any person based—in whole or in part—on race, color, national origin, or sex.

The bill's supporters saw it as an extension of the values expressed in the Equal Protection Clause. But it had its critics. Activists and politicians responded vociferously, arguing that the bill was a step backward and a turnaround from hard-earned civil rights gains. Massachusetts Democrat Barney Frank suggested that it offered "a safe haven for sophisticated bigots," while Nita M. Lowey (D-NY) called it a "unilateral disarmament in the war on racism and discrimination."

For many of the bill's opponents a Texas court case was to provide alarming evidence of the dangers of a legal system that factored out any requirement to set conditions on racial representation. In Tulia in 2000, 40 African American men were arrested and tried for drug offences. Together they represented an astonishing 17 percent of the town's black population, and several of them were first-time offenders. The juries, however, were almost exclusively white.

"Sound judgment will prevail."

—JOSEPH CANNON

Following allegations by undercover officer Tom Coleman, almost all of the accused were charged with selling small amounts of cocaine. Coleman's evidence was not corroborated, but all of the men were found guilty and given severe sentences. Had it not been for former police officer Tom Gardner, who spoke out against the improprieties in the trial, the case would probably have slipped by unnoticed.

The American Council for Civil Liberties subsequently filed a lawsuit charging local council officials with devising a plan to target members of the black community. It suggested that they had deliberately manipulated the legal system in an attempt to remove black people from the area. The lawsuit posed a significant challenge to the government because it suggested not only that the current policy failed to protect or support the civil rights of minorities, but that the judicial system was still open to blatant manipulation.

But in 1991 a Second Circuit ruling, on African Americans Lemrick Nelson Jr. and Charles Price, highlighted some of the problems of trying to ensure a fair and impartial jury. Nelson was accused of stabbing and killing a Jewish man, Yankel Rosenbaum, in a racially motivated attack. He was acquitted in the state court, but the jury's verdict was judged to have been clouded by a racial agenda rather than being an impartial and reasoned response to the evidence.

A retrial followed in federal court presided over by Judge David Trager, who attempt to avoid the pitfalls of the first prosecution by selecting a jury that included a Jewish man and an African American man. However, the Jewish man, known as juror 108, claimed to be unable to make an objective decision in the case. Judge Trager was determined to include him and struck a deal with the defense whereby juror 108 was allowed to sit on the jury after a second African American was included. The final outcome was that the Court of Appeals vacated the convictions and demanded another retrial on the grounds that the jury was neither properly chosen nor impartial.

The two articles that follow explore the ethical implications of minority representation on juries. Arianna Huffington argues that a judicial system that allows corruption of the kind seen in Tulia is flawed, discriminatory, and in need of reform. Sherry F. Colb asserts that to implement a system of minority representation does not constitute anti-discriminatory practice or pave the way for a fair and impartial trial.

TULIA'S WITCH TRIALS
Arianna Huffington

Miller wrote The Crucible *in response to Senator Joseph McCarthy's crusade against communist sympathizers, and the play first ran on Broadway in 1953. Miller based it on the witch trials that took place in Salem, Massachusetts, in 1692—although his was a liberal interpretation of the real events.*

YES

Oct. 11, 2000: As Salem was to witch-hunt hysteria, so is the little town of Tulia, Texas, to our modern version of the witch hunt, the drug war.

In his classic play *The Crucible*, Arthur Miller captured the way a mixture of fear, paranoia and bad laws led to a horrific miscarriage of justice in 17th century America. To explore the 21st century equivalent of this madness, someone—David Mamet? Anna Deavere Smith?—should dramatize what is going on in this rural community of 5,000, best known until now for its livestock auctions.

Was this justice?

In July 1999, following an 18-month undercover sting operation, 43 residents of Tulia were arrested in an early-morning drug raid. Forty of them were black—an astounding 17 percent of the town's entire African-American population of 232. Almost all were charged with selling small of amounts of cocaine—worth less than $200. But as the cases went to trial—most without a single black on the jury—and as the convictions mounted, the sentences looked like something out of the Gulag-era Soviet Union. First-time offenders with no prior convictions—a status which could have made them eligible for probation—were locked away for more than 20 years. One man with a previous drug conviction was given 435 years in prison; another got 99 years.

Do these sentences seem reasonable compared with general trends? In Ohio, for example (see www.clelaw.lib.oh. us/Public/Misc/FAQs/ Sentencing.html), the recommended sentence for murder is 15 years to life.

By the end, Tulia had become a crucible for the drug war. These were clearly not big-time drug dealers. In fact, when they were arrested, no drugs, drug paraphernalia, guns or caches of money were found. Only a few could afford to make bail; none was able to hire a lawyer.

As Miller wrote about Salem: "The human reality of what happens to millions is only for God to grasp; but what happens to individuals is another matter and within the range of mortal understanding."

Uncorroborated evidence

What happened to the 19 men and women convicted of witchcraft in eastern Massachusetts began with the accusations of children. The convictions in northern Texas

COMMENTARY: *12 Angry Men*

First released in 1957, this low-budget feature film was based on a TV play by Reginald Rose. Henry Fonda and Rose coproduced the film, Sidney Lumet directed, and like the Tulia case, it featured one man standing against the prejudices of others in the fight for justice.

It is a hot summer day, and a teenage "slum kid" with a criminal record is accused of killing his father. His alibi is flimsy, he owned a knife similar to one found at the scene, one neighbor claims to have seen him run from the scene, and another claims to have watched him commit the murder. And according to several of the jurors, the boy—who is of ethnic origin—is "one of those people," and "you know how they are."

The 12 jurors—all male, white, and generally of middle-class status—are to remain locked in the deliberating room until they come to a unanimous verdict. If the boy is pronounced guilty, he will be executed.

Initially most of the jurors are convinced of the boy's guilt and are eager to vote for a "guilty" verdict so they can all go home. Only one, an architect called Davis (Fonda), insists it is their duty to go through the evidence and consider any inconsistencies. As the debate continues, votes change and passions build as the 12 men's deep-seated prejudices, ignorance, and perceptual biases threaten to taint their decision-making abilities. The camera, shooting from all angles, captures every expression and nervous twitch, revealing each man's emotional and psychological state. Only in the final moments do they all agree on a not-guilty verdict.

After the media blitz on drugs that followed George W. Bush's victory in the 2000 election the number of people who viewed drugs as the country's biggest problem soared from 3 to 45 percent. And in early 2001 Bush sent the Taliban rulers of Afghanistan a gift of $43 million as a reward for declaring that opium growing was against the will of God.

By January 2002 there had been no successful appeals against any of the Tulia convictions. But in May 2002 the case against one of the final two defendants—facing a life sentence—was dismissed after an investigator found a record of a bank transaction she made in Oklahoma City on the day she allegedly sold drugs to Coleman.

Why does the author use these terms? Is she perhaps suggesting that Gary Gardner might have been expected to be biased, and that if he was not convinced, then things must have been very wrong?

were based on one accuser, Tom Coleman, a white undercover officer who was working as a welder when he landed the job in Tulia. His accusations were uncorroborated —he had no audio tapes or video surveillance of his drug buys and no eyewitnesses to back up his version of events.

Only in an atmosphere of drug-war hysteria could so many rules of evidence be so willfully cast aside and institutions that would normally function as watchdogs become swept up in the frenzy. The morning after the arrests, the *Tulia Sentinel* described the suspects as "known dealers," "drug traffickers" and "scumbags."

Extreme irony

So much for a free press. So much for the presumption of innocence. So much for an untainted jury pool. As happened in Salem, the powers that be defined reality—witches (drug dealers) are rampant among us!—and then identified those who had to be purged to protect all decent people. To dissent from the prevailing view was to join the outcasts.

Anything that did not fit into the preordained outcome, including the many questions about the accuser himself, was simply ignored. In the middle of Coleman's sting operation, the Tulia police received a teletype with a warrant for his arrest from Cochran County, where Coleman had previously worked as a deputy sheriff. He had been charged with theft and leaving thousands of dollars in unpaid debts in his wake when he skipped town. Unlike those he accused in Tulia, he was never jailed and, shockingly, was allowed to continue conducting the Tulia operation. In fact, his word continued to be trusted by the prosecution after he perjured himself by testifying that he had never been charged with anything worse than a traffic violation—even after one of the black men he accused was able to produce an unassailable alibi.

The lone voice of reason

Yet the world would never have heard of Tulia had it not been for another man, Gary Gardner, a rotund, self-described redneck farmer and former cop with a fondness for salty language. He alone refused to stay silent. "I just worked the facts, and the facts show that a lot of these people aren't guilty," said Gardner, who referred to one of the trials as a "lynching."

"There were moments," Miller wrote about Salem, "when an individual conscience was all that could keep the world from falling apart." In the Tulia case, Gardner's conscience led to the story breaking wide open. And in late September, the

ACLU filed a federal lawsuit. The suit—which the NAACP is joining this week—charges local officials with "a deliberate plan, scheme and policy of targeting members of the African-American community" as a way of "removing them from the area using the legal system."

Front-page news

Tulia is on its way to becoming a cause célèbre, with front-page stories appearing in major newspapers this past weekend. A protest rally was held in front of the Texas state Capitol, and the pressure is mounting on Gov. George W. Bush to take a stand.

As Evan Smith, editor of *Texas Monthly*, told me: "There was a collective gasp in the state. Then again, this is a state in which James Byrd was dragged to death behind a pickup truck. Tulia is as much a story about race as how the drug war has gone crazy."

An unfair fight

On Friday, Bush called the drug war "one of the worst public-policy failures of the '90s." This was supposed to be an indictment of the Clinton/Gore administration for not being tough enough. But as Tulia—in the governor's own backyard—chillingly proves, the problem is not that we are fighting the drug war, as he put it, "without urgency, without energy." It's that we are fighting it without logic, common sense, morality, fairness, justice—and compassion.

"People were being torn apart, their loyalty to one another crushed and ... common human decency was going down the drain." That was Miller about Salem and the witch trials. But it could have been about Tulia and the tragic consequences of the drug war.

In Jasper, on July 7, 1998, three white men offered James Byrd a ride home. They then beat him unconscious, chained him to the back of their truck, and dragged him along until bits of his body littered the road. George W. Bush condemned the racial killing but declined an invitation to come to Jasper, fueling speculation that he did not want to weaken his standing with the Christian Coalition and other right-wing groups prior to the Republican presidential nomination in 2000.

Noam Chomsky argues that drug policy has more to do with distracting the population, building support for the attack on civil liberties, and increasing repression in the inner cities. Read his comments at www.deoxy.org/usdrugs.htm.

...THE DIFFICULT ISSUE OF RACE-CONSCIOUS JURY SELECTION
Sherry F. Colb

NO

After black driver Rodney King failed to stop his car in Los Angeles, four white policemen pulled him over and beat him 56 times with their batons, fracturing his skull and damaging his brain and kidneys. A bystander captured the incident on video camera. The trial was in Simi Valley, where an all-white, suburban jury acquitted the four men, sparking six days of violent rioting. A federal grand jury later convicted two of the four men.

For a discussion of the "double jeopardy" ruling against retrial with regard to state, federal, and civil courts go to www.state.co.us/gov_dir/cdps/academylar797.htm.

On January 7, the United States Court of Appeals for the Second Circuit issued a ruling vacating the convictions of Lemrick Nelson, Jr. and Charles Price for violating the civil rights of Yankel Rosenbaum in August of 1991. Nelson was convicted of attacking and stabbing Rosenbaum to death ... after receiving encouragement from Price. The evidence showed that Rosenbaum had been selected as a victim because he was Jewish. (The attack ... followed an incident in which another Jewish man, unrelated to Rosenbaum, accidentally drove his station wagon into two African-American children, one of whom—Gavin Cato— died of his injuries. The evidence showed that in attacking Rosenbaum, Price and Nelson, who were both African-American, were exacting vengeance for Cato's death.)

Like the police officers who beat Rodney King in 1991, Nelson was first prosecuted in state court. The state jury acquitted Nelson of all charges, including second-degree murder. However, as in the Rodney King case, many in the public perceived the acquittal as an instance of racially-motivated jury nullification, rather than a reasoned response to the evidence presented at trial.

Following his acquittal, prosecutors therefore brought federal civil rights charges against Nelson in federal court.... The second trial was meant to afford both sides a fair and impartial consideration of the facts, and to guarantee them a verdict rendered upon the evidence and only upon the evidence. As it happened, however, the judge's racial gerrymandering of the jury ... resulted in verdicts of guilty that were called into question, and then reversed on appeal.

A judge's jurymandering
Judge David Trager, a federal judge in Brooklyn, selected the Nelson jury with the conscious goal of avoiding what he perceived to be the pitfalls of Nelson's first prosecution. Judge Trager stated explicitly that "[t]his trial is occurring ... because the first jury did not represent the community." ... With this objective in mind, Judge Trager went about

empanelling a jury that would ultimately include two people —a Jewish man and an African-American man—who were seated expressly because of their religion and race....

The first of the two jurors selected in this fashion—Juror 108, the Jewish man—told the judge that he was not sure he could render a fair and impartial verdict in the case. He said he had followed the first trial and was disappointed in the outcome. Juror 108 added that although he wanted to believe he could be objective, he had to admit he was not confident he could. These revelations should have disqualified the juror from serving.... When the defense properly challenged Juror 108 for cause, however, ... Judge Trager denied the challenge, stating that "I will not allow this case to go to the jury without 108 as being a member of that jury, and how that will be achieved I don't know."

Invalid "consent" to a biased juror
Judge Trager did later figure out how to include Juror 108, and also how to effectuate more generally his overall plan to empanel a racially and religiously diverse jury. The method he chose, however, was illegal, according to the appeals court.

What Judge Trager did was to convince the defense to "consent" to including Juror 108. How? ... in exchange for the assignment to the panel, of an additional African-American juror." The Appeals Court held that the court's offering the defense an African-American juror to induce them to accept a biased juror, was improper.... As a result of these holdings, the Court of Appeals ... remanded for retrial "before a properly chosen, impartial jury."

Though the Second Circuit clearly disapproved of Judge Trager's conduct, the majority did not address the question of whether the trial court violated the Equal Protection Clause of the Fourteenth Amendment, which forbids government discrimination, by deliberately manipulating the composition of the jury on the basis of race and religion. This question ... is extremely important, however, and could have profound implications for our legal system....

If the Second Circuit and other courts ultimately determine that the Constitution requires race-neutrality (or color-blindness) in jury selection, this would hardly represent a surprising development.

In a series of well-known rulings, the Supreme Court has held that the Fourteenth Amendment prohibits trial lawyers from eliminating jurors from the venire based on their race or gender. The seminal case is *Batson v. Kentucky*, which held that a prosecutor may not use race as a basis for peremptory

Is it really possible to determine someone's race in such a multicultural society? Skin color is no real indication, and even blood tests would not be infallible.

What exactly is a "properly chosen" jury? And how could total impartiality be ensured?

Although the equal protection clause is intended to ensure "equal application" of the law, there is no clear rule for deciding when a classification is unconstitutional. Neither does the 14th Amendment supposedly apply to the federal government. See www.law.cornell. edu/topics/equal_ protection.html.

For more information on the implications of these cases go to www.csamerican.com/SC.asp?r=476+U%2ES%2E+79.

After an employee of the Philadelphia District Attorney's Office lectured young rookies in 1987, a videotape revealed a deliberate policy of jury manipulation. But attempts to counteract such negative biasing also had legal implications for those who tried to redress the balance. See www1.minn.net/~meis/juries.htm.

challenges. Peremptory challenges normally permit each party to strike a set number of jurors without having to articulate any rationale for their dismissal. The holding in Batson circumscribed that potentially boundless discretion to some extent. In another important decision, *Edmonson v. Leesville Concrete Co.*, the Supreme Court extended Batson to include civil litigators' exercise of peremptory challenges. The Court said there that "if race stereotypes are the price for acceptance of a jury panel as fair, the price is too high to meet the standard of the Constitution."

Under these and the cases that followed, the anti-discrimination principle in peremptory challenges came to encompass the conduct of all trial lawyers, including criminal defense attorneys trying to increase the odds of acquittal for their clients. The logic of these cases therefore necessarily extends to the trial judge....

The judge's problem

The nation's history of all-white, male, Christian juries who brought their prejudices to bear on the cases they decided no doubt contributed to the Supreme Court's decisions to bar discrimination in the selection of criminal and civil juries. It is equally clear that Judge Trager—in his own unusual way—was also attempting to respond to this country's history of discrimination in acting as he did.

One could conclude, moreover, that had Judge Trager done so without insisting on seating a blatantly biased juror, his behavior might have been defensible. Seating Juror 108 after he had confessed his bias, though, was an error.... But would the judge have been acting in accord with the Constitution if he had exacted an agreement from the parties to seat both an unbiased Jewish juror and an unbiased African-American juror? Put another way, was the problem with Judge Trager's strategy the consensual swap of jurors, the inclusion of the biased juror, or both?

As many politically and racially charged trials have evidenced, a race-neutral approach to selecting a jury can often result in the sorts of homogeneous, insular juries that the rulings in Batson and Edmonsonwere designed, in part, to prevent. This occurs in part because of housing patterns that reflect a history of deliberate exclusion and segregation.... To ignore race, and simply draw upon the local community, can easily have the effect of producing racially-biased juries like the all-white group in Simi Valley that acquitted Rodney King's assailants. The dilemma faced by Judge Trager is a familiar one from other areas of law. Over the last several decades, businesses, schools, and public institutions have chosen on occasion to take race, ethnicity, gender, and religion into account in order to ensure an otherwise elusive diversity or balance. This raises an interesting question: Should there be some form of affirmative action for jurors, as well?

Jury diversity and the constitution

One underlying premise of affirmative action in other contexts is that were it not for a history of discrimination and segregation … there would most likely be diversity as a matter of course. Because the effects of discrimination are difficult to uproot, color-blindness or "neutrality" can therefore perpetuate an oppressive homogeneity.

The same might be said for juries. Absent a history of residential segregation and most juries would be integrated as a matter of course. But because we do have such a history, choosing a jury "neutrally" often means imposing on the jury a racial disproportion, the effects of which can be unfair to the defendant—or in some cases, to the prosecution. Judge Trager was apparently attempting to address himself … to the phenomenon by which color-blind jury selection risks jury homogeneity. Though the way he implemented his concern was in error, the impulse behind it was not.

After all, in the federal civil rights trial arising from the Yankel Rosenbaum killing, most people would probably agree that having a jury that included both unbiased African American jurors and unbiased Jewish jurors would make sense, given the nature of the case. Such a jury's unanimous verdict would be hard to criticize, likely to be supported by the evidence, and unlikely to cause any social upheaval or be perceived as jury nullification. The question, however, is how we can get such a jury without committing improprieties—including wrongful racial and religious discrimination in jury service—along the way. Judge Trager's solution did not work, but we should keep trying.

In keeping with the important objective of integrating spaces that have persistently tended toward de facto segregation, the Second Circuit and the Supreme Court should perhaps—cautiously—consider modifying the rules of jury selection. As Justice Harry A. Blackmun commented in the 1978 case of *Regents of the Univ. of Calif. v. Bakke*, it may be impossible to diversify successfully in a racially neutral way: "To ask that this be so is to demand the impossible. In order to get beyond racism, we must first take account of race. There is no other way." In criminal trials of racially motivated murder, these words continue to ring true.

For a discussion of the equal protection clause in relation to other areas go to www.constitution center.org/sections/work/educlinks.as.

How logical is this argument? Suggesting that both Jewish and African American jurors were required implies this was necessary to even out some kind of bias. If jury members were truly unbiased, would it matter what their ethnic background was?

Although Colb has argued that racial representation is far from a clear-cut issue, ultimately she is not against the actual principle of mandatory representation.

Summary

By comparing the Tulia trial to the Salem trials, Arianna Huffington suggests that the United States' judicial system is still as open to manipulation as it was in the 17th century. She likens the mood in Tulia to the atmosphere of mass hysteria and paranoia in Salem, which resulted in the execution of innocent people. Simply describing the Tulia trial as an example of the failure of the war against drugs is an inaccurate representation of events, she asserts.

For Huffington the real issue behind Tulia was the failure of the judicial system and society in general to respond swiftly to the prosecution's corrupt practices. She contends that racial issues were at the heart of the episode and sees a need for an urgent discussion about how minority groups are represented within the judicial system.

Sherry F. Colb discusses the Equal Protection Clause in relation to the Lemrick Nelson Jr. trial, which she feels has profound implications for constitutional law. Using Judge Trager's actions in the Nelson trial to highlight her point, she argues that as a representative of the state, a trial judge is subject to the dictates of the Fourteenth Amendment.

However, she also maintains that the race neutrality principle as it is currently expressed does not ensure an unbiased jury and suggests that had the judge gained agreement from both parties to seat an unbiased Jewish juror and an unbiased African American juror, he might have escaped reversal for acting unconstitutionally. So while she perceives race neutrality to be judicious in many respects, she also feels that there might be room for some cautious modifications to the existing law to encourage jury diversity.

FURTHER INFORMATION:

Books:

Baum, Dan, *Smoke and Mirrors: The War on Drugs and the Politics of Failure*. New York: Little Brown & Co, 1997.

Fukurai, Hiroshi, Edgar W. Butler, and Richard Krooth, *Race and the Jury: Racial Disenfranchisement and the Search for Justice*. New York: Plenum Publishing Corporation, 1993.

Kressel, Neil J., and F. Dorit, *Stack and Sway: The New Science of Jury Consulting*. Colorado: Westview Press, 2001.

Russell, Dan, *Drug War*. Camden, NY: Kalyx.com, 2000.

Useful websites:

www.salemweb.com/memorial/default.htm
A chronology of events at the Salem witch trials.
www.refuseandresist.org/ndp/102100tulsa.html
Web campaign supporting the Tulia suspects.

www.november.org/razorwire/july-aug-sept2001/page2.html
For the article "Tulia drug sting remembered."
www.abc.net.au/7.30/s454611.htm
January 2002, ABC News: crusade continues 10 years on.
www.blacknewsweekly.com/bin110.html
The closing chapter in the Rosenbaum story.

The following debates in the Pro/Con series may also be of interest:

In this volume:
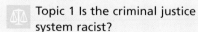
Topic 1 Is the criminal justice system racist?

Topic 10 Is racial profiling wrong?

SHOULD JURIES HAVE MANDATORY REPRESENTATION OF PEOPLE OF ALL RACES?

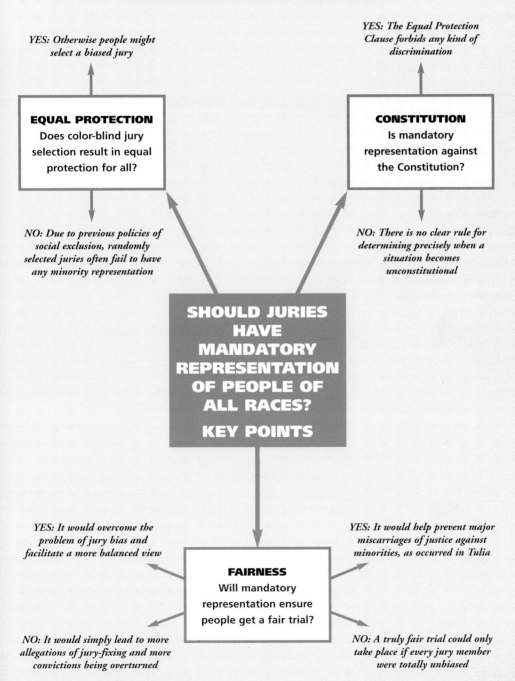

YES: Otherwise people might select a biased jury

YES: The Equal Protection Clause forbids any kind of discrimination

EQUAL PROTECTION
Does color-blind jury selection result in equal protection for all?

CONSTITUTION
Is mandatory representation against the Constitution?

NO: Due to previous policies of social exclusion, randomly selected juries often fail to have any minority representation

NO: There is no clear rule for determining precisely when a situation becomes unconstitutional

SHOULD JURIES HAVE MANDATORY REPRESENTATION OF PEOPLE OF ALL RACES?

KEY POINTS

YES: It would overcome the problem of jury bias and facilitate a more balanced view

YES: It would help prevent major miscarriages of justice against minorities, as occurred in Tulia

FAIRNESS
Will mandatory representation ensure people get a fair trial?

NO: It would simply lead to more allegations of jury-fixing and more convictions being overturned

NO: A truly fair trial could only take place if every jury member were totally unbiased

IMPROVING SPEAKING SKILLS

"Speech is after all only a system of gestures, having the peculiarity that each gesture produces a characteristic sound, so that it can be perceived through the ear as well as through the eye. Listening to a speaker instead of looking at him tends to make us think of speech as essentially a system of sounds; but it is not; essentially it is a system of gestures made with the lungs, larnyx, and the cavities of the mouth."
—R.G. COLLINGWOOD (1889–1943), BRITISH PHILOSOPHER

Speaking is the most common method of communicating ideas and knowledge. We communicate every day in conversations with friends as well as in discussions and presentations in the classroom or the workplace. Effective speech involves structuring your thoughts into a cohesive arrangement. There are some basic grammatical and presentation tips that will help you do this effectively.

SENTENCE STRUCTURE

Grammar is the study of words and their relationship to each other. The following grammatical tips will help you better structure the sentences you use in your speech. Check what you have written, and be aware that the best-communicated ideas are those that come over clearly.

Stress

Make sure you stress important content words to emphasize their meaning, such as names (*Mohammad*), nouns (*table*), and adjectives (*beautiful*). Examples of function words that do not need to be stressed are *a*, *the*, *some*, *can*, and the like.

Main and subordinate clauses

The main clause is the most important part of the sentence. Keep your sentences coherent by not adding too much additional information: *I am going home* (main clause) *because I am tired* (subordinate clause).

Use an active sentence structure

Active sentences are more concise and easier to understand than passive ones. For example, *The dog bit the man* is clearer than *The man was bitten by the dog*.

Avoid using noun forms of verbs

Do not use long words unnecessarily. This may confuse the audience and make it harder for them to understand the meaning of your words. For example, *The justification of the point was made* should be *The point was justified*.

SPEAKING SKILLS

Proper sentence structure will help you deliver a clear message, but it is also important to use your voice effectively. The following points should help you improve your speaking skills.

Diction   Enunciate your words. Use your mouth and your lips to form the words clearly. Do not mumble.

Pace   Nervousness can impair your speech. Avoid rushing through your sentences. Use pauses for effect after giving important or meaningful information.

Pitch   Speaking in a monotone voice will not engage your listeners. Vary the volume and tone of your voice.

Breathing   Take a few deep breaths before you begin. Breathe from the diaphragm rather than your throat. Make sure you give yourself time to breathe properly when you speak.

Projection   The audience must be able to hear you. Aim to project your voice to the back of the room. If using a microphone, check the sound levels before you begin to speak.

Stance   Stand straight with your shoulders back to help you breathe and project well. This will also help you feel more confident.

SPEAKING TIPS

Speaking is a communication process, and a good speaker is one who conveys his or her ideas clearly to the listener.

Remember:

- Organize your thoughts.

- Make notes or use cue cards to help.

- Think about what you want to say before you begin.

- Be confident.

Topic 3
IS THE THREE STRIKES LAW A DETERRENT?

YES

"DON'T BELIEVE THE EXPERTS: THREE STRIKES REDUCES CRIME"
CLAREMONT INSTITUTE
EDWARD J. ERLER AND BRIAN P. JANISKEE

NO

FROM "STRIKING OUT: THE FAILURE OF CALIFORNIA'S 'THREE STRIKES AND YOU'RE OUT' LAW"
JUSTICE POLICY INSTITUTE
MIKE MALES AND DAN MACALLAIR

INTRODUCTION

In 1993, 12-year-old Polly Klaas was taken from a slumber party at her home in Petaluma, California, and brutally murdered. In a state in which there were more than 11 killings each day in 1993, the news of Polly's death might have come as no great shock. Yet this case provoked widespread public outrage, not only because Polly was so young but also because it was revealed that her murderer, Richard Allen Davis, was on parole at the time of her killing. Davis was convicted of Polly's murder in 1996 and sentenced to death.

At the time of Polly's murder a ballot initiative for a so-called Three Strikes and You're Out law to deal with violent reoffenders was already under way in California. This latest tragedy gave the campaign impetus. In March 1994 California Governor Pete Wilson signed into law the new bill, and in November the voters of California ratified the Three Strikes proposition (184), making

California the second state, after Washington in 1993, to have a Three Strikes law. By 2002 about two dozen states and the federal government had enacted some form of Three Strikes legislation.

In essence the 1994 California statute directs judges to impose life sentences for defendants convicted of any felony if they have previously committed two or more "serious" or "violent" offenses. Such crimes range from drugs and firearms offenses to murder. Parole can be considered only after the prisoner has served a minimum of 25 years. In addition, defendants with one "strike" for a relevant offense who are convicted of a second such crime must receive twice the usual sentence prescribed for the second crime.

According to those in favor of Three Strikes, the logic behind the legislation is simple. Most crimes are perpetrated by a small proportion of criminals, so it seems reasonable to assume that by keeping persistent reoffenders off the streets, crime rates will fall. Proponents also believe that Three Strikes acts as a deterrent to reoffenders through the threat of longer sentences.

In 1996 the California Supreme Court amended the Three Strikes law. The amendment gave judges some discretion when passing sentence on reoffenders. Opponents of Three Strikes were quick to praise the decision. In their opinion Three Strikes was rushed through as an example of "soundbite populism."

"No punishment has ever possessed enough power of deterrence to prevent the commission of crimes."
—HANNAH ARENDT (1906–1975), GERMAN-BORN U.S. PHILOSOPHER AND POLITICAL THEORIST

A number of other criticisms have been leveled at California's Three Strikes. In many cases, it is argued, people are convicted on the third strike for an offense that does not warrant such a punitive sentence. For example, a person convicted of assault (strike one), who is then convicted of a drugs offense (strike two), and then gets caught shoplifting to fund his or her addiction (strike three) will automatically receive a life sentence. Why overcrowd prisons with minor offenders when rehabilitation is what is really needed?

Opponents of Three Strikes also believe that the law does not deter the violent reoffender. Most violent crimes

occur in the heat of the moment, often under the influence of alcohol or drugs—and violent criminals do not fear being caught. Indeed, only 10 percent of violent crimes come to trial.

An analysis of crime statistics also provides conflicting viewpoints. As Erler and Janiskee point out in their article, the statistics for homicide are generally considered to be the most reliable source of data because such a serious crime is almost always reported to the police. The homicide rate in California did show a sharp decline in the years immediately following the introduction of Three Strikes. Hence the legislation can be seen as effective.

Opponents of Three Strikes disagree. They argue that California crime rates have been falling since 1991, before the introduction of Three Strikes. In support of their claim they also point out that crime rates dropped in states in which Three Strikes had not been enacted. They suggest that other factors are behind falling crime rates. Many have proposed that the upturn in the U.S. economy may be the main reason for the decline, with fewer people being driven to crime.

In the first of the two articles that follow, Edward J. Erler and Brian P. Janiskee outline their support for Three Strikes. They believe that the sharp decline in homicide rates from 1995 to 1999 reflects the profound impact of this legislation. In response Mike Males and Dan Macallair propose that national crime rates were falling anyway, with or without Three Strikes. They present statistical evidence that suggests that older offenders, who are most affected by Three Strikes, are not deterred by the law. Similarly, counties in which Three Strikes has been most rigorously applied did not experience greater reductions in crime than elsewhere.

DON'T BELIEVE THE EXPERTS: THREE STRIKES REDUCES CRIME
Edward J. Erler and Brian P. Janiskee

This figure appears in the California Attorney General's preliminary report, "Crime 1999 In Selected California Jurisdictions January through December." To view this and other similar publications, go to http://caag.state. ca.us/cjsc/pubs.htm.

YES

✓ The recent California Attorney General's Crime Index report showed that crime declined a whopping 13.2 percent in 1999. This continues a trend that began in the early 1990s. While the news continues to be good for Californians, there is heated debate about the cause of the decline. Liberal academics generally argue that it is the good economy—during bad times, the desperate turn to crime. Other liberals are certain that it is the increased use of community policing. Yet the public seems stubbornly convinced that the cause is the Three Strikes initiative passed in 1994. This law requires judges to give enhanced sentences to second time felons, if their crime is classified as "serious" or "violent," and mandates a sentence of 25 years to life for a third felony.

Punishment not rehabilitation
The liberal antipathy to Three Strikes is simple: it is a "retributive" law; it seeks to punish criminals rather than rehabilitate them. In approving Three Strikes the public showed its intense dissatisfaction with the liberal rehabilitation theories because they had failed miserably in reducing the high rate of recidivism. The public's greatest antipathy, however, was reserved for soft-on-crime judges who refused to hold criminals individually responsible for their actions. Three Strikes gave judges no discretion to dismiss prior felonies or to sentence two and three strike criminals to probation or alternative punishment.

A 1996 California Supreme Court decision, however, overturned the prohibition on judicial discretion to strike prior felonies "in the furtherance of justice." Some anti-Three Strikes commentators praised the decision as the first step in the "restoration of democracy." In their eyes, the Three Strikes initiative was merely the result of widespread "panic" about a crime rate that was already declining, and therefore represented "soundbite" populism at its worst. After all, in the ideological universe of liberal criminologists, no one is individually responsible for his actions. Rather, it is the economy, class exploitation, an abusive childhood, low self-esteem, or an host of other causes that are the true malefactors. Yet the court decision has had remarkably little impact. Since 1994 more than fifty thousand felons have been sentenced to enhanced prison terms because of the Three Strikes law. Since it is well known that a small number of criminals commit a disproportionately large number of crimes, simple logic would conclude that increased incarceration will inevitably lower the crime rates.

With Sam Kamin and Gordon Hawkins, Franklin E. Zimring coauthored Crime and Punishment in California: The Impact of Three Strikes and You're Out, *published in 1999 by the Institute of Governmental Studies Press, University of California.*

Criminologists and legal scholars, however, would never use simple logic when complicated and abstruse statistical manipulation is available. A recent study coauthored by Franklin E. Zimring, a Berkeley law professor and one of the leading critics of Three Strikes, concludes that the legislation has not played a major role in the reduction of crime. The study, which was released amid much fanfare and world-wide publicity, even went so far as to maintain that Three Strikes produced no measurable deterrent effect upon criminals.

Whether or not the law had a deterrent effect is, of course, beside the point since its express purpose was, in the words of the California Penal Code, "to ensure longer prison

COMMENTARY: Three Strikes laws

The first state to pass a Three Strikes and You're Out law was Washington in 1993. Although the bill failed in the state legislature, the voters gave the ballot initiative a 76 percent approval in November of that year, and Three Strikes became law the next month. During the next few years about two dozen more states passed Three Strikes laws, as did the federal government for persons facing trial in a federal court.

Although all of these laws have the general aim of removing violent and serious-crime reoffenders from the streets, their specific methods vary. For example, the laws differ in exactly what they regard as a "strikeable" offense—although violent crimes are high on the list—and in what penalty they call for when a person is "out." Differences also exist over the number of strikes needed before a person is considered out. Some states operate on the straight "three strikes" principle before the top sanction (often a life sentence without parole) is invoked. Others, like California, have a two-tier system, with more serious crimes needing fewer strikes to rule a person out. South Carolina has a "two strikes" system, with a mandatory life sentence without parole following conviction for the second offense. In 2002 certain states were reconsidering their Three Strikes laws in the face of rising prison populations and shrinking budgets, while Florida's was declared unconstitutional by an appeals court and a revised version signed into law.

More than 50,000 felons have received longer prison terms since Three Strikes was passed in 1994, leading to rising prison populations.

sentences and greater punishment for those who commit a felony and have been previously convicted of serious and/or violent crimes." Yet there is overwhelming evidence that Three Strikes has been the principal factor in crime reduction as well as a significant deterrent to crime.

Zimring points out that the California crime rate began to decline in 1991, before the enactment of Three Strikes. Crime continued to decline after the passage of the law, but there is no evidence, Zimring alleges, that the rate of decline was any greater because of Three Strikes. Yet even the most unsophisticated statistical analysis indicates that there was a significantly sharper decline in crime rates in 1995-99 than before Three Strikes. Homicide rates are generally considered to be the most reliable crime statistics because homicides are almost always reported to the police because of the seriousness of the crime. Prior to Three Strikes, the homicide rate in California was increasing at a rate of 1.57 percent. In 1995-99 the average decline in the homicide rate was a dramatic 12 percent. Neither the economy nor community policing are likely to account for this sharp downward rate of decline.

Study ends too soon

One important element of the Zimring study was designed to conceal the impact of Three Strikes. The most important effects of Three Strikes could not have begun to appear before 1997 at the earliest. Had there been no Three Strikes law, felons convicted in 1994 would have received sentences that could not have put them on the streets before 1997. The enhanced sentences mandated by Three Strikes have kept many felons in prison who would have otherwise been paroled in 1997. Thus the statistics from 1997 and beyond are crucial in determining whether Three Strikes has had a significant impact on the reduction of crime rates. Where does the Zimring study end? 1996! Its conclusion: Three Strikes has had no measurable deterrent effect on crime.

Common sense and honest statistics, on the other hand, demonstrate that Three Strikes has had a profound impact. Zimring uses statistics in a dishonest attempt to bolster his ideological antipathy for laws that provide certain punishment for criminals and hold them individually responsible for their crimes. This is precisely what Three Strikes promised to do and it has delivered on its promise— and in the process has provided a powerful and an effective deterrent to crime.

The extract quoted is from Section 667 of the California Penal Code, the statute portion of the Three Strikes law. The other portions are the ballot initiative (Proposition 184) and the sections detailing the offenses covered.

According to the report of the California Attorney General's office entitled Crime and Delinquency in California, 1999, *the rate of reported homicides went down 48.7 percent from 1994 to 1999, and the 1999 homicide rate in California was the lowest since 1967. The corresponding publication for 2000, though, showed a 1.7 percent rise in the homicide rate, the first increase since 1993.*

STRIKING OUT: THE FAILURE OF CALIFORNIA'S "THREE STRIKES AND YOU'RE OUT" LAW
Mike Males and Dan Macallair

NO

Pete Wilson (born 1933) was the 36th governor of California (1991–1999). He has also served as a U.S. senator, as mayor of San Diego, and as a California state assemblyman.

Introduction

In the wake of the widely publicized Polly Klaas murder, California Governor Pete Wilson signed into law on March 7, 1994 one of the most punitive sentencing statutes in recent history. The law was dubbed "Three Strikes and You're Out" because of its provision requiring 25 to life prison terms for defendants convicted of any felony who were already convicted of two "serious" or "violent" felonies. The law was overwhelmingly affirmed by three-fourths of California voters through a statewide initiative in November of that year.

The "Three Strikes" law promised to reduce violent crime by putting repeat violent offenders behind bars for life. The severe nature of the law was intended to maximize the criminal justice system's deterrent and selective incapacitation effect. Under deterrence theory, individuals are dissuaded from criminal activity through the threat of state-imposed penalties. Selective incapacitation suggests that crime can be reduced by incapacitating the small group of repeat offenders who are responsible for a large portion of serious crime.

The Justice Policy Institute (JPI) was formed in 1997 by the Center on Juvenile and Criminal Justice (www.cjcj.org) as "a policy development and research body which promotes effective and sensible approaches to America's justice system."

In the recent California gubernatorial election, both major party candidates credited the "Three Strikes" law for reducing crime in the state. However, national crime trends show that crime was dropping in every region regardless of incarceration practices. A 1997 Justice Policy Institute [JPI] study found that California's declining crime rates were no different than states without a "Three Strikes" law. Such evidence undermines the crime control argument of the law's proponents.

The crime control impact of the "Three Strikes and You're Out" law is an important analytical subject for a variety of reasons. Under the deterrence and selected incapacitation theory, populations and geographical areas most impacted by "Three Strikes" laws should show the greatest crime rate declines. Because of its broad applications and disparate enforcement, California's "Three Strikes" law provides a rare opportunity to analyze these theories.

Methodology

Since California counties enforce the "Three Strikes" law in different ways, it was hypothesized that counties that employed a strict enforcement policy would experience higher levels of crime reduction. It was also hypothesized that age group populations (in this case the over 30 age group) most targeted by "Three Strikes" would show greater decreases in crime patterns relative to age groups less affected by "Three Strikes."

To test these theories JPI examined official county-by-county reported crime and arrest statistics. Arrest rates were disaggregated by age group subpopulations. Official county-by-county statistics for homicide, all violent crime, property crime, and all index offenses were obtained from the California Department of Justice's Criminal Justice Statistics Center. County-by-county "Three Strikes" sentencing statistics were obtained from the California Department of Corrections Data Analysis Unit. For this study, JPI compared data from California's 12 largest counties including, Alameda, Contra Costa, Fresno, Los Angeles, Orange, Riverside, San Bernardino, San Francisco, Sacramento, Santa Clara, San Diego, and Ventura.

Up-to-date county-by-county reported crime and arrest figures are available in the county and city criminal justice profiles at http://caag.state.ca.us/cjsc/pubs.htm.

Who is being sentenced under "Three Strikes?"

National studies show that older adults are accounting for a growing percentage of violent crime arrests and convictions. Between 1980 and 1990 the age specific arrest rate for robbery increased for all age groups between 24 and 44, while it decreased for the age group 23 and under. An analysis of California arrest data reveals a similar aging of the state's serious offender population. Data from California's Criminal Justice Statistics Center shows that the average age of a felon in California has risen from 21 two decades ago to 28 today. In other words, while the state's average age increased about 4 years, the average age of a convicted felon increased seven years.

The average age of the 35,363 offenders sentenced for a second strike was 32.9 while the average age for the 4,368 third-strike offenders was 36.1 at the time of admission to prison (Data Analysis Unit 1998). Two-thirds of those sentenced under "Three Strikes" were ages 30 to 45 at the time of sentencing.... Because older offenders are more likely to have prior offenses, the odds of being sentenced for a third strike increase rapidly up to age 45. Statistics reveal that felony offenders in their 30s and 40s are 8 and 10 times more likely to be sentenced under "Three Strikes" than felons in their early 20s....

43

Under deterrence and selective incapacitation theory, one would expect that the most dramatic declines would occur in the over 30 age group, since this is the population disproportionately targeted by "Three Strikes". In contrast, declines among 20–24 year old age groups would be negligible because smaller proportions of felons from this population are receiving enhanced sentences. However, age group crime patterns reveal a directly opposite effect than what would be predicted by the selective incapacitation and deterrence arguments for "Three Strikes"....

According to the official data, the largest age group crime decreases in the past six years occurred among those under age 20....

Conversely, the over 30 age groups were the only groups to display net increases in both violent crime and total felony arrests during the post "Three Strikes" period. In other words, the age group that is most likely to be sentenced under "Three Strikes" witnessed increases in felony arrests and violent crime. Therefore, the age group that should have been the most affected by "Three Strikes" showed no deterrent or selective incapacitation effect.

The 10–17 age group had a 19.1 percent decrease in felony offenses and a 9.7 percent decrease in violent crime. The decreases for the 18–19 age group were 11.2 percent and 6.2 percent respectively.

Did counties enforcing "Three Strikes" have greater reductions in crime?

According to selective incapacitation and deterrence theory, counties that most heavily enforced the "Three Strikes" law will experience greater crime declines than more lenient counties. For purposes of this evaluation, California's 12 largest counties which account for three-fourths of the state's population and four-fifths of its major crime were examined. Analysis shows that California counties have radically different rates of sentencing under "Three Strikes." The sentencing rate ranged from 0.3 per 1000 violent crime arrests in San Francisco, to 3.6 in both Sacramento and Los Angeles. Data revealed that the highest sentencing counties invoke the law at rates 3 to 12 times higher than the lowest counties....

Data clearly shows that counties that vigorously and strictly enforce the "Three Strikes" law did not experience a decline in any crime category relative to more lenient counties. The absence of any difference in relative crime rates occurred despite the fact that the six largest counties applied the law at a rate 2.2 times greater than the six counties that invoked the law least.... In fact, San Francisco, the county which uses "Three Strikes" most sparingly, witnessed a greater decline in violent crime, homicides, and all index crime than most of the six heaviest enforcing counties.

Crimes covered by the California Crime Index are homicide, forcible rape, robbery, aggravated assault, burglary, and motor vehicle theft.

Conclusion

The results of this analysis present a startling departure from popular assumptions about crime and crime control. Contemporary criminal theory assumes that most serious criminal activity declines as offenders approach the age of 28.... Advocates of "Three Strikes" assumed that the over 30 age groups would be the least likely to be represented in the "Three Strikes" population because of their declining criminal behavior. In this instance, this was the only population to show an increase in crime rates during the time "Three Strikes" was implemented. The population that showed the greatest decline was the under 24 age groups who were least affected by "Three Strikes."

Additionally, the draconian nature of the "Three Strikes" law offers a unique opportunity to test the selective incapacitation effect of massive incarceration. A selective incapacitation effect would be greatest in counties where the "Three Strikes" law was most invoked. However, this was not the case. In fact, San Francisco experienced a 32% decline in homicides, a 28% decline in all violent crimes, and a 24% decline in all index crimes. This compares to Sacramento, which had the highest rate of third strike commitments, yet it experienced a 22% decline in homicides, but only a 6% decline in violent crimes, and a 3% decline in index crimes.

Reported declines in crime rates around the country in recent years have elicited a number of theories and explanations. Crime rates, which climbed rapidly during the late 1980s, particularly violent crime, have been in steady decline since 1991. Criminologists attribute a number of explanations to this decline, such as the stabilizing of the crack trade, a stronger economy, and more incarceration. Virtually no evidence could be found supporting the law's deterrent or selective incapacitation effect on targeted populations, or jurisdictions most affected. This study suggests that researchers examining recent declines in crime rates across the country must broaden their analysis to include non-criminal justice related causes.

Based on these findings, the Justice Policy Institute feels that one of the following recommendations should be considered:

- Repealing the current version of "Three Strikes".
- Amend the "Three Strikes" law requiring the third strike to be a violent crime.
- Further research by the legislature into the crime control impact of "Three Strikes" and its financial impact on California's budget.

In the fall of 2002 the U.S. Supreme Court was due to review the California law after an appeals court overturned a 50-year third-strike sentence against Leandro Andrade for shoplifting. To read more, go to www.streetgangs. com/topics/2002/ 040202supreme. html.

Summary

Following the highly publicized murder of 12-year-old Polly Klaas in 1993, an outraged California public voiced their opinion in 1994 by passing a ballot initiative entitled "Three Strikes and You're Out." Politicians and policymakers were quick to credit the new law with the continuing decline in crime rates in California. But ever since its introduction crime experts have been divided as to whether Three Strikes really does deter reoffenders or reduce crime.

Edward J. Erler and Brian P. Janiskee lend support to Three Strikes in their article "Don't Believe the Experts: Three Strikes Reduces Crime." The authors accept that crime in California has been in decline since 1991 but point out that there was a significantly sharper decline in the years immediately following the introduction of Three Strikes. They cite the steep drop in the homicide rate, generally considered to be the most reliable crime statistic, as evidence of this trend. Erler and Janiskee also dismiss some critics of Three Strikes by suggesting that their analysis of crime rate statistics is misleading.

In the second article Mike Males and Dan Macallair provide statistical evidence to support their claim that Three Strikes is ineffective as a deterrent. According to proponents of Three Strikes, say the authors, older reoffenders should be least affected by the new law, since older people are generally less likely to commit serious crimes. Also, as Males and Macallair point out, older reoffenders are more likely to have prior offenses, which makes them more vulnerable to Three Strikes and more likely to be deterred. Yet study of the post-Three Strikes figures revealed that this population showed increases in felony arrests and violent crime. The authors also note that localities in which Three Strikes was most forcefully implemented did not experience any relative difference in crime rate compared to less frequent users of Three Strikes. In conclusion, Males and Macallair suggest that factors other than Three Strikes are the real reasons behind the fall in crime.

FURTHER INFORMATION:

Books:

Reynolds, Mike, and Bill Jones with Dan Evans, *Three Strikes and You're Out!: A Promise to Kimber.* Fresno, CA: Quill Driver Books, 1996.

Useful websites:

www.co.san-diego.ca.us/cnty/cntydepts/safety/defender/threestrikes.html
San Diego Public Defender's summary of Three Strikes law.
www.facts1.com
Families to Amend California's 3-Strikes (FACTS) site.
www.ncjrs.org/pdffiles/165369.pdf
National Institute of Justice brief on state Three Strikes laws.

The following debates in the Pro/Con series may also be of interest:

In this volume:

Topic 7 Does community policing help reduce crime?

In *Government*:
Topic 10 Should people be able to legislate directly through ballot initiatives?

IS THE THREE STRIKES LAW A DETERRENT?

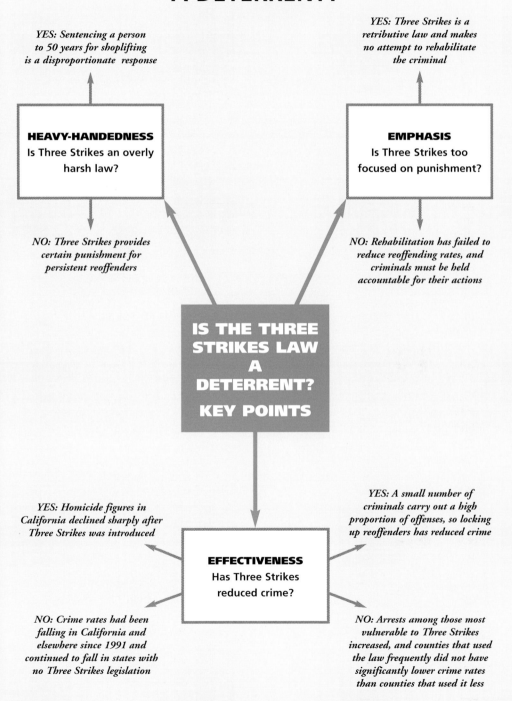

YES: Sentencing a person to 50 years for shoplifting is a disproportionate response

YES: Three Strikes is a retributive law and makes no attempt to rehabilitate the criminal

HEAVY-HANDEDNESS
Is Three Strikes an overly harsh law?

EMPHASIS
Is Three Strikes too focused on punishment?

NO: Three Strikes provides certain punishment for persistent reoffenders

NO: Rehabilitation has failed to reduce reoffending rates, and criminals must be held accountable for their actions

IS THE THREE STRIKES LAW A DETERRENT?
KEY POINTS

YES: Homicide figures in California declined sharply after Three Strikes was introduced

YES: A small number of criminals carry out a high proportion of offenses, so locking up reoffenders has reduced crime

EFFECTIVENESS
Has Three Strikes reduced crime?

NO: Crime rates had been falling in California and elsewhere since 1991 and continued to fall in states with no Three Strikes legislation

NO: Arrests among those most vulnerable to Three Strikes increased, and counties that used the law frequently did not have significantly lower crime rates than counties that used it less

Topic 4
SHOULD SOLDIERS BE PROSECUTED FOR CRIMES COMMITTED DURING WAR?

YES
"LETTER WRITTEN BY CAPTAIN AUBREY M. DANIEL TO PRESIDENT NIXON"
APRIL 8, 1970
HTTP://WWW.LAW.UMKC.EDU/FACULTY/PROJECTS/FTRIALS/MYLAI/DANIELS_LTR.HTML
CAPTAIN AUBREY M. DANIEL

NO
FROM "SUMMATION OF GEORGE LATIMER FOR THE DEFENSE:
THE COURT-MARTIAL OF LIEUTENANT WILLIAM CALLEY"
HTTP://WWW.LAW.UMKC.EDU/FACULTY/PROJECTS/FTRIALS/MYLAI/DEFENSE.HTML
GEORGE LATIMER

INTRODUCTION

"War," Michael Walzer has written, "is a world of duress." For soldiers in the field of battle war entails serious risks, hard choices, and often moral ambiguities. Indeed, war tests the capacity of soldiers to maintain even the most rudimentary moral distinctions, such as that between killing and murder. In the words of theologian Ernest Fortin: "Killing is not the same thing as murder and one does not normally look upon a soldier who kills in the legitimate exercise of his duties as a murderer."

Too frequently, the distinction between killing and murder is lost in the heat of battle, often with tragic consequences for all concerned, leading people to ask if there is such a thing as a war crime? Who should decide what is a crime and what is a justifiable action? Should soldiers really be prosecuted for actions committed during times of war?

This is currently the subject of heated debate, not least because of the number of ethnically based conflicts going on around the world and the increasing number of reports of human rights abuses committed by military forces during them. Certainly more and more people are being called on to account for their actions during war.

In the last ten years many men and women have been called before international tribunals, such as the International Criminal Tribunal for Former Yugoslavia in the Hague, South Africa's Truth and Reconciliation Committee, and an international tribunal into the planned genocide in Rwanda.

However, some people believe that there is no such thing as a war crime. If a soldier is serving his or her country for the good of the people, he or she should not be prosecuted for actions carried out during that service. Critics argue that serving one's country does not stop a soldier from behaving honorably; in fact to the contrary, soldiers have more of a duty to act in a morally responsible way. Thus crimes such as rapes, murders, and lootings must always be punished.

"To my mind to kill in war is not a whit better than to commit ordinary murder."

—ALBERT EINSTEIN (1879–1955)

But what happens if the soldier argues that he or she was simply following an order? Should they have refused to carry out orders that they felt morally or ethically suspect? Or should members of a military force always obey every order they are given, no matter how much they disagree with it? Supporters of the last argument feel that soldiers should trust the judgment of the people who are leading them however difficult that may be. Critics claim that human beings are fallible, and outside factors, such as seeing friends or colleagues killed by the "enemy," can adversely influence the decisions made, even by trained leaders. In those cases soldiers should be able to disobey orders without fear of reprisal.

The rights of citizens who may have been mistreated during war, as well as the rights of soldiers, must also be considered, though. While many people believe that the "end justifies the means" and that a certain number of civilians inevitably are injured or killed

during conflicts, others argue that there should be some form of redress for victims. That is part of the reason why international tribunals exist—to make sure that both the victim and the alleged perpetrator of the war crime are treated fairly and are tried according to international law. Some countries object, though, to having their "dirty laundry" aired in public; they believe that if crimes have been committed, the accused should be tried in their own country according to their own laws.

The following two articles look at the trial of a U.S. officer following an incident that occurred during the Vietnam War. On March 16, 1968, Lieutenant Calley and members of C company entered the village of My Lai. According to some of the unit, Calley ordered his men to enter the village firing, even though there had been no report of enemy fire. The unit had allegedly been told that by the time they attacked, only the "enemy" would be present. At the end of the operation around 500 unarmed civilians—mostly old men, women, and children—had been killed. According to eyewitness reports after the event, Calley was alleged to have killed more than 100 villagers by machine gun fire.

At his trial Calley testified that he had been ordered by his superior officer, Captain Ernest Medina, to kill everyone in My Lai. He maintained he had been told that even the children were communist sympathizers. However, there was enough photographic evidence to convict Calley alone of murder. He was found guilty and was sentenced to life in prison. But in the face of the public disapproval that was aroused by the verdict, President Richard Nixon ordered Calley's release.

LETTER WRITTEN BY CAPTAIN AUBREY M. DANIEL TO PRESIDENT NIXON
Captain Aubrey M. Daniel

YES

Sir:

…On November 26, 1969, you issued the following statement through your press secretary, Mr. Ronald Ziegler, in referring to the My Lai incident:

> *An incident such as that alleged in this case is in direct violation not only of United States military policy, but is also abhorrent to the conscience of all the American people. The Secretary of the Army is continuing his investigation. Appropriate action is and will be taken to assure that illegal and immoral conduct as alleged be dealt with in accordance with the strict rules of military justice. This incident should not be allowed to reflect on the some million and a quarter young Americans who have now returned to the United States after having served in Vietnam with great courage and distinction.*

The statement was written in 1969, before the public made its feelings known. President Nixon appears to support the moral view that it is unlawful for an American soldier to execute unarmed people. Why did he change his mind?

At the time you issued this statement, a general court-martial had been directed for a resolution of the charges which have been brought against Lieutenant William L. Calley, Jr., for his involvement at My Lai.

On December 8, 1969, you were personally asked to comment on the My Lai incident at a press conference. At that time, you made the following statement:

"What appears was certainly a massacre, and under no circumstances was it justified…. We cannot ever condone or use atrocities against civilians to accomplish that goal."

These expressions of what I believed to be your sentiment were truly reflective of my own feelings when I was given the assignment of prosecuting the charges which had been preferred against Lieutenant Calley….

I undertook the prosecution of the case without any ulterior motives for personal gain, either financial or political. My only desire was to fulfill my duty as a prosecutor and see that justice was done in accordance with the laws of this nation….

William Lawes. Calley Jr. (1943–) was born in Florida. He was posted to South Vietnam, after being commissioned as a lieutenant by the Officers Training School. He led C company into My Lai in 1968 and was consequently convicted of murdering 22 civilians during the operation. Although Nixon ordered Calley's release, some people believe that Calley was a scapegoat.

Throughout the proceedings there was criticism of the prosecution but I lived with the abiding conviction that once the facts and the law had been presented there would be no doubt in the mind of any reasonable person about the necessity for the prosecution of this case and the ultimate verdict. I was mistaken....

Throughout the trial, the entire system was under the constant scrutiny of the mass media and the public, and the trial of Lieutenant Calley was also in a very real sense the trial of the military judicial system. However, there was never an attack lodged by any member of the media concerning the fairness of the trial. There could be no such allegation justifiably made.

I do not believe that there has ever been a trial in which the accused's rights were more fully protected, the conduct of the defense given greater latitude, the prosecution held to stricter standards.... The jury selection, in which customary procedure was altered by providing both the defense and the prosecution with three peremptory challenges instead of the usual one, was carefully conducted to insure the impartiality of those men who were selected. Six officers, all combat veterans, five having served in Vietnam, were selected. These six men who had served their country well, were called upon again to serve their nation as jurors and to sit in judgment of Lieutenant Calley as prescribed by law.

From the time they took their oaths until they rendered their decision, they performed their duties in the very finest tradition of the American legal system. If ever a jury followed the letter of the law in applying it to the evidence presented, they did. They are indeed a credit to our system of justice and to the officer corps of the United States Army.

Negative reaction

When the verdict was rendered, I was totally shocked and dismayed at the reaction of many people across the nation. Much of the adverse public reaction I can attribute to people who have acted emotionally and without being aware of the evidence that was presented and perhaps even the laws of this nation regulating the conduct of war.

These people have undoubtedly viewed Lieutenant Calley's conviction simply as the conviction of an American officer for killing the enemy. Others, no doubt out of a sense of frustration, have seized upon the conviction as a means of protesting the war in Vietnam. I would prefer to believe that most of the public criticism has come from people who are not aware of the evidence as it was presented, or having

Part of the criticism of the prosecution was that although 100 soldiers took part in the massacre, only one man was tried for the crime because there was only enough reliable evidence to convict Calley. Do you think this was fair?

A telephone survey carried out at the time showed that in April 1971, 71 percent of adults in the United States disapproved of the military court's decision to give Calley a life sentence. Go to www.law.umkc.edu/faculty/projects/ftrials/mylai/Survey Results.html to see the full survey results.

COMMENTARY: My Lai

In December 1967 Charlie ("C") company arrived in Vietnam and was sent into Quang Ngai Province the following month. The province, which lay in South Vietnam, had already been targeted as a Viet Cong (VC) stronghold. By the time C company arrived, many villages in the province had been destroyed, and around 140,000 civilians were homeless.

One of the company's officers was 24-year-old Lieutenant William L. Calley, a man of mixed popularity. On March 15, 1968, the commander, Captain Medina, briefed C company that members of the VC's 48th Battalion were in the region near a small hamlet called My Lai. He allegedly told the men that the next morning they would attack the battalion and destroy My Lai. Eyewitnesses claimed they were told that by the time they attacked, all the civilians would have left the hamlet, leaving only the VC behind. The platoon reached the village at around 8 a.m., led by Calley. They found old people, women, children, and babies, who allegedly shouted, "No VC! No VC!" at them repeatedly. However, according to soldier Paul Meadlo, Calley reportedly said, "I want them dead. Waste them." By 9 a.m., when an army helicopter piloted by Hugh Thompson arrived, several hundred villagers lay dead or dying, and Thompson saw people being shot. He reported the incident to the brigade headquarters. However, it was not until 22-year-old Ronald Ridenhour began his own investigation of the events of March 16 and sent a letter to President Nixon, the Pentagon, and various other places, that a full investigation was launched.

Can it ever be justifiable for a nation that follows the "rule of law" to commit unlawful acts?

followed it they have chosen not to believe it. Certainly, no one wanted to believe what occurred at My Lai, including the officers who sat in judgment of Lieutenant Calley. To believe, however, that any large percentage of the population could believe the evidence which was presented and approve of the conduct of Lieutenant Calley would be as shocking to my conscience as the conduct itself, since I believe that we are still a civilized nation.

If such be the case, then the war in Vietnam has brutalized us more than I care to believe, and it must cease. How shocking it is if so many people across the nation have failed to see the moral issue which was involved in the trial of Lieutenant Calley—that it is unlawful for an American soldier to summarily execute unarmed and unresisting men, women, children, and babies....

In view of your previous statements concerning this matter, I have been particularly shocked and dismayed at your decision to intervene in these proceedings in the midst of the public clamor. Your decision can only have been prompted by the response of a vocal segment of our population who, while no doubt acting in good faith, cannot be aware of the evidence which resulted in Lieutenant Calley's conviction. Your intervention has, in my opinion, damaged the military judicial system and lessened any respect it may have gained as a result of the proceedings.

You have subjected a judicial system of this country to the criticism that it is subject to political influence, when it is a fundamental precept of our judicial system that the legal processes of this country must be kept free from any outside influences. What will be the impact of your decision upon the future trials, particularly those within the military?

Not only has respect for the legal process been weakened and the critics of the military judicial system been supported for their claims of command influence, the image of Lieutenant Calley, a man convicted of the premeditated murder of at least 22 unarmed and unresisting people, as a national hero has been enhanced, while at the same time support has been given to those people who have so unjustly criticized the six loyal and honorable officers who have done this country a great service by fulfilling their duties as jurors so admirably....

Great expectations

I would expect that the President of the United States, a man whom I believed should and would provide the moral leadership for this nation, would stand fully behind the law of this land on a moral issue which is so clear and about which there can be no compromise. For this nation to condone the acts of Lieutenant Calley is to make us no better than our enemies and make any pleas by this nation for the humane treatment of our own prisoners meaningless.

I truly regret having to have written this letter and wish that no innocent person had died at My Lai on March 16, 1968. But innocent people were killed under circumstances that will always remain abhorrent to my conscience.

While in some respects what took place at My Lai has to be considered a tragic day in the history of our nation, how much more tragic would it have been for this country to have taken no action against those who were responsible. That action was taken, but the greatest tragedy of all will be if political expediency dictates the compromise of such a fundamental moral principle as the inherent unlawfulness of the murder of innocent persons, making the action and the courage of six honorable men who served their country so well meaningless.

Daniel implies that the president's action was influenced by public opinion. At the time Nixon wanted the public's support for the Vietnam war. Do you think his actions were justified?

Daniel argues that Nixon's decision reflects badly on the six jurors, who had all served in Vietnam. How might the jurors' experiences make a difference?

In March 2002 prisoners taken during military action in Afghanistan were transported to Guantanamo Bay, Cuba. Do you think that action reflects United States' "humane treatment" of prisoners?

SUMMATION OF GEORGE LATIMER FOR THE DEFENSE: THE COURT-MARTIAL OF LIEUTENANT WILLIAM CALLEY
George Latimer

NO

If the prosecution in this case was necessary to prevent the image of the army from being tarnished, then in my humble judgment, conviction of one lieutenant for the ills and vices occurring in My Lai will sear the image beyond recognition. In excess of one hundred soldiers participated in this assault, and the pages of this record bear testimony of the fact that this was not a one-man carnage. Present indications are that eventually this tragedy, as such, will narrow to be a death race between Captain Medina and Lieutenant Calley, and I am here trying to stop that from happening to my client.… I am proud of the United States Army, and it grieves me to see it being pulled apart from within. Whether you consider it as such or not, I do not know, but this case is a vehicle which is hurrying along its destruction.… Someone called the wrong signals and something went wrong. Then, the second tragedy occurred. The incident was hushed up by the company commander who ordered it, and those superior to him, and the real truth was forever buried. It cannot be resurrected for memories have dulled. Self-interest has multiplied manyfold and the truth is too easy to avoid. Approximately one year later, the third tragedy occurred, and that involved this prosecution. By this time, many of the members of the company were discharged and insulated from prosecution. They, with the help of army investigators who led the way, pointed the finger of blame toward other members who remained loyal to the service, and were trying to make the army a career, some including the accused, who sought to extend his tour of duty in Vietnam.…

All of these people, or most of them, seek to avoid the charge of accomplices, that they were murderers at My Lai; because, let me suggest this to you, good gentlemen, that if Captain Medina shot any of these people or ordered them shot, he is a murderer. If Lieutenant Calley follows in his footsteps, then what about Meadlo? Where is he? He admits

Is this a facile argument? Can the lives of several hundred people be written off so easily?

Paul Meadlo was a soldier under the command of Calley. Although Meadlo took part in the massacre, he voiced remorse for what he did. Do you think that this excuses his participation in the My Lai incident?

having murdered a number of people, and use the word "murder" advisedly, because he was ordered to do it. Does the buck passing stop at Lieutenant Calley or does it go down? In my judgment, every one man who participated if there was an offense committed here, as the government alleges and seeks to prove, there are many that should suffer the same as should those who were convicted....

Should there be any difference in the treatment of Calley and Meadlo?

Unseen enemy

Let's look at the experiences of C Company. These are the experiences just before they go in: a number of reconnaissance and sweep and destroy missions, without ever seeing an enemy; losses of buddies by mines and snipers; never any security from death for it always came from unseen and unknown sources. Darkness, an inability to see, breathes fear. Now, in addition to that, the deaths that were being occasioned to the members of the platoon added to the fear because you never knew when your number was up, and you never knew when the next step might cost you a leg or your life. Always destroyed by a visionary fold, no one you could really see and take a bead on and end his chance to save your life and the life of your buddies. Women and children operating with your enemy, being used to help destroy your unit. That enemy was lethal, but it could not be seen. This is the type of warfare that fends hatred against any enemy and anyone who can aid the enemy, and when the fight starts, it is too late to reason why. It just seems to do or die and everything must go....

Go to http://www.law. umkc.edu/faculty/ projects/ftrials/mylai /mylai.htm, and look at the evidence on My Lai. Do you think that the intelligence information was so wrong?

Everybody concurs on the fact that the intelligence information was fantastically wrong. Everybody had a major force in there, and from whence that information came I cannot imagine because they were making some aerial reconnaissance near that area and surely they expected to meet the enemy, to take extra ammunition. They were told to go in aggressively and so I bring myself down to the events with Captain Medina standing in the pit with his shovel, when he starts telling his men what to do tomorrow. "The briefing that I conducted for my company was that C Company had been selected to conduct a combat assault operation into the village of My Lai beginning with LZ time 0730 hours on the morning of 16 March 1968. I told them the VC Battalion was approximately numbered, approximately 250 to 280 men, and that we would be outnumbered approximately two to one and that we could expect a helluva good fight, and we would probably be heavily engaged." The intelligence reports also indicated that innocent civilians or noncombatants would be gone to the market at 0700 hours in the morning, that this was one of the reasons why the artillery preparation was being placed on the village at 0720....

A young man, Sergeant Schiel, testified as follows: "Medina stressed we were to kill everything.... Captain Medina said, 'Everything was to be killed, men, women, and children, cats, dogs, everything that breathed.'"

> By referring to men, women, children, and animals in the same breath, the testimony implies that Medina considered the villagers as little more than animals.

Lamartina stated. "Medina said, 'Go into the village and kill everything that breathed.' On March 11, I obeyed that order as I killed everything that moved. I observed others obeying the order. We sprayed the village...."

Meadlo: "We are going to have contact with a heavily armed regiment. He said, 'Everything there is considered VC or VCS and that everybody should be destroyed.'"

Men, women, and children

Now, when you put those items all in their proper perspective, it just seems to me that despite Captain Medina's denial that he used that language, that certainly it is fair to say that every member of his group that testified, that came here to testify, either said that he said "men, women, or children"; that he was asked whether his phrase included men, women, and children, that he used words from which they inferred that that was what they were supposed to do; and lastly, those that did not testify, testified in the negative that they did not remember whether Captain Medina made the comment about that or not. Now, so you have the positive evidence on one side, the negative evidence on the other, but most of all you have the activity in connection with this extemporaneous construction by the people who heard it. They went in. They went in firing. Insofar as the evidence shows, in every sector of that village civilians were killed....

> Do you think that soldiers should have a different code of conduct from civilians? Could these soldiers just be protecting their senior officer?

Orders

Captain Medina was a man, a disciplinarian. He wanted orders obeyed. He said that and he didn't brook any denial or disobedience of orders. It may well be that the niceties of the military require that if I have a question about an order, I go to my company commander and say, "Captain, I think this is an illegal order, and I don't think I should obey it," but the other philosophy is that they were saying here, "Obey it first and then go back and find out what about the legality of it," because if you take the former in this situation, your troops might be dead; and if you don't follow out a combat order, then you sacrifice your troops. What a horrid choice to place

> Should soldiers be able to question orders from their superiors that they believe are morally unsound?

upon anybody. The court is also going to instruct on the legality and illegality of orders. You will have it in written form so there is no point in my doing anything more or less than this; that he will define an illegal order and what is an illegal order and he may tell you, in this case, that the killing of civilians—in certain situations, a given order to kill those might be an illegal order, but he also will tell you that that does not end the subject.…

It may be the difference between winning and losing and so, as you look back on the situation … I think when you put untrained troops out in areas and they are told to do certain things, they have a right to rely on the judgment and the expertise, then you are bound to give credence in effect to orders from their company commander; and so when you take that background, the laws of war were tailored in certain respects to meet this very situation, then you will understand that the Congress of the United States and other bodies feel that leeway and latitude should be given to people who were far from home and trying to save the United States of America.

Do you think "leeway and latitude" justifies the murder of innocent civilians during war?

Unique case

I do not believe that history records another incident when the United States of America ever had a similar situation, nor do I believe that we have taken collectively a group of people who were engaged in a combat mission and what they believed to be a combat mission and put them up before a court for trial. So, you gentlemen are in a situation where you must chart a course for what should be done.

The incident was originally covered up. Do you think that the government would cover up another similar incident if it happened today? Would it even be able to?

All the time, apparently, the finger pointing to Captain Medina, who himself stated that he would probably get twenty years and all of a sudden, times change. Who becomes the pigeon—Lieutenant Calley, the lowest officer. Now, I ask you good gentlemen to give, as I know you will, honest consideration (of) this kid that sits behind me and know there is a difference.

There ought to be a difference, and you ought to make the difference between errors in judgment and criminality and so I ask your serious consideration and ask that you let this boy go free. Thank you very much.

Summary

Should soldiers be prosecuted for crimes committed during war? The incident at My Lai during the Vietnam War is a good case study when considering this difficult question. Aubrey Daniel, arguing for the prosecution of the soldier held responsible for the events of My Lai, insists that Lieutenant Calley violated "the laws of this nation regulating the conduct of war" by "the premeditated murder of at least 22 unarmed and unresisting people." As a matter of justice, then, his prosecution must be carried out free from the influence of politics. In Daniel's view expediency as well as justice demand Calley's prosecution. "For this nation to condone the acts of Lieutenant Calley," he argues, "is to make us no better than our enemies and make any pleas by this nation for the humane treatment of our own prisoners meaningless."

George Latimer, in his summation for the defense of Calley, strongly denies that justice demands Calley's prosecution. Latimer does not deny that innocent civilians were killed by American soldiers, but he rejects the notion that it was premeditated murder. According to Latimer, the battlefield conditions at My Lai made it extremely difficult for the soldiers to distinguish innocent civilians from hostile combatants. Calley should not be blamed because he was simply carrying out his commander's orders. Latimer concludes that Calley was relying on what we now know was the flawed judgment and expertise of Captain Medina, but did not know this at the time. Even if he had known, it is dangerous for soldiers caught in the grip of war to disobey orders. Daniel argues that it is never right to kill innocent civilians, while Latimer suggests that the unique circumstances of war should give one pause before prosecuting such "crimes" in a court of law.

FURTHER INFORMATION:

 Books:

Angers, Trent, *The Forgotten Hero of My Lai: The Hugh Thompson Story*. Lafayette, LA: Acadian House, 1999.

Carr, Caleb, *The Lessons of Terror: A History of Warfare Against Civilians*. New York: Random House, 2002.

Articles:

Gorin, Julia, "The Dark Side of the U.N. War Crimes Court," *Insight on the News*, August 31, 1998.

Useful websites:

http://www.facts.com/icof/critic.htm
Site that provides facts on the Geneva Conventions and war trials.
http://www.law.umkc.edu/faculty/projects/ftrials/
mylai/mylai.htm
"Famous War Trials: The My Lai Court Martial."

The following debates in the Pro/Con series may also be of interest:

In this volume:

 Part 1: Criminal law in the United States, pages 8–9.

Topic 5 Do wartime laws violate civil liberties?

Topic 14 Do prisoners have rights?

SHOULD SOLDIERS BE PROSECUTED FOR CRIMES COMMITTED DURING WAR?

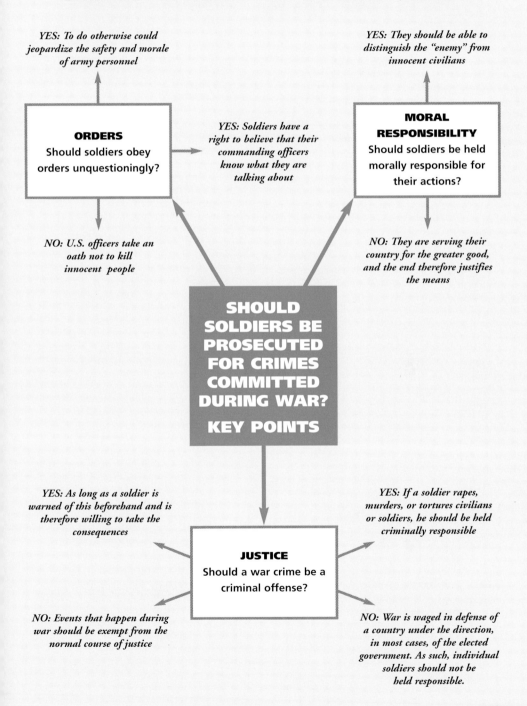

YES: To do otherwise could jeopardize the safety and morale of army personnel

YES: They should be able to distinguish the "enemy" from innocent civilians

ORDERS
Should soldiers obey orders unquestioningly?

YES: Soldiers have a right to believe that their commanding officers know what they are talking about

MORAL RESPONSIBILITY
Should soldiers be held morally responsible for their actions?

NO: U.S. officers take an oath not to kill innocent people

NO: They are serving their country for the greater good, and the end therefore justifies the means

SHOULD SOLDIERS BE PROSECUTED FOR CRIMES COMMITTED DURING WAR?
KEY POINTS

YES: As long as a soldier is warned of this beforehand and is therefore willing to take the consequences

YES: If a soldier rapes, murders, or tortures civilians or soldiers, he should be held criminally responsible

JUSTICE
Should a war crime be a criminal offense?

NO: Events that happen during war should be exempt from the normal course of justice

NO: War is waged in defense of a country under the direction, in most cases, of the elected government. As such, individual soldiers should not be held responsible.

LAW AND SOCIETY

INTRODUCTION

Laws are at the heart of society. They dictate what behavior is acceptable or not in a community. They govern the ways in which people behave toward one another and determine what they can and cannot do in that society without fear of reprisal. Certain behavior is generally considered unacceptable, including actions such as murder, rape, genocide, and incest. Other laws, however, vary from place to place and can alter over time

In the United States the Constitution is the fundamental law of the federal system of government. The Constitution's separation of legislative, executive, and judicial branches of government, the checks and balances of each branch against the other, and the explicit guarantees of individual liberty were designed to strike a balance between authority and liberty.

Each branch contributes to the rule of law: The legislative branch (the Congress) makes laws, the executive branch (the president) enforces laws, and the judicial branch (the Supreme Court) adjudicates the law.

This separation of powers exists at national, federal, and local levels of government. For example, the president (in the case of national government), the governor (in the case of each state), and the mayor (in the case of each city) are the chief law enforcers in the domain over which they preside. This separation of powers among the three branches of government was established to prevent one becoming too powerful and thus to guarantee that laws were generally fair, that they did not victimize or advantage particular sections of society over others, and that they respected as much as possible the rights and freedoms of individual Americans. At various times, however, some sections of society have felt that this has not been true.

It is generally accepted that the people who live in a society have a duty to obey its laws; in return, they enjoy the protection of those same laws. However, is there the same obligation to obey laws, for example, that contravene one's religious or moral beliefs? Can people pick or choose what laws they obey? The answer might be clear in a case such as drunk driving—no one has the right to drive drunk and thus endanger other people—but what about laws that said that escaped slaves had to be returned to their owners? By the same token, if enough people disagree with a law—say, a law against smoking marijuana—should that law be scrapped? The topics in this section examine important issues in law and society.

Special laws

When a society is under threat, governments sometimes introduce special laws that override individual rights for the greater good of its citizens. Topic 5 examines this issue with respect to the aftermath of the September 11, 2001, attacks on New York City and Washington, D.C., when some citizens were imprisoned without trial. The two debaters see such imprisonment from opposite sides: as an infringement of basic liberties and as a necessary surrender of certain rights to preserve greater freedoms.

Topics 6 and 7 discuss different approaches to community policing. Tarek Tannous in Topic 6 suggests that in tackling minor misdemeanors, the "Broken Windows" policy can prevent

serious crimes. Topics 8 and 9 examine two key issues in this regard.

The PBS online article in Topic 8 argues that juveniles should be tried as adults. The Child Welfare League, however, supports the rehabilitation of young offenders in most cases.

Josh Rubak in Topic 9 takes a different tack, claiming that juveniles deserve to be sentenced to the death penalty if they commit murder. But Steven A. Drizin and Stephen K. Harper counter that young offenders cannot be held responsible for their actions.

"I shall pass through this world but once.... Any good therefore that I can do, or any kindness that I can show to any other human being, let me do it now. Let me not defer or not neglect it, for I shall not pass this way again."
—ANONYMOUS

---

more serious crimes from occurring, but Bruce Shapiro states that it may result in police abuses. Michael Crowley, the author of the "yes" article of Topic 7, disagrees, claiming that when police officers liaise with residents, community policing works. Debra Dickinson, on the other hand, claims that residents resent police presence in their neighborhoods.

Juveniles
Advocates of "Broken Windows" and community-based policing argue that they help reduce juvenile crime and stop offenders from graduating to serious crime. This is a problem area; in 2000 more than two million Americans under the age of 18 were arrested for

Race, drugs, and TV
Certain issues come up repeatedly when one looks at law and society. The last three topics in this section examine racial profiling, drugs, and the media. In Topic 10 David A. Harris and Heather Macdonald examine the pros and cons respectively of racial profiling, or judging the likelihood of someone breaking the law by their race. Topic 11 probes whether decriminalizing soft drugs, such as marijuana, would help reduce drug-related crime. Debra Mackenzie and Larry Collins argue this issue; and finally, Topic 12 discusses the question of whether televising trials helps preserve justice. The articles look at the Lockerbie bombers' and O.J. Simpson's trials, respectively.

Topic 5
DO WARTIME LAWS VIOLATE CIVIL LIBERTIES?

YES

FROM "FREE SPEECH R.I.P.: THE GOVERNMENT DECLARES WAR ON CIVIL LIBERTIES"
NEW HAVEN VALLEY ADVOCATE, NOVEMBER 20, 2001
HANK HOFFMAN

NO

"SECURITY VERSUS CIVIL LIBERTIES"
THE ATLANTIC MONTHLY, DECEMBER 2001
RICHARD A. POSNER

INTRODUCTION

The Constitution guarantees certain civil liberties—such as freedom of expression and freedom from arbitrary arrest and prosecution—that protect citizens against government's abuse by restricting powers over the people. The government must also protect national security, however, and at times that may require it to take unusual security measures—such as passing laws that infringe on people's freedom.

In the wake of the terrorist attacks of September 11, 2001, the federal government enacted special legislation to combat terrorism. The move has since been the subject of much heated debate between those who worry that an overzealous government will trample citizens' civil liberties and those who want to see government powers expanded.

Civil libertarians are concerned that the new laws will lead to a repeat of past abuses, when exaggerated concerns over threats to national security led to some of the most notorious violations of civil liberties in history. During World War I, for example, fears that many German Americans were spies and that radicals were seeking to overthrow the government led Congress to narrow the limits of permissible speech and activity. The Espionage and Sedition Acts threatened imprisonment for anyone "advocating or urging treason, insurrection, or forcible resistance to any law of the United States," or uttering or writing any disloyal, profane, or abusive language intended to incite resistance or hinder war production. Under the new laws, more than 2,000 people were prosecuted (about half were convicted), and thousands more were rounded up and deported.

Similarly, during World War II President Franklin D. Roosevelt ordered the Army to move more than 112,000 Japanese Americans—most of them citizens who were born in the United States—from their homes on the West Coast to inland "relocation centers." Although this action was unprecedented in U.S. history, the Supreme Court upheld Roosevelt's decision on the grounds that—in times of war with Japan—people of Japanese ancestry might pose a threat to internal security. Since then, public attitudes have changed, and the 1988 Civil Liberties Act ordered Congress to pay reparation to the victims of this "grave injustice."

> *"Are all the laws, but one, to go unexecuted, and the government itself go to pieces, lest that one be violated?"*
>
> —ABRAHAM LINCOLN, 16TH PRESIDENT

However, history also reveals times when the restriction of civil liberties was necessary. During the Civil War, for example, President Abraham Lincoln suspended the writ of *habeas corpus* (the constitutional requirement that law officials bring people in custody before a judge and show sufficient cause for their detention), enabling government officials to detain people suspected of rebellious activity and helping the Union quash the rebellion. Lincoln contended that in times of national emergency the Constitution permitted the government to exercise discretionary powers. He argued that a domestic rebellion obstructed the law "by combinations too powerful to be suppressed by the ordinary course of

judicial proceedings" and claimed that his responsibility to suppress treasonous activity justified his actions.

The government's current efforts to combat terrorism have again raised the issue of the legitimacy of restricting civil liberties during wartime. After the September 2001 attacks Congress passed the USA PATRIOT Act, which (among other things) permits law-enforcement officials gathering intelligence to listen in on lawyer-client conversations.

The Federal Bureau of Investigation (FBI) has also issued new guidelines expanding its authority to monitor libraries, the Internet, political groups, and religious organizations—even without due reason to suppose a crime is being committed. These guidelines overturn those issued by the Ford administration (1974–1977) to stop investigative abuses by the FBI in its efforts to disrupt the civil rights and anti-Vietnam War movements.

The government has also quietly detained hundreds of noncitizens without allowing them to stand trial and has called for special military tribunals to try some suspected terrorists. It has justified its actions on the grounds that the fight against terrorism should no longer be considered a matter for the ordinary criminal justice system, with all its restrictions on intelligence gathering and court practice, but a matter of vital national security.

Hank Hoffman disagrees with this viewpoint. In the following article he argues that the government should not violate the Constitution in the fight against terrorism. Richard Posner, on the other hand, argues that in times of trouble, the imperatives of public security trump those of civil liberties.

FREE SPEECH R.I.P.
Hank Hoffman

✓ The American Airlines ticket clerk at Bangor International Airport in Maine handed Nancy Oden her ticket. She had waited what she says was an 'inordinate amount of time' while the ticket agent typed and responded to computer prompts. Oden thought it odd that the clerk never asked for any identification after she gave her name. It was Thursday, Nov. 1, and Oden—a longtime peace and environmental activist, organic farmer and leader in Green Party USA (the more radical wing of the American Green movement)—was heading for a party confab in Chicago. She was scheduled to speak the next night on biochemical warfare....

Would you consider someone like Nancy Oden to be a threat to national security? For more information on her politics see www.greenparty. org/Platform.html.

Oden's ordeal

Oden's experience and the anecdotal accounts of political oppression from people like her ... indicate we face the worst crisis in civil liberties in almost half a century.

After accepting her ticket, Oden noticed it was marked with a big 'S'. When she asked the clerk what the 'S' stood for, he told her she had been picked to have her bags searched. That's fine, Oden thought. I'm as subject to a random search as the next person. But then she paused. "I looked him in the eye and said, 'This wasn't random, was it?'" recalls Oden in a phone interview several days later. 'He looked at me for a second and said, 'No, you're flagged in our computer. You were going to be searched no matter what.''

Do you think it is acceptable for officials to search the luggage of political activists? And if so, what kind of activists do you think are legitimate targets?

It got worse. After passing through the X-ray machine without setting off any alarms, Oden settled herself in the boarding area. According to Oden, a young National Guardsman yelled at her to 'Bring those bags over here!' and 'Hurry up!' when she didn't move fast enough. When she reached out to help undo a recalcitrant zipper for one of the women searching her bags, the Guardsman barked, 'Get your hands out of there!'

A difficult situation

The ... Guardsman then grabbed Oden's arm and started 'spouting pro-war stuff in my face,' she says. She found this odd. How did he know her antiwar views? She wasn't wearing any buttons. He went on and on, saying 'Don't you

Do you think it is acceptable for officials to manhandle people who have shown no signs of resistance?

know we have to get them before they get us? Don't you understand what happened on Sept. 11?' She pulled her arm away, telling him he couldn't do that to her. She said to him, 'I'm not going to stand here and listen to you about why we should bomb poor women and children and starving people in Afghanistan.' He went to grab her again but she stepped back, saying, 'Don't touch me.'

The Guardsman would not let Oden board the plane, claiming she didn't cooperate with the search. Oden insists she did. At one point … the 61-year-old, conservatively dressed Oden was surrounded by six machine-gun-toting Guardsmen. The military men told all the airlines servicing the Bangor airport not to allow Oden to fly on that day (and possibly other days). An airport policeman escorted her off the premises….

Oden has never been arrested in 30 years of activism. She bought her ticket online six weeks in advance, using a personal credit card—not a terrorist profile. She believes she was singled out for political reasons….

Terrorists are more likely to book their tickets a few days in advance and to pay in cash.

A growing problem

Oden's ordeal isn't unique. The disturbing signs accumulate:

If the government is acting in the public's interest, do you think there is any need for this kind of secrecy?

* Several hundred people have been detained secretly by the government since Sept. 11. A coalition of civil liberties, human rights and Arab-American groups charge that a growing number of reports 'raise serious questions about deprivations of fundamental due process, including imprisonment without probable cause, interference with the right to counsel and threats of serious bodily injury….'

* …Neil Godfrey, a 22-year-old Philadelphia man, was barred from a flight to Phoenix to visit his parents because officials didn't like his choice of reading material. Godfrey had a copy of the Edward Abbey novel *Hayduke Lives!*, about a radical environmentalist; the cover shows a man's hand holding sticks of dynamite…. About a dozen officers from airport, city and state police forces interrogated Godfrey for 45 minutes and pored over the book….

* Several nonviolent antiwar demonstrators arrested at an unpermitted march in Hartford on Oct. 25 were charged not with the usual misdemeanor offenses common in these instances but with felonies carrying multi-year prison terms on conviction. The bonds in some cases were set at punitive levels of $35–50,000….

This is a reference to the author George Orwell, who wrote 1984, a satire on political tyranny. His book describes a world where everyone is monitored by the government, which uses brainwashing and torture to control people's thoughts, beliefs, and emotions.

The term "kangaroo court" is used to describe a mock or illegal court in which the accused's rights are disregarded. The term originated in the United States in the 1850s and may refer to the way Australian claim jumpers were often tried or to the way the action jumps from accusation to sentencing without due process.

With the enactment of the Orwellian-named USA PATRIOT Act, these cancers on the democratic body politic threaten to metastasize. The new law grants law enforcement and intelligence agencies a decades-old wish list of surveillance and detention powers. It expands the ability of the government to conduct secret 'black bag' searches. It restricts the oversight powers of the court system, a necessary check on the abuse of power. It creates a new crime called 'domestic terrorism.' The definition is so broad and vague that much legitimate dissent in this country could now be considered criminal....

An executive order

On Nov. 13 [sic], President Bush signed an executive order allowing special military tribunals, possibly operating in secret, to try foreigners charged with terrorism. Vice President Dick Cheney defended the policy. According to the *New York Times*, Cheney said terrorist suspects do not deserve the same guarantees of due process as American citizens. A military tribunal, Cheney said, 'guarantees that we'll have the kind of treatment of these individuals that we believe they deserve.' There's a term for the type of trial where the result is decided in advance: kangaroo court. Cheney, Ashcroft and others in the administration are asserting the prerogatives of dictatorship. We can, they are saying, bypass fundamental liberties, rule by executive order without consulting Congress and operate in secrecy.

The attack on fundamental liberties—like the downturn in the economy—didn't begin on Sept. 11. What changed with the attacks was the ability of the Bush administration to extend and codify their assault on democratic freedoms.

Over the past two years, the global justice movement, known in the mainstream press as the 'anti-globalization movement,' has been subjected to increasing official attacks. In Washington, D.C., during the April 2000 protests against the International Monetary Fund and World Bank, numerous federal and District of Columbia law enforcement agencies engaged in wholesale violations of civil liberties. They harassed activists on the street. They used conspicuous surveillance as an intimidation tactic. The protesters' headquarters was raided and closed on a flimsy fire code pretext. Later that same day, riot police trapped some 600 demonstrators. Closing off both ends of a city block without warning, the police penned the protesters—who believed they were in a legal demonstration —in the rain for two hours before arresting the lot of them. They were held with their wrists in plastic handcuffs and their arms behind their backs for periods of 10–17 hours.

The nonviolent civil disobedience that occurred the next morning-—blocking intersections to try to prevent delegates from getting to the IMF or World Bank meetings—was met with targeted brutality…. Baton beatings. Charges into crowds with motorcycles and other vehicles…. Beatings and homophobic threats from police, guards and U.S. marshals. Over 1,000 people were arrested that weekend. There were no convictions on any charges other than misdemeanors….

Michael Ratner, a human rights lawyer and vice president of the Center for Constitutional Rights, worries the type of scattershot repression witnessed the last two years may now be systematized. The key is the 'domestic terrorism' provision in the USA PATRIOT Act. Under Sec. 802, domestic terrorism is defined as an activity that involves acts dangerous to human life that violate the laws of the United States or any of the individual states and appears to be intended to either 'intimidate or coerce a civilian population,' 'influence the government by intimidation or coercion' or 'affect the conduct of government by mass destruction, assassination or kidnapping.' In addition, the government can now charge anyone who provides assistance to a person or organization charged with domestic terrorism….

Kit Gage, director of the First Amendment Foundation, says the changes are 'clearly comprehensive….' Gage is also concerned about the expansion of secrecy and what is known as 'court-stripping,' or denying courts the power to oversee and approve or reject government actions. The essential checks and balances of court oversight, Gage argues, are being eviscerated when they are needed most….

Michael Ratner's human rights site can be found at www.human rightsnow.org/.

For details of the USA PATRIOT Act see www.epic. org/privacy/ terrorism/ hr3162.html.

According to this definition, could officials such as those who stopped Nancy Oden be legitimately accused of domestic terrorism themselves?

A threat to us all

The very concept of the right of the individual to have his or her day in court is under systematic attack. The edifice of due process protections is designed to curtail arbitrary and illegitimate exercises of authority. The idea is that if government officials or police believe they may have to answer for their actions in a court of law, they will be less likely to abuse their power. But now, officials need no longer justify their intrusions on privacy or personal freedom … the definition of criminality [has become] so broad as to be meaningless….

If the government's raison d'être is to find and punish subversives, subversives will be found-—even if subversives end up being defined as anyone exercising a constitutional right to question the government. What looms before us is the possibility that the singular encounters … of people like Nancy Oden … may become the general experience of us all.

SECURITY VERSUS CIVIL LIBERTIES
Richard A. Posner

NO

X   In the wake of the September 11 terrorist attacks have come many proposals for tightening security; some measures to that end have already been taken. Civil libertarians are troubled. They fear that concerns about national security will lead to an erosion of civil liberties. They offer historical examples of supposed overreactions to threats to national security. They treat our existing civil liberties—freedom of the press, protections of privacy and of the rights of criminal suspects, and the rest—as sacrosanct, insisting that the battle against international terrorism accommodate itself to them.

If rights are not sacrosanct, does that mean that they are not rights? And who should decide what they are at any time?

I consider this a profoundly mistaken approach to the question of balancing liberty and security. The basic mistake is the prioritizing of liberty. It is a mistake about law and a mistake about history. Let me begin with law. What we take to be our civil liberties—for example, immunity from arrest except upon probable cause to believe we've committed a crime, and from prosecution for violating a criminal statute enacted after we committed the act that violates it—were made legal rights by the Constitution and other enactments. The other enactments can be changed relatively easily, by amendatory legislation. Amending the Constitution is much more difficult. In recognition of this the Framers left most of the constitutional provisions that confer rights pretty vague. The courts have made them definite.

For more information about the Constitution see Volume 7, Constitution.

Concretely, the scope of these rights has been determined, through an interaction of constitutional text and subsequent judicial interpretation, by a weighing of competing interests. I'll call them the public-safety interest and the liberty interest. Neither, in my view, has priority. They are both important, and their relative importance changes from time to time and from situation to situation. The safer the nation feels, the more weight judges will be willing to give to the liberty interest. The greater the threat that an activity poses to the nation's safety, the stronger will the grounds seem for seeking to repress that activity, even at some cost to liberty. This fluid approach is only common sense. Supreme Court Justice Robert Jackson gave it vivid expression many years ago when he said, in dissenting from a free-speech decision he thought doctrinaire, that the Bill of Rights should not be made into a suicide pact. It was not intended to be such, and the present contours of the rights that it confers, having been shaped far more by judicial interpretation than by the literal text (which doesn't define such critical terms as 'due process of law' and 'unreasonable' arrests and searches), are alterable in response to changing threats to national security.

If it is true, therefore, as it appears to be at this writing, that the events of September 11 have revealed the United States to be in much greater jeopardy from international terrorism than had previously been believed—have revealed it to be threatened by a diffuse, shadowy enemy that must be fought with police measures as well as military force—it stands to reason that our civil liberties will be curtailed. They should be curtailed, to the extent that the benefits in greater security outweigh the costs in reduced liberty. All that can reasonably be asked of the responsible legislative and judicial officials is that they weigh the costs as carefully as the benefits.

> By using these terms, what does the author suggest about his concept of the situation?

What can history teach us?

It will be argued that the lesson of history is that officials habitually exaggerate dangers to the nation's security. But the lesson of history is the opposite. It is because officials have repeatedly and disastrously underestimated these dangers that our history is as violent as it is. Consider such underestimated dangers as that of secession, which led to the Civil War; of a Japanese attack on the United States, which led to the disaster at Pearl Harbor; of Soviet espionage in the 1940s, which accelerated the Soviet Union's acquisition of nuclear weapons and emboldened Stalin to encourage North Korea's invasion of South Korea; of the installation of Soviet missiles in Cuba, which precipitated the Cuban missile crisis; of political assassinations and outbreaks of urban violence in the 1960s; of the Tet Offensive of 1968; of the Iranian revolution of 1979 and the subsequent taking of American diplomats as hostages; and, for that matter, of the events of September 11.

> It can be very effective to take an opposing argument and contradict it directly, as Posner does here.

It is true that when we are surprised and hurt, we tend to overreact—but only with the benefit of hindsight can a reaction be separated into its proper and excess layers. In hindsight we know that interning Japanese-Americans did not shorten World War II. But was this known at the time? If not, shouldn't the Army have erred on the side of caution, as it did? Even today we cannot say with any assurance that Abraham Lincoln was wrong to suspend habeas corpus during the Civil War, as he did on several occasions, even though the Constitution is clear that only Congress can suspend this right. (Another of Lincoln's wartime measures,

> Posner admits that there are cases when the government has overreacted to a perceived threat. Did U.S. activities after September 11, 2001, constitute an overreaction?

Mechanical diggers clear wreckage in the aftermath of the devastation caused by the September 11 terrorist attacks in New York City.

the Emancipation Proclamation, may also have been unconstitutional.) But Lincoln would have been wrong to cancel the 1864 presidential election, as some urged: by November of 1864 the North was close to victory, and canceling the election would have created a more dangerous precedent than the wartime suspension of habeas corpus. This last example shows that civil liberties remain part of the balance even in the most dangerous of times, and even though their relative weight must then be less.

Lincoln's unconstitutional acts during the Civil War show that even legality must sometimes be sacrificed for other values. We are a nation under law, but first we are a nation. I want to emphasize something else, however: the malleability of law, its pragmatic rather than dogmatic character. The law is not absolute, and the slogan 'Fiat iustitia ruat caelum' ('Let justice be done though the heavens fall') is dangerous nonsense. The law is a human creation rather than a divine gift, a tool of government rather than a mandarin mystery. It is an instrument for promoting social welfare, and as the conditions essential to that welfare change, so must it change.

So, does this mean that people should always be subject to the will of the nation—even when it is decided by a few individuals?

A time to reassess

Civil libertarians today are missing something else—the opportunity to challenge other public-safety concerns that impair civil liberties. I have particularly in mind the war on drugs. The sale of illegal drugs is a 'victimless' crime in the special but important sense that it is a consensual activity. Usually there is no complaining witness, so in order to bring the criminals to justice the police have to rely heavily on paid informants (often highly paid and often highly unsavory), undercover agents, wiretaps and other forms of electronic surveillance, elaborate sting operations, the infiltration of suspect organizations, random searches, the monitoring of airports and highways, the 'profiling' of likely suspects on the basis of ethnic or racial identity or national origin, compulsory drug tests, and other intrusive methods that put pressure on civil liberties.

The author seems to be suggesting that civil libertarians have done little to challenge the war on drugs. Do you think this is true? Try reading Noam Chomsky's comments at www.deoxy.org/usdrugs.htm.

The war on drugs has been a big flop; moreover, in light of what September 11 has taught us about the gravity of the terrorist threat to the United States, it becomes hard to take entirely seriously the threat ... that drug use is said to pose. Perhaps it is time to redirect law-enforcement resources from the investigation and apprehension of drug dealers to the investigation and apprehension of ... terrorists. By doing so we may be able to minimize the net decrease in our civil liberties that the events of September 11 have made inevitable.

If the drug war has already proved to be a big flop, do you think similar tactics will prove any more effective in the war on terrorism?

Summary

The question of whether the government should restrict civil liberties during wartime has gained renewed significance since the events of September 11, 2001, and these articles help us consider some of the most important issues.

Hank Hoffman argues that civil liberties are under attack from an overzealous government exercising "arbitrary and illegitimate" authority in the name of national security. He is worried, for example, that the knowledge that the government is monitoring political activity will restrict the free discussion that has traditionally formed an integral part of American democracy. He also expresses concern that any extra surveillance—introduced in the name of gathering of intelligence vital to national security—will in fact be used as a political intimidation tactic. "If the government's raison d'être is to find and punish subversives," he contends, "subversives will be found—even if subversives end up being defined as anyone exercising a constitutional right to question the government."

Richard Posner, however, argues that civil liberties should be curtailed as part of the current war on terrorism because "the benefits in greater security outweigh the costs in reduced liberty." The lesson of history, Posner writes, is not that government officials have exaggerated possible threats to security to justify illegitimate restrictions, but that they have "repeatedly and disastrously underestimated" the dangers citizens face. In sharp contrast to Hoffman, Posner feels that if the government pays too much attention to the criticisms of civil liberties campaigners, that will hinder its ability to respond adequately to the unprecedented dangers posed by international terrorism.

FURTHER INFORMATION:

Books:
Rehnquist, William H., *All the Laws but One: Civil Liberties in Wartime*. Vancouver, WA: Vintage Books, 2000.

Useful websites:
www.aclu.org
American Civil Liberties Union site, which includes information on recent special legislation.
www.hrw.org
Human Rights Watch site.
www.refuseandresist.org/big_brother/113001ratner.html
"Moving Toward A Police State." This article discusses the government's changes to the law following the terrorist action of September 11.
http://thomas.loc.gov/home/terrorleg.htm
The Library of Congress's comprehensive list of federal legislation relating to September 11.

http://www.whitehouse.gov/response/
White House site with links to articles, press releases, and other material relating to the U.S. response to the terrorist attack.

The following debates in the Pro/Con series may also be of interest:

In this volume:
 Topic 10 Is racial profiling wrong?

 Topic 14 Do prisoners have rights?

DO WARTIME LAWS VIOLATE CIVIL LIBERTIES?

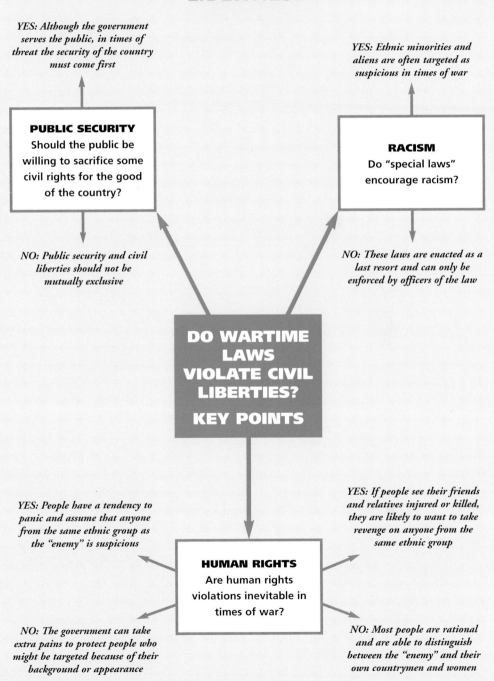

YES: Although the government serves the public, in times of threat the security of the country must come first

PUBLIC SECURITY
Should the public be willing to sacrifice some civil rights for the good of the country?

NO: Public security and civil liberties should not be mutually exclusive

YES: Ethnic minorities and aliens are often targeted as suspicious in times of war

RACISM
Do "special laws" encourage racism?

NO: These laws are enacted as a last resort and can only be enforced by officers of the law

DO WARTIME LAWS VIOLATE CIVIL LIBERTIES?
KEY POINTS

YES: People have a tendency to panic and assume that anyone from the same ethnic group as the "enemy" is suspicious

YES: If people see their friends and relatives injured or killed, they are likely to want to take revenge on anyone from the same ethnic group

HUMAN RIGHTS
Are human rights violations inevitable in times of war?

NO: The government can take extra pains to protect people who might be targeted because of their background or appearance

NO: Most people are rational and are able to distinguish between the "enemy" and their own countrymen and women

Topic 6
DOES THE "BROKEN WINDOWS" POLICY WORK?

YES

"STUDY PRAISES POLICING STRATEGY"
INTERCOUNTYNEWS.COM, AUGUST 12, 2002
TAREK TANNOUS

NO

FROM "BRUTAL VERDICT"
SALON.COM, FEBRUARY 26, 2000
BRUCE SHAPIRO

INTRODUCTION

In 1982 crime experts James Q. Wilson and George L. Kelling published a report in which they proposed a new crime-fighting theory. The authors suggested that public order offenses, no matter how trivial, lay the foundations for more serious crime in a community. Put simply, they argued that one unrepaired broken window in a building acts as a signal to potential window breakers that no one in the community cares. Soon all the windows in the building will be broken.

In the context of Wilson and Kelling's theory the term *broken window* relates to any minor public order offense—for example, dropping litter or dodging fares. A rise in such offenses sends out messages to the community and to potential lawbreakers. A neighborhood full of "broken windows" is more likely to attract teenage gangs, drunks, and other "unwelcome" visitors. The community thinks that crime is on the rise, and residents take steps to avoid the streets and each other. As this so-called urban decay extends, minor offenders might try their luck at more serious crimes. The process also leaves the community vulnerable to hardened criminals. Very quickly, drugs change hands, cars are stolen, and violent crime increases.

To break the link between crime and disorder, Wilson and Kelling urged the police to adopt a tough approach to law enforcement—increased vigilance for minor offenses, foot patrols to replace ineffective squad-car policing, and increased contact with the community. If the police fostered a safe environment by increasing their presence on the streets, people would take pride in their community, challenge unruly behavior, and help the police maintain order.

Soaring crime rates at the end of the 20th century meant that many police departments seized on the idea of "Broken Windows" policing. New York City led the national drive. In 1994 Mayor Rudolph W. Giuliani and Police

Chief William Bratton began an initiative to crack down on minor public order offenses. At first glance the policy seemed to be hugely successful. Statistics credited the new police tactics with a 27 percent drop in crime in the first two years. Many crime experts were quick to endorse Wilson and Kelling's theory.

> *"If you pay attention to the first window that was broken and you fix it, and you try to find who did it and say, 'You can't do that. That isn't right,' you protect the building at the first, easiest, and earliest possible moment."*
>
> —RUDOLPH W. GIULIANI,
> MAYOR OF NEW YORK CITY
> (1993–2001)

As more cities in the United States and around the world embraced "Broken Windows," many crime experts began to have their doubts. Critics pointed out that crime rates in New York City peaked around 1990, well before the introduction of "Broken Windows" policing. They also noted that crime declined just as rapidly in cities such as San Francisco and San Diego, where law-enforcement policies were less rigorous. In addition, they suggested that the policy did not address the root causes of crime, such as poverty, discrimination, and a lack of economic opportunities in the inner cities.

The most worrying aspect for critics of "Broken Windows" was the increasing number of high-profile allegations of police misconduct. In a 1998 article in the *Michigan Law Review* Bernard Harcourt, a professor of law at the University of Arizona, noted: "'Broken Windows' is an essay about creating order. But the order is achieved in part through disorder."

Harcourt highlighted fears about the police reasserting their authority in "extralegal" ways—by "roughing up" gang members or arresting people "on suspicion" of certain offenses. As one police officer in Wilson and Kelling's report put it: "We kick ass." But can the police justify the use of tough tactics when no obvious law has been broken?

The most controversial cases are those in which someone is killed by the police. In February 2000, for example, four New York Police Department officers were acquitted in the killing of Amadou Diallo, a 22-year-old immigrant. The jury believed there was no criminal intent to kill Diallo and that the officers operated fairly and within New York Police Department guidelines. Many critics believe cases such as the killing of Amadou Diallo highlight the shortcomings of "Broken Windows" tactics. So, too, do the soaring numbers of police complaints and the millions of dollars in out-of-court settlements in suspected cases of police misconduct.

The first of the following two articles focuses on a California State University research study that concluded that the "Broken Windows" theory can be an effective tool in reducing serious crime in California. In the second article journalist Bruce Shapiro responds by arguing that such a policing approach is in fact a precursor to police brutality.

STUDY PRAISES POLICING STRATEGY
Tarek Tannous

YES

☑ According to a new study, the "Broken Windows" approach to policing that has become popular in recent years may actually work better than initially suggested, giving more weight to proponents of the community policing model of law enforcement utilized in many Chester County municipalities.

"Quality of life" policing attempts to make neighborhoods more pleasant and livable.

Quality of life

"You have to buy into the quality of life argument, where police address quality of life issues and not just crime issues," said Chief Eugene Dooley of the East Whiteland Police Department. "You can't do it if you're just hovering around in a holding pattern waiting for someone to call you, then you swoop in after the fact."

The study was conducted by Professor John L. Worall of the California Institute for County Government. To read the study in full, go to www.cicg.org/publications/CICG_Brief_Aug_2002.pdf ?PHPSESSID=fb2010 b56bc4940002db59 0a66e6538e.

The study, "Does 'Broken Windows' Law Enforcement Reduce Serious Crime?"—larger and more in-depth than previous examinations of the topic—concludes that there is a significant link between targeting minor crime and a drop in serious crime.

Conducted by the California Institute for County Government at California State University in Sacramento, the study is one of the few to examine the strategy on a large scale rather than at a neighborhood or community level. Researchers examined all California counties from 1989 to 2000 and concluded that there existed a notable tie between so-called "Broken Windows" policing and a drop in felony property crime.

"Broken Windows" policing assumes that serious crime can be reduced by strongly enforcing minor crimes such as graffiti, property damage, prostitution, public drunkenness and the like.

Under Mayor Giuliani's leadership (1993-2001), New York City experienced a 44 percent reduction in overall crime.

"It addresses quality of life issues, the small things," said Coatesville Police Chief Dominick Bellizzie. "It's the mind-set that it puts people in. They see police going after people who litter, or graffiti, open containers. The community starts to buy into the idea that they're not going to tolerate these things."

"I think it works really well. It was the cornerstone of (former Mayor Rudolph) Giuliani's strategy in New York," Bellizzie said.

"Broken Windows" explained

The approach was named after an article that first appeared 20 years ago in *The Atlantic Monthly* and has since been credited with revamping mainstream thoughts on urban police strategy.

To read the article "Broken Windows: The Police and Neighborhood Safety" by James Q. Wilson and George L. Kelling, go to www.theatlantic.com/politics/crime/windows.htm.

"Broken Windows," written by university professors George L. Kelling and James Q. Wilson, published in the March 1982 issue of the magazine, argued for a return to the "long-abandoned view that the police ought to protect communities as well as individuals."

The strategy's success should not come as a surprise to Chester County residents, Dooley says, since it is really an urbanization of the community policing strategies that have long been employed by smaller, municipal departments.

"Theoretically, Chester County has always had a community policing model. Police officers are doing things in North Philadelphia now that they've been doing in Chester County for 30, 40 years," said Dooley.

Dooley, who spent the vast majority of his career with the Philadelphia Police Department, says that the "Broken Windows" approach is a repudiation of what he considers an outdated and inefficient style of policing.

"In the '60s and '70s, a police department was a manpower pool—because they were all men back then—who were there to respond to a demand for service. They focused only on hard crimes, like robberies, burglaries, auto theft," he said. "There was a financial, organizational and political benefit to keep this 'crime only' approach."

What benefits do you think the speaker is referring to in relation to a "crime only approach"?

Before the arrival of "Broken Windows" and other community policing strategies, a police officer's job was to be there only in response to a crime, and to not be concerned with what was considered "social work." Community order and engaging in the day-to-day concerns of a neighborhood were not in the job description.

"If all you have are the 911 call-chasers, you can't do the community policing," said Bellizzie. "There was a time when people thought police work meant you just ran around locking up the guy with the gun doing the burglary. But 99.9 percent of the time, these issues are not going to come up on a daily basis."

"The abandoned car, left on the street with two tires missing, people care about that just as much as the burglary up the street," he said.

Do you agree with the speaker? Are people as worried about abandoned cars as burglaries?

Like Dooley, Bellizzie, himself a former Philadelphia officer, has seen the effects of the "Broken Windows" campaign on an urban setting.

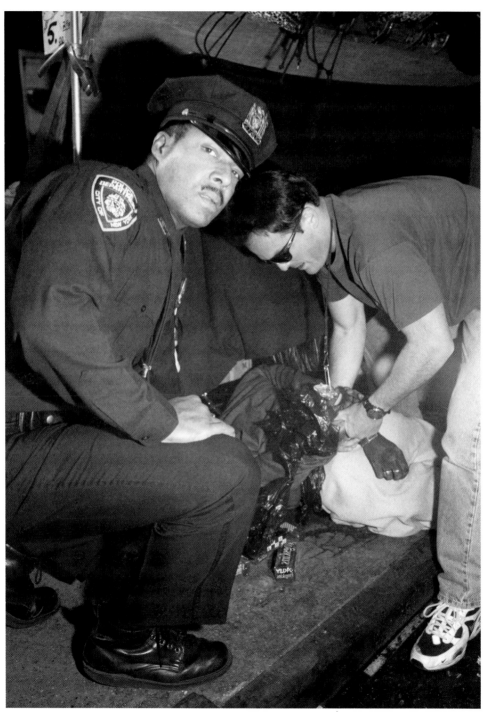

Under the "Broken Windows" strategy embraced by Mayor Rudolph Guiliani, a street vendor is arrested for selling counterfeit goods in Times Square, New York City, in 1999.

"It changes not only the mind-set of the police department, but the mind-set of the community," he said. "In New York, it got to the point where the community expected it."

Since the article's publication two decades ago, the strategy has been the subject of heated debate—many police departments have adopted it, but critics charge that it leads to police harassment.

In what ways do you think the "Broken Windows" strategy could lead to police harassment?

Limits of previous research

Previous studies have tended to focus on single jurisdictions, and have not been able to discount numerous other possible factors when they discovered drops in serious crime.

This new study compared both misdemeanor arrests and misdemeanor charges filed to the overall number of arrests and charges. It also controlled many social and economic factors, such as unemployment rates and neighborhood demographics.

More misdemeanor arrests and charges were taken to indicate a local law enforcement tendency to engage in "broken window" policing. That tendency was then compared to the felony property crime rate to see if a link existed.

A misdemeanor is a minor crime, as compared to a felony, which is a major crime. A misdemeanor is usually punished by a fine or a prison term of less than one year, or both. Unlike the committing of a felony, committing a misdemeanor cannot cancel citizenship or lead to deportation in the case of a noncitizen.

"We've tested the spirit of the 'broken windows' theory, and we've found a relationship between targeting misdemeanors and reducing serious crime," said John L. Worrall, the California State University San Bernardino criminal justice professor who authored the study.

The study, however, only focused on finding a statistical link between enforcing minor crimes and a drop in serious crime, Worrall said. It does not conclusively prove a cause-and-effect relationship, nor does it estimate how much of a drop in crime is seen when a community pursues a "broken windows" strategy.

"What makes this study unique is all the other factors we controlled for, and that even after we did that we still found a strong statistical relationship between 'broken windows' policing and a reduction in serious crime," Worrall said. "This is by no means the last word on the 'broken windows' theory, but it is an important contribution."

BRUTAL VERDICT
Bruce Shapiro

On February 4, 1999, West African immigrant Amadou Diallo was shot dead by police officers who mistook him for a rape suspect. For more information go to www. washingtonpost. com/wp-dyn/ nation/specials/ aroundthenation/ nypd.

NO

X Shortly after an Albany jury acquitted four New York City police officers of all charges in the shooting death of unarmed immigrant, 22-year-old Amadou Diallo, Mayor Rudolph Giuliani tried, for a few minutes, to play the diplomat. He expressed "deep, heartfelt sympathy" for the Diallo family and the officers alike. "I would ask everyone in New York to reflect on the evidence and the facts," he told a City Hall press conference. "We might be able to grow by that."

But Giuliani's own personal growth soon gave way to a barely-concealed sense of vindication. While 150 miles away in Albany the Rev. Al Sharpton was imploring that "not one brick or bottle be thrown," the mayor took the occasion to lash out at "people who protest against the police, and blame them for every ill in society."

Giuliani's sense of vindication is premature. Far from a repudiation of the NYPD's critics, the criminal acquittal of those four officers—Kenneth Boss, Sean Carroll, Edward McMellon and Richard Murphy—contains, paradoxically, a far more sweeping indictment.

Key testimony

Here is why Mayor Giuliani should take little comfort from today's verdicts. Central to the jury's decision, it appears, was the testimony of police brutality expert James Fyfe, a former New York police officer, now a professor at Temple University. I've spoken with Fyfe often over the years. He is the most precise and acerbic critic of police brutality I know. This time, Fyfe testified—without any witness fee—in the four officers' defense. Hours before coming down with its acquittals, the jury asked to have Fyfe's testimony read back to them.

What Fyfe testified—simply but forcefully—is that the officers did not have a criminal intent. Rather, he said, they followed standard police procedure when they asked Diallo to halt, and when—thinking the wallet in his hand might be a gun—they fired 41 times.

And standard procedure—not premeditated brutality by rogue officers—is the real crime in Diallo's death. Fyfe himself underscored that point the day after his testimony in the *New York Times*. The Diallos, he said, "were dealt a great wrong and deserve to be compensated" in a civil trial. The problem, he said, was not criminal intent but NYPD policy. Given the officers' hair-trigger training and their high-powered 16-round weapons, Diallo's death was "an accident waiting to happen."

The Diallo case is a mirror image of the last celebrated police case, the trial of four Brooklyn officers in the brutalization of Abner Louima. In Brooklyn, enraged officers systematically raped and beat Louima, a suspect in their custody, and their precinct tried to cover it up.

But in the Diallo case, there was no sadism, no rage, no cover-up. Instead, there was just standard operating procedure: plainclothes officers accosting a civilian who might well have mistaken them for gangbangers, firing their guns in confusion and fear at the first mistaken hint that he might be armed, hitting Diallo 19 times.

Around the country, it is not rogue officers but standard operating procedure which has turned police brutality into the civil rights issue of the decade. In that sense, Diallo's case, not Louima's, goes to the heart of the matter.

Abner Louima, a Haitian immigrant living in Brooklyn, was assaulted by police officers on August 8, 1997. For further detail see pages 86–87.

Casual defiance can mean death

Studies by the U.S. Justice Department and the University of North Carolina have documented that fatal police encounters are likely to begin not with major crime but with a citizen's casual defiance of an officer on a minor public-order matter. Take, for instance, a traffic stop, which led to the asphyxiation death of Johnny Gammage while in police custody in Pittsburgh in 1995, a case which brought the Justice Department into its most sweeping police-brutality investigation; or intoxication, the condition in which Archie Elliot of Prince George's County, Maryland was shot 14 times in the back the same year.

Behind the standard operating procedures—and behind these deaths—is a profound debate over policing philosophy.

The plainclothes neighborhood-sweeping squad known as the Street Crimes Unit, to which Boss, Carroll, McMellon and Murphy were assigned, was established as a vehicle for Giuliani's crime-reduction strategy—a strategy he claims is responsible for a reduction in crime so drastic that the city is now among the safest in the U.S. After being elected in November 1993, Giuliani and his new police chief William Bratton declared that no offence was too small—not begging in doorways, single-joint marijuana sales in public parks, squeegee hustles in traffic—and no offender too low-level to escape police attention.

William J. Bratton (1947–) was commissioner of the New York Police Department from 1994 to 1996. He previously headed the Boston Police Department (1993) and the New York Transit Police (1992).

More than a strategy, their approach has become a law-enforcement faith, variously known as zero-tolerance policing, broken-windows policing, or quality-of-life policing (depending on whether the speaker wants to appear tough, intellectual or socially concerned). It is emulated by police departments from New Orleans to London.

Diallo's death is the dark side of the zero-tolerance movement—as are New York City's soaring numbers of police brutality complaints and $25 million annually in out-of-court settlements in brutality cases.

In his press conference after the Diallo verdict, Giuliani inveighed against those who hold "different standards for cops." Yet for months New York's Civilian Complaint Review Board has been at odds with the NYPD over the small number of legitimate complaints which even rise to disciplinary hearings. It is still the NYPD, not the critics of brutality, which evades an even standard for officers' behavior.

It's not too much to say that Diallo's death can be traced back to the founding document of the zero-tolerance faith, its Sermon on the Mount: a 1982 article in *The Atlantic Monthly* entitled "The Police and Neighborhood Safety," written by James Q. Wilson, a conservative political scientist, and George Kelling, a criminologist who had studied foot patrols in Newark.

Disorder from broken windows

Wilson and Kelling's central argument was simple, centered on what they called their "Broken Windows" hypothesis. If a factory or office window is left broken, passers-by will conclude that no-one cares, no-one is in charge—and will soon shatter the other windows as well. Soon that decay will extend to the surrounding street, which will become menacing and hostile. Said Wilson and Kelling, it is the small, seemingly insignificant signs of disorder—graffiti, loitering by the homeless, subway fare-jumping by teenagers—which lay the groundwork for more serious street crime and social decay.

The graffiti artists and fare-jumpers themselves, getting the message that social norms will not be enforced, become likely candidates for more dangerous lawbreaking; while citizens, feeling threatened by homeless beggars and squeegee-men, withdraw from the civic arena. So police, Wilson and Kelling argued, should go back into the business of aggressive order maintenance.

With its vivid central image and its implied rejection of economic or social explanations of crime, the broken windows hypothesis proved instantly appealing to politicians

New York City's Civilian Complaint Review Board (www.nyc. gov/html/ccrb/home. html) "is an independent, non-police city agency with the authority to investigate allegations of police misconduct filed by members of the public against New York City police officers."

like Giuliani. And it is grounded in a sensible core perception: an environment of physical safety is one important element of any civil society. Few urban dwellers have not raged against the absentee landlord down the block whose crumbling tenement shelters crack dealers in the cellar. Few have not felt some relief when a police officer quietly intervened with a deranged, intoxicated stranger.

The only problem is that on the New York streets, "order maintenance" quickly became a synonym for brutal neighborhood sweeps and generous employment of the truncheon. One of New York City's first broken-windows success stories, for instance, the cleanup of streets around Grand Central Station, was soon discredited after large-scale beatings of the area's homeless by a privately-employed goon squad were exposed by the press.

Are such illicit acts an acceptable price if they improve the life of the majority?

Erosion of police legitimacy

And as the huge gulfs in political perception opened by the Diallo case show, such zero-tolerance strategies brought another unintended consequence: vast erosion of police legitimacy. "The larger concern about zero tolerance," warned a 1998 study commissioned by the decidedly law-and-order U.S. Congress, "is its long-term effect on people arrested for minor offenses ... The effects of an arrest experience over a minor offense may permanently lower police legitimacy, both for the arrested person and their social network of family and friends."

Indeed, Giuliani himself gave a backhanded acknowledgement of such consequences in his press conference Friday night: "We have already had a great deal of examination regarding police procedures" as a result of Diallo's shooting: "Relationships with communities. Reaching out to communities. Dealing with people in a more respectful way."

Neither Guiliani's assurances, nor the acquittal of the four officers, are likely to bridge the zero-tolerance divide which Diallo's shooting has turned into a political chasm in New York.

On the law, the jury had it right: Those officers did not set out to kill an unarmed immigrant on the streets. But as a political matter, Al Sharpton, for all of his notorious theatricality, made the case in plain and simple language Friday night. "Any man has the right to expect the police are protecting him, not shooting at him." The Diallo criminal trial is over, but the Diallo case will haunt the politics of zero-tolerance policing for a long time to come.

Born in Brooklyn, New York, the Reverend Alfred (Al) Sharpton Jr. is a Pentecostal minister and civil rights activist. He has run for the Senate and contested the Democrat nomination for mayor of New York City.

Summary

Maintaining law and order is essential to every democratic society, so finding effective ways to police the community is a priority for all policymakers. In "Study Praises Policing Strategy" Tarek Tannous looks at a study that examined the effects of the "Broken Windows" policing strategy on all California counties from 1989 to 2000. It concluded that the strategy was eventually effective in reducing the number of serious crime offenses. The author notes that "Broken Windows" policing is a preventative approach to crime and is therefore effective because it treats the first signs of criminal activity rather than reacting after a serious crime has been perpetrated, when it is already too late. Tannous claims that crime only escalates in communities that neglect the minor signs of public disorder. He believes that the goal of the police should be to respond not just to individuals who have already been the victims of serious crime but to protect whole communities from the effects of criminal activity in order to enhance the general quality of life.

In "Brutal Verdict" Bruce Shapiro questions the "Broken Windows" theory. He backs up his argument by focusing on the killing of Amadou Diallo by four police officers from the New York Police Department. Although he concedes that the officers did not set out to kill Diallo—they acted in accordance with standard operating procedures—Shapiro believes that Diallo's death "can be traced back" to Wilson and Kelling's 1982 article. The author cites evidence that fatal police encounters are less likely to begin with major crime than with a citizen's attitude when confronted over a minor public order offense. Shapiro also cites the growing number of complaints and out-of-court settlements in police brutality cases. He agrees that a safe environment is important to a civil society. When people start to question the legitimacy of "Broken Windows" policing, however, the author concludes that it does not foster feelings of security within the community.

FURTHER INFORMATION:

Books:

Harcourt, Bernard E., *Illusion of Order: The False Promise of Broken Windows Policing*. Cambridge, MA: Harvard University Press, 2001.

Kelling, George L., and Catherine M. Coles, *Fixing Broken Windows: Restoring Order and Reducing Crime in Our Communities*. New York: Martin Kessler Books, 1996.

Useful websites:

www.cjcj.org/jpi/windowsex.html
Justice Policy Institute study on San Francisco crime policies.
www.ncjrs.org/pdffiles1/nij/178259.pdf
National Institute of Justice report on Broken Windows.

The following debates in the Pro/Con series may also be of interest:

In this volume:

Topic 1 Is the criminal justice system racist?

Topic 7 Does community policing help reduce crime?

Topic 10 Is racial profiling wrong?

DOES THE "BROKEN WINDOWS" POLICY WORK?

YES: Crime follows on the heels of urban decay and community neglect, which are the targets of "Broken Windows"

YES: Rates of serious crime have fallen dramatically in cities such as New York that have introduced public order policing

ROOTS

Does "Broken Windows" address the causes of crime?

PREVENTION

Is public order policing responsible for falling crime rates?

NO: The root causes of crime are poverty, inequality, and lack of opportunity

NO: Cities such as San Francisco, which do not have zero tolerance policing, have also seen a dramatic decline in levels of serious crime

DOES THE "BROKEN WINDOWS" POLICY WORK?

KEY POINTS

YES: An increased police presence on the streets fosters a sense of safety in the community

YES: The public applauds police zero tolerance of "undesirable" elements such as drug dealers

DESIRABILITY

Does "Broken Windows" give the public what it wants?

NO: People question the legitimacy of using "extralegal" methods to maintain order

NO: If the price of zero tolerance is to be brutality and the deaths of innocent people, then it is too high

ABNER LOUIMA

"Some say hate's what caused this crime
Some say Giuliani time
But blame hate or mayor or blame police
All of us must hold the peace."
—FROM THE POEM "ABNER LOUIMA" BY STEPHAN SMITH

In 1997 Haitian immigrant Abner Louima was arrested outside a New York nightclub. He was physically and sexually assaulted while in custody; five NYPD police officers were later tried for the assault. The case generated heated criticism of the "broken-windows," "three strikes," and "stop and search" measures employed by U.S. law-enforcement agencies to reduce crime, especially as they often involved the targeting of minority groups through racial profiling. This timeline lists the key events leading up to and during the Louima trial.

August 1997 9: Haitian immigrant Abner Louima (33) is arrested outside Club Rendezvous, allegedly for being involved in a street fight. Louima is beaten by officers during the journey to the 70th Precinct station. He is later sodomized with a broken broom handle by Officer Justin Volpe, while another officer holds him down. **10:** At 8.00 a.m. Louima is taken to hospital with a torn rectum and bladder. One of the nurses there reports his condition to NYPD Internal Affairs. Louima's relatives also complain to the police department. **13:** Officer Justin Volpe is charged with aggravated sexual abuse and first-degree assault. Officer Thomas Bruder is given desk duty. **15:** Volpe and Officer Charles Schwarz are indicted on charges of aggravated sexual abuse and first-degree assault. **18:** Officers Thomas Wiese and Thomas Bruder are charged with assaulting Louima in their patrol car. The Louima family announces plans to file a $55 million lawsuit against the city. **29:** Several thousand Haitians march through New York to protest Louima's treatment.

October 10, 1997 Louima leaves Brooklyn Medical Center.

February 26, 1998 The federal government takes over prosecution of the case, and the four officers charged are indicted on a variety of federal civil rights charges. A fifth officer, Michael Bellomo, is also charged with obstructing justice.

March 26, 1998 New York mayor Rudy Giuliani dismisses most of the recommendations of the specially formed task force formed following Louima's attack to study relations between New York City residents and the police department.

November 16, 1998 Schwarz, Wiese, and Bruder are charged with conspiracy and obstruction of justice as a grand jury finds that they tried to stop Justin Volpe from being charged.

May 1999 4: The trial of Volpe, Schwarz, Wiese, Bruder, and Bellomo begins in the

Federal District Court in Brooklyn. Johnny Cochrane is Louima's lawyer. **12:** Fellow officers testify against the five accused. Detective Eric Turetzky says Louima's pants were "down below his knees." **25:** Volpe pleads guilty to his role in the attack in the face of overwhelming evidence.

June 8, 1999 The jury finds Schwarz guilty of helping to torture Louima; Wiese and Bruder are acquitted of the beating and Bellomo is also found innocent of conspiring to hide the incident. All three officers are still charged with obstructing justice.

July 28, 1999 Schwarz's lawyers motion for a dismissal, but a new trial is rejected.

August 1999 Volpe tells officials that the second officer in the bathroom when he attacked Louima was Thomas Wiese, not Charles Schwarz, although Louima has always insisted it was the driver of the police car— Schwarz. Volpe says Wiese watched but did not participate in Louima's assault.

December 13, 1999 Volpe is sentenced to 30 years in prison.

February 7, 2000 The trial of Schwarz, Wiese, and Bruder on the grounds of conspiracy to cover up the attack on Louima begins .

March 6, 2000 Schwarz, Wiese, and Bruder are convicted of covering up the attack on Louima.

April 17, 2000 Former police officer Rolando Aleman pleads guilty to making false statements about what he saw on the night Louima was attacked.

June 2000 5: Officer Francisco Rosario's trial begins. He is charged with lying about what he saw inside the 70th Precinct on the night of the attack. **21:** Rosario is found guilty of

making false statements. **27:** Bruder and Wiese are sentenced to five years for conspiring to obstruct justice, and Schwarz to 15 years and 8 months for participating in the attack on Louima and for conspiring to cover it up.

July 2001 12: Louima is awarded the largest settlement by the City of New York in a police brutality case. The city pays him $7.125 million and the Patrolmen's Benevolent Association (PBA) pays $1.625 million. **19:** An affidavit appears containing testimony by "Officer F" that throws doubt on whether Schwarz can be tried. The Second Circuit Court of Appeals orders Judge Nickerson to consider the evidence.

September 5, 2001 Judge Nickerson denies Schwarz's bid to win a new trial, saying Sergeant Walsh's (Officer F's) testimony was inconsistent.

February 28, 2002 Schwarz's conviction is overturned on the basis that he had ineffective counsel and that jurors were exposed to prejudicial information. The appeals court also overturns Wiese and Bruder's convictions on grounds of insufficient evidence.

March–April 2002 Schwarz is indicted on perjury charges for stating that he did not help Justin Volpe torture Abner Louima. He pleads not guilty.

May 15, 2002 Schwarz is to be retried on charges that he assisted in Justin Volpe's torture of Abner Louima. Wiese and Bruder are free to apply for reinstatement to the NYPD and possibly for back pay. Louima's family ask the police not to reinstate them.

June–September 2002 Schwarz is retried. He is sentenced to five years in prison.

Topic 7
DOES COMMUNITY POLICING HELP REDUCE CRIME?

YES
FROM "THE FALSE TRADE-OFF"
SALON.COM, APRIL 27, 1999
MICHAEL CROWLEY

NO
"COPS IN THE 'HOOD"
SALON.COM, JUNE 14, 1999
DEBRA DICKERSON

INTRODUCTION

In the last 20 years or so in the United States there has been a shift toward community policing, away from more "reactive" policing. "Reactive policing" involved law-enforcement officers responding to incidents of crime rather than trying to prevent them. Among the techniques used in community policing are putting higher numbers of police on visible patrol, many on foot or on bicycle; police consultation with local people about problems that may affect their quality of life and may lead to crime; recruiting civilians and other agencies to help tackle problems such as drugs or vandalism; and arresting more small-time offenders. The effectiveness of this method of law enforcement has stirred much debate in the United States. The increased police presence on the streets, harsher punishments for minor crimes, and "stop and searches" have led to accusations of police brutality, racism, and First Amendment offenses.

At the same time, however, advocates of community policing argue that crime rates have fallen in areas where it is in place. But does this type of law enforcement work? Or does it, as critics claim, create more problems than it solves?

The origins of community policing in the United States can be traced to August Vollmer, former police chief in Berkeley, California. In response to rising crime in the Prohibition era of the 1920s Vollmer identified the need to bolster community law enforcement to prevent crime. However, it was only really in the 1980s that theories of modern community policing began to emerge. In 1982, in *The Atlantic Monthly* academics James Wilson and George Kelling wrote about "broken windows" policing, which theorized cracking down on minor offenders to prevent further public disorder and more serious crimes. "Broken windows" policing subsequently became a byword in any discussion of the shift in law-enforcement policy toward community policing.

In his 1994 State of the Union address President Bill Clinton pledged to put 100,000 more police officers on the streets. The Violent Crime Control and Law Enforcement Act (VCCA), further authorized $8.8 billion over six years for grants to beef up police patrols, and Attorney General Janet Reno introduced the Community Oriented Policing Services (COPs) program to build on this initiative.

Supporters credit the policy with reducing crime. In Chicago, for example, police link a 53 percent drop in gun crimes to community policing tactics introduced in 1994.

"The main political problem is how to prevent the police power from becoming tyrannical."

—LUDWIG VON MISES (1871–1973), AUSTRIAN ECONOMIST

However, critics argue that there is no convincing correlation between policing strategies and crime rates. They see such policing as violations of individual freedom and democracy because, they claim, it leads to the police using aggressive techniques that target certain groups. They also claim that the 1994 Three Strikes Law in California, under which offenders receive a mandatory 25 years to life sentence for a third felony, is unfair.

"Broken windows" policing effectively means that a three-times offender can be sent to jail for life for minor offenses. Statistics, however, suggest that crime has fallen in California.

New York is often cited in discussions on community policing. In the mid-1990s the city's police commissioner, William Bratton, endorsed a strategy of arresting small-time offenders and increasing the presence of officers on the streets. Bratton claimed that his methods accounted for a 50 percent drop in crimes such as murder, rape, and robbery between 1990 and 1996.

Opponents, however, point to the high number of complaints against New York's police since the policy was adopted. Some argue that racial tension has increased because minorities feel targeted. The 1996 brutalization of Haitian Abner Louima in police custody and the 1999 shooting of unarmed African Amidou Diallo by police have fueled criticism. In response, Bratton claims that complaints against the police are a fair exchange for safer streets.

In the first article Michael Crowley argues that New York is not a good example of community policing since its strategy is one of intimidation. But Crowley believes that community policing does help reduce crime when officers work alongside the local community. In the second article Debra Dickerson focuses on a different aspect of community policing: programs that encourage police officers to live in the inner-city neighborhoods they patrol. Her article suggests that these programs are likely to fail because many officers do not want to live where they work. She also cites the large number of inner-city residents who resent the idea of having police officers as neighbors.

THE FALSE TRADE-OFF
Michael Crowley

Rudolph (Rudy) W. Giuliani (1944–) became mayor of New York City in 1993. He began a much publicized war on crime. Between 1993 and 1998 the city's crime rate dropped by 40 percent.

On February 4, 1999, Amidou Diallo, a 22-year-old African immigrant was shot dead by four policemen who believed he was about to shoot them. The officers fired 41 shots. They were cleared of the offense. Similarly, Abner Louima, a Haitian immigrant, was arrested outside a New York nightclub. He was physically and sexually assaulted by police officers. See pages 86–87 for more information on his case.

YES

✓ … By now, New York's dilemma is familiar: Under Mayor Rudy Giuliani, the city's crime rate has plunged, with homicides down 70 percent and felonies down by half since 1994. At the same time, police brutality and harassment complaints have risen alarmingly. New York registered about 5,000 complaints about its officers' conduct in 1998, up from about 3,600 in 1993. Racial tension is peaking as minorities feel especially targeted by the department's aggressive tactics —a concern crystallized in such high-profile incidents as the Diallo shooting and the brutal beating of Haitian immigrant Abner Louima last year. To some, the lesson is that stamping out crime means stomping on civil liberties.

A tale of a happier city
Less publicized, however—as good news always is—is a happier story to the north. In Boston, not only has crime dropped even faster than in New York, but complaints about police tactics have fallen as well—by an astonishing 50 percent. Like New York, Boston has adopted new crime-fighting strategies in the 1990s, but there has been no backlash against its police force—no street protests, no cries of racism, no expletives hurled at the mayor. As people try to figure out what New York did wrong, they should look first at what Boston has done right.

Where the New York police have acted like an occupying force in the city's neighborhoods, Boston's police have succeeded through partnerships. Where New York has relied on an aggressive strategy that cultivates fear and intimidation, Boston's police have worked with local clergy and community leaders to identify and target actual criminals, rather than wantonly sweeping neighborhoods. Next to New York's archetypal "NYPD Blue" approach, Boston's strategy might sound wimpy. But don't snicker. President Clinton has called on "communities around the country [to] follow the example of Boston." And New York Sen. Charles Schumer recently proclaimed: "The Boston model will work in New York, and we should move quickly to implement it here." …

New Yorkers may think of Boston as a quaint, provincial New England capital. But a decade ago, the city was an urban nightmare, with drugs, guns and gangs terrorizing residents.… In the late 1980s, according to one Boston police superintendent, "there was a lack of trust, there was no communication" between the police and the neighborhoods. Now the traditional rivals needed one other. The police wanted to shed their reputation for racism, and the clergy wanted to stop the killing. The result was a partnership between the police department and neighborhood leaders that allowed the cops to crack down on minority offenders without being resented in minority neighborhoods.

Working with communities

"That is the approach of neighborhood policing," says Boston Police Commissioner Paul Evans. "It's the idea that the police cannot solve the problems themselves. They have to work with the communities to solve problems."…

Ironically, New York and Boston both owe their 1990s police department overhauls to the same man, William Bratton. It was Bratton who changed the Boston police force's mission by placing an emphasis on selective crime prevention over haphazard response. Bratton left Boston for New York, where he served as that city's acclaimed police chief from 1994 to 1996, before ego clashes with Giuliani forced him out.

Since replacing Bratton in Boston, Evans has become hailed as an innovator in his own right. A modest, low-key product of South Boston, a tightly knit Irish neighborhood, Evans has been less of a publicity hound than Bratton. He has been willing to cede his power, for instance, decentralizing the police force by breaking up the department's five jurisdiction zones into 10 smaller districts, and is quick to share credit for his department's successes.

Like Boston, New York also practices neighborhood (or community) policing, which gets officers out of their patrol cars and onto the streets. But Boston police have given a higher priority to building relationships with neighborhood residents than to the "zero tolerance" crime prevention strategy that prevails in New York. Better known as "broken windows" policing, the strategy is to crack down on small offenses like jaywalking or public drinking, which are often used as an excuse to "stop and frisk" thousands of people in a hunt for guns.

The result is that thousands of innocents are harassed: More than 27,000 New Yorkers, largely minorities, were frisked by the NYPD's street crimes unit last year; only about 4,600 were arrested.

Should a professional law-enforcement body require extra help in solving crime?

When William Bratton was sworn in as New York police chief, he pledged to reduce New York's crime by 10 percent in the first year and 16 percent the year after. He managed to do that using a computer mapping system he helped develop. The system is still used by police in the city.

See Topic 6 Does the "Broken Windows" policy work? pages 74–85.

Do minority rights matter if the majority benefits from reduced crime rates?

In 1989 Carol Stuart, a pregnant white woman, was stabbed to death, according to her husband, by a young black man. His evidence led to a citywide manhunt in which dozens of black males were arrested. The police arrested someone, only to let him go when the real killer—Stuart's husband—was apprehended. The case affected Boston's race relations for some time.

In Boston, the guiding principle has been integration, not intimidation. Ministers, street workers and community leaders have made an explicit compact with the police: They will identify lawbreakers in their neighborhoods and accept decisive police action against those criminals. In return, however, the police refrain from the kind of sweeping and indiscriminate stop-and-frisk tactics that bred such anger during the 1989 Stuart manhunt....

Commissioner Evans cites curfews as an example of this strategy. Although youth curfews are in vogue in troubled cities like Baltimore and New Orleans, Evans says they clash with his department's philosophy. "Instead of those types of enforcement tactics that go across the board and target everyone, we do focused intervention," Evans says. "We put area restrictions and time curfews on young people who earn them instead of every young person in the city."

Nontraditional tactics

Evans has also focused on nontraditional crime-prevention tactics. He recalls a 1994 meeting with officers in his department's gang unit at a moment of rising violence in Boston's low-income Roxbury neighborhood. "I asked them what we could do," Evans says. "And I expected them to say, 'More cops, tougher judges and more jail space.' But what they said to a person was, 'We need jobs and alternatives for these people. We need to provide them with hope.'" The result has been a network of programs for youths and young adults, from business-sponsored summer jobs to "midnight basketball" to whitewater rafting trips.

Is it right that the police should be involved in such funding initiatives?

Evans is particularly proud of his department's new practice of using federal block-grant money—dollars traditionally used for salaries and overtime—to award its own grants to local community groups who submit specific plans for assisting in crime-prevention. (This year the department will give out $1 million to 20 local groups.)

Leroy Stoddard, director of community services for Urban Edge, a Roxbury community development corporation that has received grant money, says the work can be as simple as shooing unwanted loiterers off building stoops and moving illegally parked cars—tasks that are "below the threshold of police attention." As someone who works on the city streets every day, Stoddard can attest to the larger success of Boston's cooperative approach. "It's important to educate people and ready them for police enforcement," he says. "It's better for residents to be aware that the police are coming rather than be surprised by a crackdown."

What does this all amount to? Not just a plunging crime rate—homicides are down from 152 in 1990 to 34 last year, and all violent crimes and robberies are down more than 80 percent since 1990—but also a steady drop in complaints about officer misconduct, by more than 50 percent since 1990.

Arguably, New York was asking for its recent troubles. Police Commissioner Howard Safir has been less enthusiastic about community policing than his predecessor, Bratton. Safir has cut back the number of officers on neighborhood beats, a move criticized by Bratton....

The author wrote this article in 1999. According to the FBI's Uniform Crime Reporting Program annual report, homicide figures for that year in Boston were the lowest in 38 years at 31 murders. This had risen to 68 killings by the end of 2001.

Resisting the community

[T]here is no doubt that under Giuliani, New York police have resisted cooperative efforts with the community. Shortly after the Diallo shooting, according to *New York Times* columnist Bob Herbert, some 100 clergy members met with the Bronx borough president to discuss response strategies. A Bronx official told Herbert, "The one thing everybody at the meeting said was: 'We could be a resource. But they're not using us. The police don't even know us. They don't come and talk to us.'"

Boston's not perfect either, of course. In February, for instance, the city paid $900,000 to settle the case of a black plainclothes police officer who was beaten by colleagues who thought he was a criminal. Some critics say that when complaints are registered, the department doesn't deal decisively with its problem officers. And finally, it's not clear whether acts of harassment and brutality have actually decreased, or whether a more trusting community is less likely to report them. Still, there's a consensus that life on Boston's streets—and the relationship between Boston's police officers and its neighborhood residents—is as good as anyone can remember.

Do you think it is likely that people who are part of a trusting community are less likely to report police harassment and brutality?

"Ten years ago you wouldn't see young kids—five, six, seven years old—out playing, riding bikes, in the parks. The parents wouldn't let them out of the house. There was a lot of fear," says Lt. Gary French, who runs the Boston police's antigang unit. "Now we have a very good relationship with a lot of the inner-city neighborhoods. The community leaders know they can call us if there's a problem." Instead of alienating whole neighborhoods, he says, "we're ticking off the right people." ... Just as it took a pair of watershed tragedies to awaken Boston's police and community leaders to the need to cooperate, perhaps some good can come of the Diallo shooting and the Louima beating....

COPS IN THE 'HOOD
Debra Dickerson

NO

X "OK, this one," the detective says as we pull slowly past a neat clapboard house in a run-down neighborhood. "Vietnamese guy is out watering his bushes. Knucklehead comes up, whips it out, gets to peeing right on them. Vietnamese guy yells at him." The detective narrates calmly, eyes both on the road and on the wary people watching the strangers go by. "Knucklehead goes on up the block home, gives his kid brother $20, $25 to go back down and shoot the guy. Kid rides his bike down, shoots at the Vietnamese guy but hits his brother sitting on the porch. Dead. The first guy, the guy ain't shot, runs in the house, gets his gun, shoots kid brother in the back of the head as he rides off on the bike."

My driver almost displays anger. Almost. "They actually tried him. The Vietnamese guy." He allows himself a little disgusted snort of a laugh.

I crane my neck to keep the house where something so awful happened in view as long as possible.

"But he was acquitted, right? The Vietnamese guy?"

"Yes! but ... Yeah. He got off. OK, this one." He might have been giving me the baseball scores. "Old guy. Lived here forever. Knucklehead grandson's a doper. Goes to jail. He gives evidence on some more knuckleheads. They decide to rob his house. Now, he's in jail, don't even live there no more, but the grandfather's there, so once they get into the house...." I listen and find myself wondering what size chalk outline a wizened old man leaves, and what it's like to hear gunshots in the night.

The Officer Home Loan Program

Never let a homicide detective show you around his city. You don't see neighborhoods; you see crime scenes. You don't see residents; you see witnesses who refuse to come forward and knuckleheads who the cops know, but can't prove, have literally gotten away with murder. So where does a cop live? What's his take on his neighbors? Is he supposed to mediate disputes on his own time? What's his duty when the guy in 4B lights up a blunt at a neighborhood barbecue? Do they make neighborhoods better? Safer? Or do they invite retribution? Should they live in the cities they patrol?

New York's police brutality problem has focused attention on getting more cops to live in the neighborhoods they patrol. There have been many such efforts. Since 1997, the Department of Housing and Urban Development's [HUD] Officer Next Door Program has made 2,511 police officers urban homeowners, with 50 percent discounts on foreclosed homes and $100 down payments. The catch is that they have to stay at least three years and the homes have to be in "designated revitalization areas"—aka the 'hood. Working with private lenders, the program so far includes 36 states and the District of Columbia....

> Why do you think private lenders are eager to encourage police officers to settle in inner-city neighborhoods?

Here in Charlotte, the Officer Home Loan Program takes the same approach. Law enforcement officers willing to live in areas designated "threatened" or "fragile" receive interest-free loans of $10,000 to $15,000, which are forgiven entirely after five years. So far, four Charlotte officers have taken advantage of the year-old program.

I wonder what my homicide guide thinks of Charlotte's program.

"Would you live here if you could get a low—"

"No."

"Not even with a fif—"

"No. I live way out where its almost rural. I have a wife, a daughter. No. I go to the mall and run into bad guys I've dealt with. I don't need them down the block, too."

But these programs didn't exist when my guide was a younger, struggling and maybe less world-weary rookie officer. For some of them, home-ownership help could make a difference....On the other hand, Memphis and Tulsa's programs, according to press reports, have few takers. "[The success of the programs] all depends on local conditions," says Lemar Wooley of HUD.

Officers living next door to criminals

And when policemen live so close to crime, what do they see? One officer in South Carolina moved into a home he'd once raided. He found bullet holes in the walls and the previous tenants' (who were crack dealers) drug-hiding places. A D.C. cop coming home from his morning workout recognized a loiterer in his stairwell as a man he had a case pending against. A records check revealed him to also be a Virginia fugitive; the cop made an arrest on his own front door step. The same officer also seized drugs from a neighbor who pleaded guilty and was never seen again. His neighbors may be safer, but is this officer? What if a previous arrestee recognizes some grocery-toting off-duty cop first?

> If the police and their families are potentially in danger, is it worth the risk? Do you think that law-enforcement officers have a duty to reduce crime at any cost?

I wondered what residents might think about having cops as neighbors, so I wandered around some "fragile" and "threatened" neighborhoods in Charlotte without my police escort—as their families, and the locals, have to do. "There go the neighborhood!" crowed one man, perched on an upturned crate, when I asked about having cops live in the 'hood. "There it go!" He laughed so hard at his own wit he coughed and sputtered.

"But seriously, would you or wouldn't you like to have cops here? Do you think they'd hassle you or help you? You know, community policing?" But he just kept braying at his joke.

The unsmiling man next to him cut in. "Ain't no cop coming here." Whether a prediction or a promise, I couldn't tell.

Women snatched up their children and retreated from their porches as I approached, preferring their un-air-conditioned houses (I could see fans whirring inside) to a stranger with a pad and pencil bearing down on them. But I know from reporting on gangs that the presence of cops and cop cars after a shooting makes the innocent feel safe; it's the one time when women, children and old people in bad neighborhoods can claim their sidewalks and playgrounds. Even if they have to share them with an ambulance or a corpse, they feel safer. Sure, the women distrust me and back off as I approach, but they might feel differently about an officer who was a homey.

Police forces that reflect their communities

New York's mayor and police chief think so. Or maybe they just hope so. In any event, only 54 percent of New York's beleaguered police force lives in the city, according to the *New York Times*. Less than half of the white officers do, while 78 percent of both black and Asian officers and 73 percent of Hispanics do. So, increasing the percentage of city-dwelling cops would probably also help to diversify a police force that is currently 67 percent white. Though they oppose mandatory city residency for cops, Mayor Rudy Giuliani and Commissioner Howard Safir are trying to increase the number of city residents on the force—through intensive recruiting and exam preferences—in the wake of the Amadou Diallo killing and the Abner Louima brutality case. "Certainly the Diallo shooting raised our consciousness," Safir told the *Times*. "As we recruit more city residents, the department will more adequately reflect the city." But will that mean greater stability for distressed neighborhoods?

Columbia, S.C., claims a 16 percent decrease in crime in neighborhoods where police officers came to live and that

The author acknowledges that more community policing makes certain sectors of the public feel safer. But in the previous paragraph she quotes other people who do not want a greater police presence. Some people find community policing intrusive and a denial of their liberties. Does her evidence make sense?

See the timeline on Abner Louima on pages 86–87 for further information on this case.

houses nearby that had languished on the market for years sold. Officers report being consulted by neighbors to settle disputes and to give home safety demonstrations. They spearhead neighborhood watch groups and shepherd locals through regulatory agencies to get their properties up to code.

"A cheap solution based on stereotypes"

Not everyone is impressed though. The Justice Department's Gil Kerlikowske told the *Times*, "There's nothing that I know of that supports the idea that a police officer living in the city vs. living outside the city provides better service, is more caring." "It's a cheap solution that's based on stereotypes," Samuel Walker of the University of Nebraska said in the same article. A Charlotte patrolman I approached at random put it rather more bluntly, "I'm tired of all of it when I get home," she said. "I don't want to deal with anybody's problems but my own. I'm not a priest."

My guide to homicide in Charlotte also shows me some "nice," neither fragile nor threatened, areas where senseless violence has also taken place. He talks freely about violent crime and the criminal mind as we drive. But he says little about my attempts to "put crime in its sociological context," though he occasionally chuckles without malice at what I say. One of the times he chuckles is when I talk about how much lower murder rates are now. "Can't tell it by Charlotte," he quips. There had been two murders in Charlotte the night before. "Whoo," he says. "That was a 30 hour shift for somebody. Glad it wasn't me."

He drops me off at the Criminal Courts Building and I'm nearly inside when I hear tires screech. He's hanging out his window. "Be careful. Lots of bad guys in there." He's not laughing. He's not scowling. All I know for sure is, this is one cop who won't be moving to the 'hood any time soon.

> Do you think that initiatives such as the Officer Home Loan Program make too great a demand on police officers? Or do you think that officers have a responsibility to "deal with ... problems" at all times?

> The author's "guide" feels that "senseless violence" can occur anywhere. Do you believe it is important for the police to focus their attention on neighborhoods where crimes are most likely to occur?

Summary

The question of whether community policing works in the United States has caused much heated debate. Michael Crowley looks at the situation in New York, where he claims that increases in both the numbers of complaints against the police and racial tension have been attributed to aggressive policing tactics in the name of community policing. Crowley compares the situation to Boston, where the police have worked with local churches and community leaders to crack down on crime. Crowley asserts that New York's approach to community policing was flawed, but that Boston shows that the concept itself works. Crime has fallen in the city, and the relationship between the police and the local community is the best in living memory.

Debra Dickerson's article has a more gloomy assessment of the relationship between police officers and local residents. She focuses on the Department of Housing and Urban Development's Officer Home Loan Program to encourage police officers to live in the inner-city neighborhoods they patrol. Dickerson acknowledges that a greater police presence in "bad neighborhoods" can make some people—particularly women and the elderly—feel more secure. However, she cites other residents who do not want police officers for neighbors, as well as a number of officers who do not want to be surrounded by the problems of their jobs when they go home. Consequently, Dickerson's article suggests that this aspect of community policing does not work.

FURTHER INFORMATION:

Books:

Kleining, John, *The Ethics of Policing*. New York: Cambridge University Press, 1996.

Nelson, Jill (editor), *Police Brutality*. New York: W. W. Norton, 2001.

Useful websites:

http://www.communitypolicing.org/about3.html
Lists articles and other useful information on community policing.
http://www.ojp.usdoj.gov/bjs/
The Bureau of Justice Statistics site contains information on crime rates in the United States.
http://www.thesmokinggun.com/torture/torture.shtml
Lists primary source material surrounding the Abner Louima case, including original police reports.
http://www.usdoj.gov/cops/
The Community Oriented Policing Services (COPS) site.
http://www.villagevoice.com/issues/0010/serpico.php
Article on Amidou Diallo on the *Village Voice* site.

The following debates in the Pro/Con series may also be of interest:

In this volume:

Topic 1 Is the criminal justice system racist?

Topic 3 Is the three strikes law a deterrent?

Part 2: Law and society, pages 60–61.

Topic 6 Does the "Broken Windows" policy work?

Abner Louima, pages 86–87.

DOES COMMUNITY POLICING HELP REDUCE CRIME?

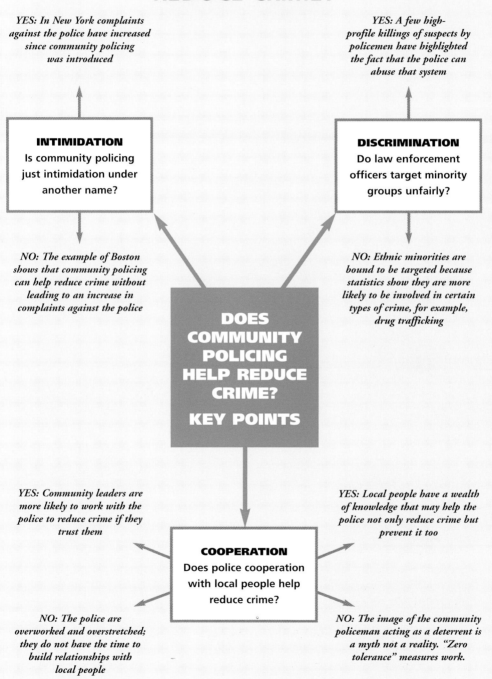

YES: In New York complaints against the police have increased since community policing was introduced

YES: A few high-profile killings of suspects by policemen have highlighted the fact that the police can abuse that system

INTIMIDATION
Is community policing just intimidation under another name?

DISCRIMINATION
Do law enforcement officers target minority groups unfairly?

NO: The example of Boston shows that community policing can help reduce crime without leading to an increase in complaints against the police

NO: Ethnic minorities are bound to be targeted because statistics show they are more likely to be involved in certain types of crime, for example, drug trafficking

DOES COMMUNITY POLICING HELP REDUCE CRIME?

KEY POINTS

YES: Community leaders are more likely to work with the police to reduce crime if they trust them

YES: Local people have a wealth of knowledge that may help the police not only reduce crime but prevent it too

COOPERATION
Does police cooperation with local people help reduce crime?

NO: The police are overworked and overstretched; they do not have the time to build relationships with local people

NO: The image of the community policeman acting as a deterrent is a myth not a reality. "Zero tolerance" measures work.

Topic 8
SHOULD JUVENILE OFFENDERS EVER BE TRIED AS ADULTS?

YES
"JUVENILE JUSTICE: SHAWN"
HTTP://WWW.PBS.ORG/WGBH/PAGES/FRONTLINE/SHOWS/JUVENILE/FOUR/SHAWN.HTML
PBS ONLINE

NO
"TESTIMONY SUBMITTED TO THE HOUSE JUDICIARY SUBCOMMITTEE ON CRIME FOR
THE HEARING ON PUTTING CONSEQUENCES BACK INTO JUVENILE JUSTICE AT THE
FEDERAL, STATE, AND LOCAL LEVELS"
MARCH 10–11, 1999
CHILD WELFARE LEAGUE OF AMERICA

INTRODUCTION

This topic examines whether juvenile offenders should ever be prosecuted as adults. Advocates of a separate juvenile system of prosecution quote grim statistics: Children in adult institutions are 500 percent more likely to be sexually assaulted than juveniles confined within a juvenile facility, 200 percent more likely to be beaten by staff, and 50 percent more likely to be attacked with a weapon. Critics of the existing system quote rising crime statistics, with increasing incidents of violent or sexually related crime among juvenile offenders. But when does a child attain the responsibilities of an adult? Although the question arises frequently in the case of under-age drinking or the age of consent, it is seldom discussed more heatedly than over the issue of juvenile crime.

Until the 19th century children as young as seven could be prosecuted in the criminal courts. It was only in 1825 that any distinction was made between adult criminals and juvenile offenders, when the New York House of Refuge, established under the auspices of the Society for the Prevention of Juvenile Delinquency, became the first U.S. institution designed specifically for juvenile felony offenders and advocated rehabilitation rather than punishment. Other states followed suit. The first juvenile court, based primariliy on the British legal system, was established in Cook County, Illinois, in 1899. It became the responsibility of the state both to protect public interest and to consider the interests of the children themselves. Judges acted in a parental role, and strict confidentiality was observed to protect the minor's interests. By 1925 there were juvenile courts in 48 states. However, as juvenile crime increased, influenced by such factors as the rise in unemployment, immigration, street gangs, consumerism, and the growing divide between rich and poor, people began to question the effectiveness of the juvenile justice system.

During the 1960s the juvenile justice system came under further attack from civil libertarians concerned that it was being used merely to confine juveniles rather than rehabilitate them. After a series of rulings during the 1960s and 1970s the Supreme Court agreed, maintaining that there was evidence that young offenders were receiving the worst of both worlds; Justice Abe Fortas in *Kent v. United States* summed up the system as "neither [providing] the protections accorded to adults nor the solicitous care and regenerative treatment postulated for children."

"Juveniles transferred into adult criminal court have a significantly higher rearrest rate and commit more serious crimes than those retained in the juvenile justice system."

—AMERICAN CIVIL LIBERTIES UNION (ACLU) OF FLORIDA

As the media focused on the rising rate of violent crime, people began to call for tougher measures on youths involved in crime. In 1995 a Gallup poll found that 72 percent of Americans advocated the death penalty for juveniles who commit murder, as opposed to only 24 percent in 1957.

Between 1992 and 1997, 44 states and the District of Columbia passed laws making it easier to try juveniles within the adult system. Vermont and Kansas also introduced legislation to make it possible to try children as young as 10 years old in adult criminal courts. A Justice Department report showed that the criminals under the age of 18 sent to adult prisons more than doubled between 1985 and 1997. By that date every state carried at least one provision allowing juvenile defendants to be tried in adult courts. Recent studies suggest, however, that adopting a tougher stance has little effect on reducing juvenile crime. A 1996 Florida study found that young people transferred to adult prisons had roughly a 30 percent higher rate of backsliding than those who remained within the juvenile system. The effects of New York's 1978 Juvenile Offender Law, which lowered the age of criminal court jurisdiction to 13 for murder and 14 for rape, robbery, and other crimes of violence, was also evaluated and found to be ineffective in reducing levels of serious juvenile crime. Yet justice authorities face a dilemma when dealing with offenders such as 17-year-old Tyrone Beane, for example. One of the prosecutors in this 2002 case said that it showed the failure of Maryland's juvenile justice system. Described by Maryland's police department in January 2002 as their most-wanted fugitive, Beane had a serious history of drug and assault charges. Critics of the juvenile system blamed it for being ineffectual in monitoring his movements and for failing to report violent behavior, including a claim by police that he had killed a man in Baltimore.

The following two articles discuss the pros and cons of this issue.

JUVENILE JUSTICE: SHAWN
PBS online

The first sentence of the article is a grim account of a crime. This is an effective opening, since it grabs the reader's attention immediately.

✓ On Christmas night 1998, in the affluent neighborhood of Los Altos, California, 16-year-old Shawn attacked his sleeping father, stabbing him repeatedly in the arms, head and neck with a knife. The reason for the attack remains unclear. Though there had been tension in the family over Shawn's marijuana use and expulsion from school, his family says that his relationship with his father had not been a violent one.

Shawn himself claims to have no memory of stabbing his father. His mother describes waking up to her husband screaming; his father remembers being unable to identify his attacker at first, then realizing it was his son and eventually tackling him to the ground. Police and medical help arrived, and both were taken to the hospital. Shawn didn't realize what had happened, he says, until a police officer approached him at the hospital: "The cop … said, 'You're gonna get charged with attempted murder, and if he dies, you're gonna get charged with first degree murder.' I said, 'If who dies?' He said, 'Your dad.' And it was then that I knew."

Juvenile vs. adult criminal systems
Shawn was charged with attempted murder. Prosecutors filed fitness papers to try Shawn in adult criminal court rather than in the juvenile system. If convicted in adult court of attempted murder, Shawn would have faced a mandatory sentence of 15 years to life.

After much discussion with his parents, Shawn decided to plead guilty to the charges and receive his punishment from the juvenile system, rather than risk the substantial prison sentence. By staying in the juvenile system, he avoided an adult criminal record, and would get a shorter sentence since the juvenile system could only hold him until he was 25.

Factors leading to the crime

The article implies that drinking alcohol leads to marijuana use. Do you think this is a fair assessment to make?

Prior to this incident, there had been signs that Shawn was troubled. He had been arrested and charged with strong-arm robbery when he and a friend stole money from a smaller boy. Shawn says his drinking had escalated into serious marijuana use, and he was asked to leave two schools. At the juvenile court dispositional hearing which would determine

COMMENTARY: Historical trends of juvenile vs. adult criminal justice systems

Debate about whether juveniles should be tried through a separate juvenile justice system or through the adult justice system has been raging for two centuries, when the first psychologists and sociologists of the 19th century began to recognize adolescence as a distinct developmental stage of life with different characteristics and needs from those of adulthood.

Child savers

The first juvenile justice reformers, known as "child savers," believed that juvenile crime was the result of a lack of moral education and that the best way to treat the problem was to set up separate juvenile institutions to teach such unfortunates the moral standards that would keep them away from a life of crime. By the turn of the century juvenile courts began to spring up under the British legal doctrine of *parens patriae* (Latin for "the state as parent"), in which the state acted as the guardian of the juvenile offender's interests, instead of acting as the offender's prosecutor, as it did in adult courts. The judge played a paternal role in which the goal was the juvenile's rehabilitation into society.

Juvenile institutions under attack

In the 1960s and 1970s the juvenile justice system came under attack from critics who believed that it was not only failing to rehabilitate juveniles, but that there was little difference between juvenile and adult institutions and that juvenile offenders lacked even the most basic protections afforded to adult criminals. By the 1970s legislation was introduced to address these problems. The Juvenile Justice and Delinquency Prevention Act of 1972 required that juvenile criminals be separated from adult criminals and offered state grants for community-based programs that introduced group homes and halfway houses as an alternative to conventional juvenile institutions. Yet this approach was shortlived as juvenile crime rates began to soar, and a tougher approach to crime became the order of the day.

The return of juveniles to the adult justice system

Since the mid-1970s most states have passed laws allowing juveniles to be tried in adult courts and reducing confidentiality, originally intended to protect juveniles from being stigmatized by their crimes. The judge's role as guardian has greatly diminished, while the prosecutor's role has increased. Many states have introduced mandatory minimum sentencing for juveniles, as well as mandatory waivers and statutory exclusions that force juveniles who have reached a certain age and committed a serious crime to be automatically transferred to adult courts. Some people have even begun to question whether there is any need for a juvenile justice system at all.

FRONTLINE is a public-affairs series broadcast on PBS (Public Broadcasting Service) since 1983. It is the longest-running documentary series of its kind.

his sentence, it became clear that there were serious problems in the household which had contributed to Shawn's drug use and troubled behavior. His mother had a drinking problem. Shawn told FRONTLINE that it was she who had introduced him to drinking at an early age. His father was often away on business trips, leaving Shawn and his mother alone.

Evaluating the behavior of the accused

In an effort to understand Shawn's behavior, the court ordered a psychological evaluation. The report found no significant psychiatric disturbances, but instead it proposed that the attack stemmed from "an altered state of consciousness" coming from "a disturbance of sleep." Based on this report, Shawn's public defender Bridgett Jones prepared a stunning new argument in his defense: he was sleep walking when he attacked his father, and therefore did not intend to do it.

Do you think that had the report found significant psychiatric disturbances, it should have influenced whether the case would be tried through the juvenile system?

At the hearing, attorneys for each side presented sleep research experts. Dr. Rafael Pelayo, of Stanford University's sleep clinic, agreed that "parasomnia" was a plausible explanation for Shawn's behavior. In his interview with FRONTLINE, he noted that family dysfunction often plays a role in parasomnia in children. The prosecution's expert disagreed, saying that parasomnia was not a likely explanation for the attack.

Since Shawn's case was so unusual and the testimony in such conflict, Judge Thomas Edwards postponed his determination of Shawn's sentence and sent him for a 90-day evaluation at the California Youth Authority, the state's most restrictive juvenile detention facility. During his first week there, Shawn says he was pressured by a white gang member to force his cellmate to perform oral sex. He says he didn't want to do it, but complied because he was frightened for his own safety.

Shawn suffered sexual abuse even in the state's most restrictive juvenile detention facility. Do you think his experience would have been different in an adult prison?

A surprise verdict

When Shawn returned, Judge Edwards handed down a sentence that surprised some people in court. After the incident with his cellmate, it seemed likely that Shawn would receive at least some time in the California Youth Authority. However, Judge Edwards ruled that Shawn remain in the Santa Clara County's Juvenile Hall until he turns 19. In addition, Shawn would be allowed to leave the facility during the day to attend community college classes, private counseling sessions, and Narcotics Anonymous meetings.

Eventually he was even allowed to go home for meals with his family.

The prosecutor was surprised, and troubled, by the outcome. He said, "At the end, I think everyone in that courtroom was ready to fall out of their chairs. And I think that it was a tremendous injustice that was done in this case. Not just the fact that we didn't treat this individual the way that he should have been treated—in my opinion—but that we have created the perception in the community that certain people are going to be treated differently in the system, because of where they come from."

Inequity in the juvenile justice system

He is not the only one. Many of the kids serving time in Juvenile Hall think Shawn got a break, and that had he not been white and from an affluent neighborhood, he would have received a much harsher sentence. Even his attorney Bridgett Jones says that this case reminds her: "There is inequity in the juvenile justice system . . . . There is inequity in terms of race, there is inequity in terms of socioeconomic status. . . . You know it and you see it, but to actually have a case like this, it really brings it to the forefront."

Whether Shawn will take advantage of the break he has been given remains to be seen. At the end of October he got into trouble again—he smoked pot. When he thought his probation officer knew and had proof, he took off. When he was arrested four hours away in another town, he was high and belligerent, and officers had to use force to restrain him. In February Judge Edwards is due to sentence him for the probation violation. He can send him to the California Youth Authority, or sentence him to additional time in a local facility.

A study of juvenile offenders by the Justice Institute in California in 2000 found that compared to white youths, minority youths are 2.8 times more likely to be arrested for a violent crime, 6.2 times more likely to appear in adult court, and 7 times more likely to be sent to adult prison.

To find out what happened, go to www.google.com.

TESTIMONY SUBMITTED TO THE HOUSE JUDICIARY SUBCOMMITTEE ON CRIME ...
Child Welfare League of America

The Child Welfare League of America begins its article by introducing its credentials. This can be an effective method of persuading the reader that the views and information that follow are from a reputable source.

For more statistics on juvenile crime see the Commentary box on page 108 of this article.

For more information on The Juvenile Justice and Deliquency Prevention Act (JJDPA) see www. cdfactioncouncil. org/jjdpa_act.htm.

NO

The Child Welfare League of America is a membership association of over 1,000 public and private, non-profit agencies throughout the country. Our member agencies serve some three million children, youth, and families every year, many of whom confront significant challenges including adjudication, incarceration or other involvement with the justice system.

Recent crime trends
As Congress considers juvenile justice legislation again this year, CWLA urges close scrutiny of the issues raised in recent proposals, especially in light of recent crime trends and increasing information about the value of prevention and early intervention. The most recent crime data highlighted that in 1997, for the third year in a row, the total number of juvenile arrests for Violent Crime Index offenses—murder, forcible rape, robbery, and aggravated assault—declined. Evidence also continues to mount that early intervention and treatment can be successful and cost-effective in preventing and reducing crime.

Early intervention and prevention treatment
We firmly support early intervention and treatment as the best juvenile crime prevention policy. Too many children grow up without adequate family and community support or the opportunity to build productive futures. We need to create a multifaceted response to youth violence that begins by restoring hope for the youngest children in the most troubled families and communities. At the same time, we need more thoughtful responses to address the problems of juvenile offenders who have records of serious violence.

The JJDPA
The Juvenile Justice and Delinquency Prevention Act (JJDPA) provides federal leadership in juvenile justice, encouraging community-based alternatives to incarceration and requiring states to deinstitutionalize status offenders and nonoffenders

and remove youths from adult jails and lockups. The law is based on the premise that a separate system of courts and intervention services is needed to serve the vast majority of delinquent youths.

Incarceration vs. rehabilitation

One major problem with the juvenile justice system is that it incarcerates youths who would have been better served by community-based rehabilitative services. Most youths sent to correctional facilities should not be there.

A U.S. Department of Justice analysis of 28 state corrections systems found that less than 14 percent of the youths committed to these facilities were detained for serious or violent crimes. More than half of those in the facilities were serving time for property or drug crimes and were experiencing their first commitment to a state institution. Another study found that an average of 31 percent of juveniles housed in state facilities could be placed in less secure settings and at much less cost to taxpayers based on objective public safety risk factors.

Do you think that drug and property-based crimes could be more adequately dealt with through community-based rehabilitation services rather than correctional facilities?

Providing alternatives

We should invest in proven and promising strategies for intervention and the rehabilitation of young people in the juvenile justice system. We should expand programs that help at-risk and disadvantaged youths succeed and reduce the chance that they will be involved in violence. Such activities for at-risk and disadvantaged youths include gang diversion; specialized Job Corps, job placement, employment and vocational training, and national and community service; substance abuse prevention and treatment programs; special education; specialized family foster care; day treatment; mentoring; family dispute resolution; and after-school, weekend, and evening youth programs with academic, vocational, athletic, and arts exploration to provide supervised learning opportunities for young people. These kinds of programs offer life-enhancing alternatives to criminal activity.

Job Corps is the largest residential education and job-training program in the United States for at-risk and disadvantaged young people between the ages of 16 and 24. It was established in 1964.

Juvenile protection strategies

In addition to increasing support for sound prevention strategies, the four core requirements in the Juvenile Justice Delinquency Prevention Act provide critical protections for youths in custody and must be retained in any new legislation. The following are of immediate concern in the current debate.

COMMENTARY: Statistics on juvenile justice

Juveniles in the adult justice system

• 44 states and the District of Columia passed laws between 1992 and 1998 enabling juveniles to be transferred to the adult justice system.

• Vermont and Kansas have passed statutory provisions to try children as young as 10 in adult criminal courts.

• In 1994, 11,700 juvenile cases were transferred to adult courts. By 1997 only 8,400 juvenile cases were transferred.

• A 1996 Florida study found that juveniles transferred to adult prisons were 30 percent more likely to backslide into a life of crime than juveniles who remained in the juvenile justice system.

• A 1996 Texas study found that juveniles sentenced in adult courts received longer sentences than those tried in juvenile courts but only served an average of 27 percent of their sentences.

• A 1996 Columbia University study showed that 76 percent of juveniles prosecuted for robbery in adult courts were reoffenders, compared to 67 percent of juveniles processed in juvenile courts.

• In 1997, 26 percent of juveniles sentenced to more than one year in state prison were between 13 and 16 years old.

• In 1985, 3,400 offenders under the age of 18 were sent to adult prisons. By 1997 this figure had more than doubled to 7,400.

Juvenile crime figures

• In 1999 juveniles accounted for 16 percent of violent crime arrests, 31 percent of larceny theft arrests, 32 percent of property crime arrests, 33 percent of burglary arrests, 42 percent of vandalism arrests, and 54 percent of arson arrests.

• Less than half of serious juvenile violent crime is reported to law enforcers.

• Juvenile violent crime fell 30 percent from 1994 to 1998. In 1999 juvenile violent crime reached its lowest level since 1987—339 out of the 100,000 arrests were of juveniles. This shows a 36 percent drop from 1994, the peak year for juvenile arrests.

- "Sight and sound separation" requires that juveniles may not have (regular) contact with adult offenders. We must not allow "incidental" contact between children and adult inmates, which in many jails will mean that children will be walked down hallways past adult cells and thereby subjected to verbal abuse.
- "Disproportionate confinement of minority youth" requires that states determine the existence and extent of the problem in their state and demonstrate efforts to reduce it where it exists. In virtually every state, minority youth are over-represented at every stage of the juvenile justice system, particularly in secure confinement. Current law directs states generally to "address" this issue, without requiring release of juveniles or incarceration quotas or any other specific change of policy or practice. Deleting all reference to "minority" or "race" and instead referring to "segments of the juvenile population" minimizes an important issue, is offensive to many, and hinders efforts to remedy the disparate treatment of minority youth.

> *In what ways do you think that a state can address the issue of a disproportionate confinement of minority youth?*

Careful judicial evaluation

We urge the committee to ensure that young people in the juvenile justice system are afforded the rights and protection they are due. Young people, with few exceptions, should be treated as juveniles rather than as adults in the justice system. Careful judicial evaluation should precede each decision about whether a juvenile offender is placed in a locked facility, a community-based program, or a residential program.

Prosecutors should not be the sole decision-makers in determining whether to prosecute juveniles 16 and over as adults. It is our firm belief that judges can best determine whether adult court is appropriate. It is essential that judges maintain this function in juvenile cases.

> *Why do you think that the CWLA believes it is essential that judges be the ones to determine whether adult court is appropriate for a juvenile offender?*

We urge you to support these recommendations and to work with your colleagues to make sure there is needed reform in the juvenile justice system that focuses on prevention and maintains the core protections for youths in trouble.

Summary

In what is seen as a return to the values of the mid-1800s, an increasing number of states throughout America are calling for young felony offenders to be tried in adult courts. But is this the way to reduce juvenile crime rates?

Illustrating the case for the adult courts, the first article quotes the case of Shawn, a 16-year-old from an affluent, middle-class neighborhood in California who, for no explicable reason, attacked his sleeping father. It claims that despite a history of family problems, drinking, and marijuana use, the youngster escaped trial within the adult court system (with its mandatory sentence of 15 years to life on conviction) because he was white and middle-class. Even his attorney claimed that within the juvenile justice system there was inequity in terms of race and socioeconomic status. This is seen as a weakness of the juvenile court system.

In the second article the Child Welfare League of America makes a case against trying juvenile offenders as adults—"with few exceptions." It encourages an examination of recent crime trends and supports early intervention and treatment of young offenders, particularly those from disadvantaged and minority communities, as a successful and cost-effective way of reducing crime. It suggests that rehabilitation should also be carried out within the community itself, since too many youngsters, especially from minority backgrounds, are institutionalized for first offenses or nonviolent crimes. Learning and leisure facilities—such as job placement, vocational, arts, and athletic training—together with specialized family foster care, day treatment, and family dispute resolution should provide life-enhancing alternatives to a life of crime or custodial sentences. The CWLA acknowledges that it is sometimes necessary to try juveniles as adults, but it believes that strict and extensive procedures must be established first.

FURTHER INFORMATION:

 Books:

Ashford, Jose B., et al (eds.), *Treating Adult and Juvenile Offenders with Special Needs.* Washington, D.C.: American Psychological Association, 2001.

 Useful websites:

www.cjcj.org

Website of the Center on Juvenile and Criminal Justice.

www.fas.pps.k12.or.us/gilkeystudents.libtech/jokvrh/whoarejuvenileoffenders.htm

Articles about juvenile offenders and juvenile crime.

www.heritage.org/library/categories/crimelaw/bg1097.html

Heritage Organization article "How State and Local Officials Can Combat Violent Juvenile Crime."

The following debates in the Pro/Con series may also be of interest:

In this volume:

 Topic 9 Should juveniles be sentenced to death?

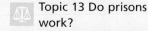 Topic 13 Do prisons work?

Topic 14 Do prisoners have rights?

SHOULD JUVENILE OFFENDERS EVER BE TRIED AS ADULTS?

YES: Juveniles have different needs than adults that deserve to be addressed by a separate system. They are also easy prey to adults in prisons and should be protected from them.

YES: Juveniles who commit rape and murder need to be punished severely to reflect the seriousness of their crimes

SEPARATE SYSTEMS
Do we need a separate juvenile justice system?

SERIOUS CRIMES
Should juveniles who commit very serious crimes be tried as adults?

NO: There is no longer much difference between the juvenile and the adult systems, and it would be more efficient and cost-effective to make it one system

NO: The focus should be on the juvenile's age and different invidual needs, not on the type of crime that they have committed

SHOULD JUVENILE OFFENDERS EVER BE TRIED AS ADULTS?

KEY POINTS

YES: Juveniles must learn to take responsibility for their actions and that bad behavior will be met with appropriate punishment

YES: Their attitudes and morals have not yet reached maturity, and they are more open to change

RESPONSIBILITY
Should juveniles be held responsible for their crimes on the same level as adults?

REHABILITATION
Should we seek to rehabilitate young offenders rather than punish them?

NO: Juveniles are in the process of developing and cannot be expected to have the same maturity and capacity for judgment as adults

NO: The crime is the same no matter what age the criminal is who commits it, and the offender should be punished according to the crime

SHOOTINGS IN U.S. SCHOOLS, 1996–2001

"Violence has become increasingly prominent ... in the United States, which has the highest youth homicide and suicide rates among 26 wealthiest nations in the world and one of the highest rates of homicide worldwide."

—AMERICAN ACADEMY OF PEDIATRICS, 1999

During the 1990s many people became concerned about the amount of juvenile crime in the United States. Several violent shootings in schools around the country have resulted in heated debate about the causes of and solutions to juvenile crime. As communities struggle to deal with the aftermath of these devastating events, increasing numbers of people are asking what drives young people to commit such terrible crimes. Does the fault lie with society as a whole? Do the media bear some responsibility? Should the parents of killers take the blame? Or are some people just innately evil? The following is a timeline of some of the shootings that took place between 1996 and 2001.

February 2, 1996 Barry Loukaitis (14) opens fire on his algebra class in Moses Lake, Washington. He kills one teacher and two students. His lawyers later claim that he was influenced by a video for the Pearl Jam song "Jeremy," in which shots of band member Eddie Vedder are interspersed with images of a boy leaving his classmates with their clothes splattered in red. Loukaitis's mother also reveals that she told her son about her dreams of killing herself in front of her estranged husband and his girlfriend. Loukaitis is convicted of two counts of aggravated first degree murder and sentenced to two mandatory life terms without parole.

February 19, 1997 Evan Ramsey (16) kills two people and wounds two others in Bethel, Alaska. Ramsey's homelife was difficult: His mother was an alcoholic, and Evan and his

brothers were brought up in a series of care homes, where he was sexually abused; his father was also involved in a similar violent incident in 1986. However, other people testify at his trial that Evan has always been an outsider who preferred playing the violent video game *Doom* to mixing with his peers. Evan Ramsey is sentenced to 200 years in prison. He says, "There will be other people that will commit other offenses and I'll be considered yesterday's news."

October 1, 1997 Luke Woodham (16) kills two students, including his ex-girlfriend, and wounds seven more in Pearl, Mississippi. He and his friends are reported to worship Satan. His lawyers plead that he was temporarily insane when he carried out the crimes. He is sentenced to two consecutive life sentences for the murder convictions and seven 20-year sentences for the aggravated assault convictions. He is also sentenced separately to life imprisonment for the murder of his mother, who was killed a few hours before the school shootings.

December 1, 1997 Michael Carneal (14) opens fire on the crowded lobby of Heath High School in West Paducah, Kentucky. He kills three girls. Carneal, the son of a prominent attorney, says the *Basketball Diaries*, a movie in which actor Leonardo DiCaprio fantasizes about carrying out a similar shooting spree, influenced his plan. Carneal is given a life sentence, with no chance of parole for 25 years.

March 24, 1998 Mitchell Johnson (13) and Andrew Golden (11) set off the fire alarm at their school in Jonesboro, Arkansas. They shoot and kill four students and one teacher and wound 10 others. Less than a month later *Time* magazine runs a picture of Golden as a toddler dressed in camouflage gear and clutching a high-powered rifle. Among the theories explaining the boys' behavior are the U.S. gun laws, the fact both boys watched "violent" films, such as *Terminator*, and Johnson's extreme reaction to being jilted by a girlfriend. Both boys are sentenced to life imprisonment.

May 21, 1998 Kipland Kinkel (15) is expelled from school in Springfield, Oregon, for carrying a gun to class. He returns with a semiautomatic rifle and goes to the cafeteria, where he starts shooting. He kills two students and wounds seven others. Police officers later discover that he has killed both of his parents and booby-trapped their house with five homemade bombs— one placed beneath his mother's corpse. Kinkel's mother took him to a therapist, concerned about his unhealthy fascination with guns. Kinkel's father bought him a gun during the same period. Kinkel is sentenced to 111 years in prison.

April 20, 1999 Eric Harris (18) and Dylan Klebold (17) kill 13 students and one teacher, and wound 23 others, before killing themselves at Columbine High School in Littleton, Colorado. The boys also booby-trap the school with homemade bombs. Evidence subsequently found shows that the boys planned the shooting for almost a year and planned to kill at least 500 people. The date they chose was the anniversary of Adolf Hitler's death. They wore long black trenchcoats, like those worn by Keanu Reeves in *The Matrix*, bringing criticism of the influence of violent films on the young.

December 6, 1999 Seth Trickey (13) shoots students in Fort Gibson, Oklahoma. He wounds four people. The motive remains a mystery. Trickey is apparently a model student and is intelligent and well liked. The school board welcomes Trickey back into the school after the shooting. Parents block the decision.

May 16, 2000 Nate Brazill (13) kills a teacher on the last day of classes at Lake Worth Middle School, Florida. Brazill is tried as an adult and is convicted of second-degree murder.

March 5, 2001 Charles Andrew Williams (15) kills two and wounds 13 after firing on a crowd from a bathroom window at Santana High School, Santee, California. He was reportedly bullied by other students and had told his friends what he planned to do, though they thought he was kidding. He is charged with two counts of murder. The shooting raises questions about the behavior of his fellow students after the event, as some took pictures and videos of the incident and tried to put them on websites. It also brings criticisms of the media coverage, as a spate of "copycat" incidents and threats occur afterward.

Topic 9
SHOULD JUVENILES BE SENTENCED TO DEATH?

YES
"SHOULD JUVENILE OFFENDERS GET THE DEATH PENALTY"?
HTTP://WWW.RUBAK.COM/ARTICLE.CFM?ID=5
JOSH RUBAK

NO
"OLD ENOUGH TO KILL, OLD ENOUGH TO DIE"
SAN FRANCISCO CHRONICLE, APRIL 16, 2000
STEVEN A. DRIZIN AND STEPHEN K. HARPER

INTRODUCTION

The appropriateness of sentencing juvenile offenders (those under the age of 18) to death in the United States is the subject of much current debate. It raises questions of whether such a penalty is in accordance with the principles on which the justice system was founded, or whether its use can be justified as a deterrent in extreme crimes such as murder.

The use of the death penalty for crimes committed by juveniles is prohibited under international human rights standards by a virtually worldwide consensus that favors different responses to juvenile crime. The United States is one of a handful of countries that have chosen not to go along with these views, and it does carry out executions for certain crimes. Since 1990 six countries—Iran, Nigeria, Saudi Arabia, Pakistan, the United States, and Yemen—have imposed the death penalty on 19 juvenile offenders, although Yemen has now outlawed this

practice. The United States accounts for 10 of the 19 executions of young offenders who are under 18.

In the United States periods of increased violent crime prompted corresponding moves toward stronger punishments and revised death penalty statutes in the last quarter of the 20th century. They led to the death penalty being reinstated in 1973. From 1985 to 2000, 17 men were executed, and another 74 still wait on death row for crimes they committed when they were juveniles.

Advocates of juvenile offender death sentencing believe it serves as an effective deterrent against similar crimes, and that furthermore it is necessary for public safety. They argue that many young offenders would rather get life imprisonment without parole than be executed, and that life imprisonment would not be a deterrent for a certain sort of offender, whose life expectations are limited.

After the case of *Stanford v. Kentucky* (1989) the Supreme Court added legal weight to the advocates of juvenile execution. They found that capital punishment of juveniles aged 16 or 17 did not offend society's standards of decency and was not prohibited by the Eighth Amendment (a provision in the Constitution that prohibits cruel and unusual punishment).

Those who agree with death sentences for children think that the fear of death should have prevented them committing a crime in the first place. Thus, if they are old enough to kill, they are old enough to die for their crime.

"I have always found that mercy bears richer fruits than strict justice."

—ABRAHAM LINCOLN,

16TH PRESIDENT (1861–1865)

Opponents of the juvenile death penalty believe that it fails as a deterrent. They are also concerned about the risk of wrongful conviction. Interested international bodies, such as Amnesty International and the Sub-Commission on Human Rights, assert that the death penalty is wrong in every case, but particularly so for children. They do not seek to minimize the crimes that have been committed by juveniles or to belittle the victims' suffering, but they believe that young people are less mature and responsible than adults, and that they can be rehabilitated. To that end, Amnesty International wants the response to child offenders to be a positive one that culminates in their reintegration into society. The United Nations Commission on Human Rights has stated that "…the imposition of the death penalty on persons aged under 18 years at the time of the offence is in contravention of customary international law."

A report compiled by the Coordinating Council on Juvenile Justice and Delinquency Prevention in the Department of Justice describes how, in 1988, U.S. researcher D. O. Lewis and colleagues conducted diagnostic evaluations of 40 percent of the 37 juvenile offenders on death row. They found that all of the prisoners had received head injuries as children. More than half had major neuropsychological disorders, some had psychotic disorders, and others had severe psychiatric problems. Only two had IQ scores above 90, only three had average reading abilities, while 12 of them had been abused physically, sexually, or both, and five had been sodomized by relatives. The researchers concluded that these issues should have been taken into account at trial.

The two articles that follow look at the issue of the juvenile death penalty. In the first article Josh Rubak argues that for extreme cases of murder the death penalty should be invoked. He feels that the death penalty is an effective deterrent without which violent crime will still occur.

In the second article authors Steven A. Drizin and Stephen K. Harper contend that children, especially adolescents, do not have the same judgment and control that adults have, since they are still in the process of cognitive development. Thus their very malleability means that they are ripe for rehabilitation.

SHOULD JUVENILE OFFENDERS GET THE DEATH PENALTY?
Josh Rubak

YES

This subject is difficult at best for the simple reason that it combines three very troublesome issues:

From the start Rubak makes clear each of the three issues that shape his piece.

1. Crime
2. The death penalty
3. Children

These are each emotional issues in and of themselves and even more so when they are placed together. However, the fact is that these three topics are bound together more often then we care to admit for reasons that I will explain below.

In order to better see this situation in a more understanding light we must realize that these are emotional issues and that many (if not most) people do NOT share the same viewpoints as ourselves. To enter into debate assuming that the others involved should feel the same about the situation that we do is counterproductive. Having said that, I'll state my stance on this situation and why.

First off we must remember that the death penalty is meant for extreme cases where every other option (such as short term incarceration, and/or financial fines) does not appear viable in deterring this criminal from creating another atrocious crime (usually murder).

Go to www. deathpenaltyinfo. org/history1.html, to find out more about the history of the death penalty.

Historically speaking, the death penalty has been an option in almost every known society since the dawn of human kind. Let's face it: Normally, people don't want to die. It has been proven time and time again that when there is no sufficient deterrent against an action then that action will occur even if it is considered "bad." How often have you broken a rule to get something knowing full well that nothing would happen to you even if you did get caught? (The historical situation of the 1992 Los Angeles riots where normally law-abiding people stole simply because they felt that they could get away with it in all the confusion is a perfect example.) The severity of the action is not important. The important thing to realize is that people will cheat if they think that they can get away with it. That fact is the

Do the circumstances in which a crime is committed make it more or less severe?

reason rules are created in the first place. Your conscience is simply your internal self-policing system punishing you for not following the laws of the land. When that internal system fails, external rules and threats of punishment are needed.

And in fact it is in children where this fear and respect for the laws and their consequences are aimed first, strongest and most importantly. Every child that comes to this world does so with no preconceived notions and no experience. This also means that they inherently have no clue between the differences of right and wrong. These are lessons that are taught as we grow up. Some learn these lessons better than others. Sometimes, situation arise due to incorrect parent reactions, changes in laws, and/or societal "hiccups" that create a lack of respect and no fear for the possible backlashes of breaking major rules.

Rubak argues that children learn what is "right" and what is "wrong" from society. Does that mean that if children commit crimes, society has failed? If so, should the child be blamed?

Learning process

Historically, we have found that these situations start off in small "tests" as the child checks the waters to see what they can and can't get away with. This is natural for all children and is a normal part of the growing/learning process of human life. The problem begins when a test (such as bullying a kid during recess) does not conclude with any harsh punishment, or punishment that is not sufficient to persuade the child from trying it again, then the actions increase in some manner to see if they can get away with it at the next level. If left unchecked, eventually a mentality is acquired stating "Who cares what I do? I can get away with it. And if they do catch me then so what? I know what the penalty is and it doesn't faze me at all." It is this thought pattern that opens the door to major problems.

Does Rubak's argument imply that corporal punishment is a good thing? Do you think it really acts as a deterrent?

(I specifically remember a time when I was 17 and a "friend" was trying to get me to cash stolen checks and tried to justify it to me by saying "Hey you're not 18 yet. They can't do anything to you. If you get caught you'll just spend the night in jail and that's it. They seal your records when you become 18 anyway so no one will ever know. Come on. This may your last chance to be able to absolutely get away with breaking the law." Truth be told, I almost did it, and I've never broken the law in my life. I'm just lucky I came to my senses before we got to the check cashing place. I can fully understand why other kids would fall for that line if I almost did.)

Unfortunately it is children (especially at the teenage years) that are most prone to start this type of mentality. By the time most people become adults their major outlook on laws and rules has already been created and tends to stay that way barring any traumatic occurrence that forces them to reevaluate their views.

This is not a mental illness as some attorneys and anti-death penalty activists have tried to reason. A mental illness indicates that something highly irregular has occurred in the brain, presumably before or during birth, not with the child rearing process. Trying to compare people who have been raised wrong somehow and do not care about rules, regulations and life to the truly mentally sick is a true example of stupidity and a simple exercise to rewrite the English language in order to achieve a goal.

Is this true? Does the fear of death prevent people carrying out immoral actions?

The fear of death has always been a strong deterrent from doing highly immoral actions … even organized crime knows this fact.

An eye for an eye

The occasional murder of someone who did not follow the rules of that crime family has long been used as a reminder to the others that they need to obey the rules under risk of harsh penalty. In all fairness even crime families do not use the death penalty too often. The punishment for breaking the rules usually involved some form of physical pain and/or banishment in a way that would truly stick with the criminal for years to come and teach them to never double cross anyone again.

If we truly have a society where the death penalty is not an option, then the next worst case scenario is life imprisonment without the possibility of parole. Let's look at this. Is life in prison really a harsh deterrent?

Rubak argues that life imprisonment is not such a bad option to many criminals. Is this a cynical way of looking at the matter? Look at the Campaign for Criminal Justice Reform's site at http://justice.policy. net/cjreform/wrong, and see if you can find information on this issue.

Well to most of us the answer is yes, but if we remember that not everyone feels the same way about these subjects, we then remember that there are those who don't care about the thought of being in a small room and being fed and looked after everyday. As long as they are still alive, that's OK with them.

Think about this: The typical criminal on death row fights in the legal courts for years in order to postpone the death penalty. Most try to simply have life in prison without the possibility of parole (even the courts admit that this is a less harsh punishment) and when this occurs the criminal feels they won. Now under what situation would someone take the worst of two punishments? None. Life in prison allows the criminal to live and feel occasional joy. This is not a harsh punishment to someone who didn't have big plans for their life anyway.

The fact is that of 13 people executed for crime as a juvenile since 1973, the person [who] committed the crime(s) at the age of 17 … was able to hold off the ultimate punishment until they were over 29 years old. They extended their life span over 70 percent as opposed to being executed within a year of the crime.

I know that the race issue is not as important considering that we are talking about juvenile offenders but just to make things fair, let's look at the facts: From 1930 to 1998, 4,361 people were put to death. Of those, 2,064 were white 2,246 were black and 51 were other races. Now bringing those statistics to more recent years gives us a similar picture so we know nothing has changed too much in recent times (1977–1998 500 killed. 313 were white 180 were black and 7 other another race. Of course most were men).

Therefore having the most threatening punishments available for crimes committed during this "pre-adult" stage is the most beneficial thing we can do. It is a deterrent. If we take away punishment options, no matter how harsh, then we simply tie our hands.

Rubak argues that the death penalty acts as a deterrent for other young people. Go to The Penalty Information Center at www. deathpenaltyinfo. org/deter.html, and see if this is actually the case.

The ultimate deterrent

I must stress again that the death penalty (whether juvenile or not) should be used only under extreme cases. It is never meant to be an option for someone who commits a petty crime. There are other punishments available for those situations. The death penalty has typically been used as a deterrent for one particularly heinous crime: Murder. Almost all other crimes should be punished in other ways.

What other crimes might merit the death penalty?

So should the death penalty be an option for juvenile criminals? My answer is yes. The death penalty, when used correctly and in conjunction with other punishments, has proven time and time again to be effective against deterring crime. In fact I submit that if it is taken out as a possible option against juvenile criminals then you will find more crime not less.

Money is not the issue

Oh and by the way, for those who argue the death penalty issue on the issue of whether it's cheaper to use the death penalty or life imprisonment: WAKE UP!

First off determining the best course of action against criminals shouldn't be treated as a monetary issue. The axiom "You get what you paid for" can not be more truer than in this situation. Sometimes the cheaper option is not the correct one. Remember that.

Should a monetary issue be taken into consideration when it's a question of someone's life?

OLD ENOUGH TO KILL, OLD ENOUGH TO DIE
Steven A. Drizin and Stephen K. Harper

See "Dead Man Walking in Virginia" at http://www. apbnews.com/ cjsystem/ justicenews/2000/01/ 12/roach_main0112 _01.html for more information on both these cases.

Civil rights organizations, such as the American Civil Liberties Union at www. aclu.org, argue that death sentencing in the United States is racist. Do statistics back this up?

"Proposition 21" was a California ballot initiative to make sentences for juvenile offenders over the age of 14 harsher by giving prosecutors the power to move "violent" felony cases (such as first-degree murder and rape) into adult criminal court. See http://www. 4children.org/news/ 100pr21.htm for further information.

NO

The Commonwealth of Virginia rang in the new millennium by executing Douglas Christopher Thomas on January 10 and Steven Roach just three days later. Texas, which has executed eight juvenile offenders since 1973 and currently has 28 youthful offenders on death row, executed Glenn McGinnis on January 25. These executions were carried out notwithstanding appeals from numerous organizations, including the European Union and the American Bar Association. Even Pope John Paul II sent a plea to Gov. George W. Bush asking that he commute McGinnis' sentence to life in prison.

About 73 other juvenile offenders are awaiting execution on death rows throughout the United States. More than two-thirds of them are minorities. Fifty-one percent are black, 18 percent are Latino and 31 percent are white. All are male.

Other juveniles will continue to take up temporary residence on death rows. Out of the 38 death penalty states, 19 execute 16- and 17-year-olds and four execute those 17 and older. In 1988, the U.S. Supreme Court held that executing children under the age of 16 violated the Eighth Amendment's ban against "cruel and unusual punishment" because it is contrary to "evolving standards of decency that mark the progress of a maturing society."

If not for this decision, some states would be executing even younger offenders. Former Gov. Pete Wilson, the architect of California's recently passed Proposition 21, has floated the idea that the age for the death penalty should be lowered to 14. In the wake of the Jonesboro, Ark., school shooting two years ago, Texas legislator Jim Pitts proposed lowering the age to 11.

Children are different

America's unforgiving attitude toward youth in the justice system is a stunning indication of just how far our country has tumbled from its leadership role in treating troubled children. More than a century ago, America led the world in its thinking about how to treat young people in trouble with the law by creating the world's first juvenile court.

Outraged by the treatment of children in adult prisons and jails and following the lessons of the nascent human sciences, reformers created a system and laws that recognized that children and adolescents were different than adults. Policymakers recognized that childhood, especially adolescence, was a transitional period of life where cognitive abilities, judgment, impulse control, identity and emotions are still being developed. They recognized that the malleability of youth makes juvenile offenders inherently capable of rehabilitation. In creating juvenile courts, Americans also understood the basic truth that adolescents are simply less culpable than adults for their misdeeds. ...

The last two decades, however, have witnessed enormous changes in the way our justice system treats offenders, first in the adult system and more recently, in the juvenile justice system. As a result of punitive measures such as "three strikes" laws, "sexual predator" laws, the abolishment of parole and mandatory prison sentences, currently more than 2 million Americans are behind bars. The adult system is now focused on punishing and incapacitating offenders and has all but given up on trying to rehabilitate them. In the last decade, these "get tough" measures have also come to drive juvenile justice policy, destroying much of the historical differences between the two systems and placing the juvenile court's rehabilitative ethos in jeopardy. Between 1992 and 1997, 47 states passed laws making it easier to try children as adults.

Is this true? Are juvenile offenders less likely to reoffend if they have been imprisoned? Go to www.google.com and find out if recent crime statistices back up this argument.

Superpredator myth

What spurred these changes? The late 1980s and early 1990s did see an alarming increase in the number of juveniles charged with murder. As crack cocaine hit the streets in America's urban areas, adult gang leaders and drug dealers recruited and armed youngsters in their battle to control the lucrative drug trade. This spike in homicide arrests was almost exclusively confined to the inner cities and virtually all of the increase was gun-related....

Go to http://crime.about. com/cs/statistics/ for links related to crime statistics. See if you can find exact figures for this time period.

The truth is that less than one-half of 1 percent of America's kids were arrested for a violent crime last year. And even though we've had seven straight years of declining juvenile crime during a time when the overall population of youth has grown—trends that completely discredit the superpredator myth—juvenile crime remains a hot-button political issue today. California's Proposition 21 is the most recent example of this trend and signals that there may be no end in sight.

The effect of these changes has altered the landscape of juvenile justice. Twenty-three states now have no bottom age limit for kids to be tried as adults. Last year, Nathaniel Abraham, a Michigan boy who was only 11 at the time he was charged with murder, became the youngest boy in modern American history to be prosecuted as an adult. According to Amnesty International, Nathaniel was just one of more than 200,000 youngsters under the age of 18 who were prosecuted in our adult courts last year....

Perhaps the most disturbing result of these changes, however, is the increase in the number of children housed in adult prisons. Just this month, the Bureau of Justice Statistics reported that the number of youths under the age of 17 who were committed to adult prisons has more than doubled, rising from 3,400 in 1985 to 7,400 in 1997. More than a quarter of these youths in adult prisons are between the ages of 13 and 16.

Nathaniel Abraham was the youngest American child ever to be tried and convicted as an adult for murder. He was 11 when he fatally shot Ronnie Greene Jr.

U.S. shuns international standards

America's changing visions of punishment and childhood—most dramatically illustrated by this practice of executing juvenile offenders—are increasingly out of step with international standards of decency and established international law. All but the United States and the collapsed state of Somalia have ratified the 10-year-old U.N. Convention on the Rights of the Child, which forbids the death penalty against youths under 18. Similarly, the International Covenant on Civil and Political Rights, which has more than 144 signatory countries, also bans the execution of those who commit crimes under the age of 18. Deferring to the rights of its individual states, the United States specifically reserved its right to ignore the covenant's ban on executing juveniles.

Go to the UNICEF site at www.unicef. org/crc/crc.htm to find out more about the UN Convention on the Rights of the Child and the International Covenant on Civil and Political Rights.

Over the last decade, only six other countries are known to have executed juvenile offenders—Yemen, China, Iran, Nigeria, Pakistan and Saudi Arabia. China and Yemen have recently outlawed the practice. In the 1990s, Amnesty International documented 19 cases of child offenders who were executed. Ten were executed in the United States alone – more than all the remaining countries combined. In this fundamental area of human rights, the United States has gone from a leader to an outlaw.

What will it take to get the 23 remaining states to stop executing minors? Appealing to the hearts and minds of legislators and governors doesn't seem to work in an age where playing upon fears and getting "tough on crime" have big political payoffs and mercy is seen as a sign of weakness rather than a strength. Such efforts failed to stop the executions of children and the mentally retarded in the past and likely will not prevail in the future.

Economic pressure and sanctions

…Already the 15 countries of the European Union, all of whom have abolished the death penalty under all circumstances, have begun to exert both diplomatic and economic pressure. In July 1998, in a letter to Gov. Bush of Texas, the chairman of the European Parliament's Delegation for Relations warned that many European companies, under pressure from their shareholders, were considering restricting their investments in states that have the death penalty.

Would sanctions pressure the United States to abandon legislation on the juvenile death penalty?

The European Parliament, which ratifies foreign trade accords and has final authority over the European Union's budget, controls billions of dollars in foreign investment. European investment in Texas, for example, supports 184,500 jobs, 39 percent of which are high-paying manufacturing jobs. Of the $67.5 billion invested in the Texas economy from around the world, 56 percent—or $38.1 billion—comes from Europe. Europe is also Texas' No. 2 export market, with $8.8 billion worth of goods bought in 1996.

The authors published this article in April 2000.

…Just last month, French President Jacques Chirac, French Prime Minister Lionel Jospin and former French Minister of Culture Jack Lang became actively involved in trying to halt the execution of Odel Barnes, an adult offender in Texas. Lang visited Barnes and took his case to the world press while Chirac reportedly took the unusual step of calling former President Bush, urging him to assert his influence on his son. Although these efforts to save Barnes' life failed, they demonstrate the commitment of the Europeans to this cause and suggest that they aren't going to go away quietly.…

Fyodor Mikhaylovich Dostoyevsky (1821–1881) was a Russian novelist most famous for writing Crime and Punishment.

The great Russian novelist and philosopher, Fyodor Dostoevsky, once wrote that a society should be "judged not by how it treats its outstanding citizens but by how it treats its criminals." We believe that an even better barometer of a nation's soul is how it treats its most troubled children. In executing juvenile offenders, America has fallen from grace.

By stopping this shameful practice, America can take a significant stride toward once again establishing itself as a beacon for the world in the area of children's and human rights. Until that happens, we'll have to look to the Colosseum for our hope and inspiration.

Summary

The issue of whether juvenile offenders should be sentenced to death is an emotional one. Josh Rubak believes that in extreme cases when a juvenile has committed violent murder, other punishments would not act as effective deterrents, and to prevent further offending behavior, the death penalty is the only appropriate option. He believes that the alternative, life imprisonment, is not a harsh enough deterrent for people whose aspirations in life are reduced to living in prison without parole. Being alive and looked after every day, albeit in captivity, is a better option for some people than death. Rubak feels that without the threat of the death penalty, offenders do not care about punishments or reprisals for their crimes. He sees no way to change this mentality unless a traumatic occurrence causes them to rethink their attitude.

Steven A. Drizin and Stephen K. Harper feel that the United States has gone astray in this matter. From a position as exemplary leader in the treatment of young offenders by creating the world's first juvenile court, they feel that the policy over the last two decades is retrograde. The tough measures seem to incapacitate rather than rehabilitate young people. No extenuating factors are taken into account, and a child is treated as an adult. The authors are also concerned at the maverick stance that the U.S. has taken. By defying the UN Commission on Human Rights, they are out of step with the international community on this issue. Because of this the 15 countries of the European Union have begun to talk of economic pressure and sanctions on the U.S.

FURTHER INFORMATION:

Books:

Day, Nancy, *The Death Penalty for Teens: A Pro/Con Issue*. Berkeley Heights, NJ: Enslow Publishers, Inc., 2000.

Woodhouse, Lauren J., *Shooter in the Sky: The Inner World of Children Who Kill*. Mt. Pleasant, SC: Corinthian Books, 2000.

Articles:

Streib, V., "Imposing the Death Penalty on Children" in *Challenging Capital Punishment*, edited by Kenneth Haas, James Inciardi, et al. Newbury Park, CA: Sage Publications, Inc., 1988.

Useful websites:

www.aclu.org/death-penalty
American Civil Liberties Union site on the death penalty.
http://deathpenaltyinfo.msu.edu/
An interactive site dealing with the death penalty.

www.inmatecentral.com/juvenile.html
A comprehensive site that examines all the issues.
www.prodeathpenalty.com
Information and resources supporting the death penalty.

The following debates in the Pro/Con series may also be of interest:

In *Individual and Society*:

Topic 13 Is the death penalty ever justifiable?

In *Constitution*:

Topic 16 Is the death penalty constitutional?

SHOULD JUVENILES BE SENTENCED TO DEATH?

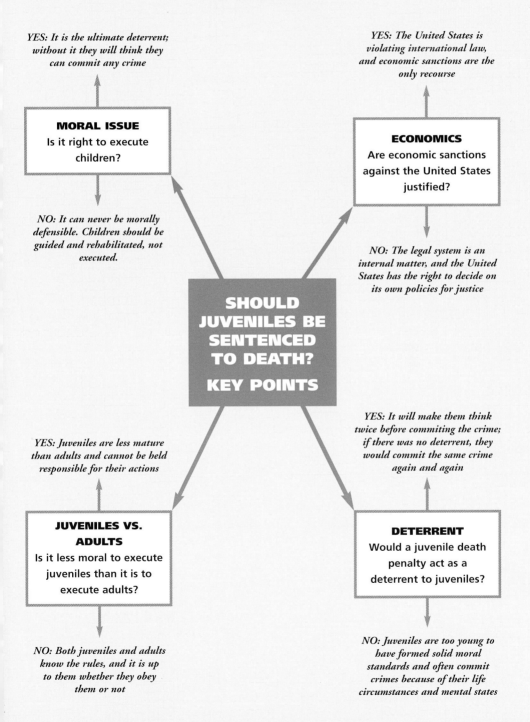

YES: It is the ultimate deterrent; without it they will think they can commit any crime

MORAL ISSUE
Is it right to execute children?

NO: It can never be morally defensible. Children should be guided and rehabilitated, not executed.

YES: The United States is violating international law, and economic sanctions are the only recourse

ECONOMICS
Are economic sanctions against the United States justified?

NO: The legal system is an internal matter, and the United States has the right to decide on its own policies for justice

SHOULD JUVENILES BE SENTENCED TO DEATH?
KEY POINTS

YES: Juveniles are less mature than adults and cannot be held responsible for their actions

JUVENILES VS. ADULTS
Is it less moral to execute juveniles than it is to execute adults?

NO: Both juveniles and adults know the rules, and it is up to them whether they obey them or not

YES: It will make them think twice before commiting the crime; if there was no deterrent, they would commit the same crime again and again

DETERRENT
Would a juvenile death penalty act as a deterrent to juveniles?

NO: Juveniles are too young to have formed solid moral standards and often commit crimes because of their life circumstances and mental states

Topic 10
IS RACIAL PROFILING WRONG?

YES

FROM "DRIVING WHILE BLACK: RACIAL PROFILING ON OUR NATION'S HIGHWAYS"
AMERICAN CIVIL LIBERTIES UNION SPECIAL REPORT, JUNE 1999
DAVID A. HARRIS

NO

FROM "THE MYTH OF RACIAL PROFILING"
HTTP://WWW.CITY-JOURNAL.ORG/HTML/11_2_THE_MYTH.HTML
CITY JOURNAL, SPRING 2001, VOL. 11, NO. 2
HEATHER MACDONALD

INTRODUCTION

Racial profiling involves the use of particular ethnic characteristics to determine whether someone is a likely suspect for committing a crime.

Profiling was originally developed in the early 1970s to help police officers identify drug couriers arriving at U.S. airports. Officers were trained to look for people using large amounts of cash, who had come from places known to be important to the drug trade, and who exhibited specific behavioral indicators such as nervousness.

In 1986 the DEA launched "Operation Pipeline," instructing some 27,000 police officers across 48 states in how to use drug courier profiling when stopping motorists for traffic law violations. As part of its instruction, the DEA included extra information about the likely ethnicity of drug-traffickers on particular routes.

Since the proportion of African Americans arrested for drug offenses rose from 25 percent in 1980 to 37 percent in 1995, civil rights activists have argued that racial profiling discriminates against ethnic minorities. Other commentators maintain that crime statistics simply reflect the truth —that ethnic groups are more heavily involved in drug trafficking than whites.

Racial profiling was brought to the public's attention by a notorious case in April 1998, when state troopers pulled over a van on the New Jersey Turnpike. As the troopers approached the van, it reversed into them, so they opened fire, injuring three of the four occupants. The police insisted they had stopped the van because it was breaking the speed limit; the occupants argued that they were pulled over because they were African American and Hispanic— their race making them automatic targets of suspicion. In a report issued the following year New Jersey officials admitted to using racial profiling as part of their law-enforcement strategy.

Since President Reagan's 1982 announcement of a "War on Drugs" several new approaches to law enforcement have been introduced to help fight crime. One of them is "zero-tolerance" policing—famously adopted by New York City lawmen after Mayor Rudolph Guiliani's election in 1994—which has led to a crackdown on minor crimes such as jaywalking, vandalism, public intoxication, and vagrancy, enforcing the message that no level of criminal activity is acceptable. Another is "three strikes and you're out" legislation, which means that anyone guilty of committing three felonies—however minor—can be sentenced to up to 25 years or even life. "Community policing," a more proactive method of crime control, has led to more foot patrols and community programs and decentralized police stations.

"Stopping or searching individuals on the basis of race is not effective law-enforcement policy."

—BILL CLINTON,

42ND PRESIDENT (1993–2001)

Supporters of such initiatives argue that they produced significant reductions in crime in the 1990s. Opponents claim that crime levels have declined throughout the whole of the United States. They argue that levels have fallen even in cities like San Francisco, where policing methods are far less assertive, the focus is on rehabilitation rather than punishment, and many offenders are sentenced to community service rather than prison.

Civil rights activists also maintain that new policing methods such as racial profiling unfairly target ethnic minorities in poor neighborhoods.

There are two main types of racial profiling. "Hard" profiling uses race as the determining factor in establishing suspicion. In "soft" profiling race is only one of several factors used to decide whether someone is under suspicion.

According to its critics, hard profiling contravenes both the Fourth Amendment—which guarantees "the right of the people to be secure … against unreasonable searches" unless there is "probable cause"—and the Fourteenth Amendment, which guarantees every citizen the right to "equal treatment under the law" and to "due process." However, the Supreme Court has ruled that soft profiling may be used if it is narrowly targeted on achieving a "compelling governmental interest."

Following the terrorist actions of September 11, 2001, the ruling on soft profiling is at the heart of the renewed debate over racial profiling at airports. Many people argue that to prevent similar attacks in the future, there is now a compelling need for travelers of Arab descent to be searched more thoroughly at airports than other ethnic groups. Opponents argue that since Al Qaeda is known to exist in some 40 countries ranging from Malaysia to Latin America, stopping Arab-looking people at airports will do nothing to improve security but simply increase the level of harassment suffered by Arab American citizens.

The following two articles by David A. Harris and Heather MacDonald respectively look at the issue of racial profiling in the United States today.

DRIVING WHILE BLACK: RACIAL PROFILING ON OUR NATION'S HIGHWAYS
David A. Harris

On a hot summer afternoon in August 1998, 37-year-old U.S. Army Sergeant First Class Rossano V. Gerald and his young son Gregory drove across the Oklahoma border into a nightmare. A career soldier and a highly decorated veteran of Desert Storm and Operation United Shield in Somalia, SFC Gerald, a black man of Panamanian descent, found that he could not travel more than 30 minutes through the state without being stopped twice: first by the Roland City Police Department, and then by the Oklahoma Highway Patrol.

During the second stop, which lasted two-and-half hours, the troopers terrorized SFC Gerald's 12-year-old son with a police dog, placed both father and son in a closed car with the air conditioning off and fans blowing hot air, and warned that the dog would attack if they attempted to escape. Halfway through the episode—perhaps realizing the extent of their lawlessness—the troopers shut off the patrol car's video evidence camera....

A war on drugs or minorities?

From the outset, the war on drugs has in fact been a war on people and their constitutional rights, with African Americans, Latinos and other minorities bearing the brunt of the damage. It is a war that has, among other depredations, spawned racist profiles of supposed drug couriers. On our nation's highways today, police ostensibly looking for drug criminals routinely stop drivers based on the color of their skin. This practice is so common that the minority community has given it the derisive term, "driving while black or brown" —a play on the real offense of "driving while intoxicated."

One of the core principles of the Fourth Amendment is that the police cannot stop and detain an individual without some reason ... to believe that he or she is involved in criminal activity. But recent Supreme Court decisions allow the police to use traffic stops as a pretext in order to "fish" for evidence. Both anecdotal and quantitative data show that nationwide, the police exercise this discretionary power primarily against African Americans and Latinos.

For more details on this incident go to www. commondreams.org/ pressreleases/ may99/ 051899a.htm.

Video cameras were installed in trooper cars in response to political pressure following the Turnpike shooting in April 1998 (see page 126).

For information and links to other sites about the Fourth Ammendment go to http://caselaw.lp. findlaw.com/data/ constitution/ amendment04/.

No person of color is safe from this treatment anywhere, regardless of their obedience to the law, their age, the type of car they drive, or their station in life. In short, skin color has become evidence of the propensity to commit crime, and police use this "evidence" against minority drivers on the road all the time.

A self-fulfilling prophecy?

Racial profiling is based on the premise that most drug offenses are committed by minorities. The premise is factually untrue, but it has nonetheless become a self-fulfilling prophecy. Because police look for drugs primarily among African Americans and Latinos, they find a disproportionate number of them with contraband. Therefore, more minorities are arrested, prosecuted, convicted, and jailed, thus reinforcing the perception that drug trafficking is primarily a minority activity. This perception creates the profile that results in more stops of minority drivers. At the same time, white drivers receive far less police attention, many of the drug dealers and possessors among them go unapprehended, and the perception that whites commit fewer drug offenses than minorities is perpetuated. And so the cycle continues.

> *Is this statement correct? For up-to-date statistics on drug use from the Department of Health and Social Services go to www.samhsa.gov/oas/NHSDA/2kNHSDA/chapter2.htm.*

This vicious cycle carries with it profound personal and societal costs. It is both symptomatic and symbolic of larger problems at the intersection of race and the criminal justice system. It results in the persecution of innocent people based on their skin color. It has a corrosive effect on the legitimacy of the entire justice system. It deters people of color from cooperating with the police in criminal investigations. And in the courtroom, it causes jurors of all races and ethnicities to doubt the testimony of police officers when they serve as witnesses, making criminal cases more difficult to win....

The road to "driving while black"

The pervasiveness of racial profiling by the police in the enforcement of our nation's drug laws is the consequence of the escalating so-called war on drugs. Drug use and drug selling are not confined to racial and ethnic minorities in the U.S.; indeed five times as many whites use drugs. But the war on drugs has, since its earliest days, targeted people of color. The fact that skin color has now become a proxy for criminality is an inevitable outcome of this process....

> *Statistics from other sources contradict these claims. For example, the Sixth Triennial Report to Congress, found at www.drugabuse.gov/STRC/Forms.html#Cocaine, reports that past-month national rates of cocaine use were 0.6 percent for non-Hispanic whites, 0.8 percent for Hispanic whites, and 1.4 percent for blacks.*

According to the government's own reports, 80 percent of the country's cocaine users are white, and the "typical cocaine user is a middle-class, white suburbanite...." Today, blacks constitute 13 percent of the country's drug users;

For a discussion on the discrepancies between drug prosecutions and the sentencing of minorities and whites go to www.civilrights.org/ publications/cj/ prosecutorial.html.

37 percent of those arrested on drug charges; 55 percent of those convicted; and 74 percent of all drug offenders sentenced to prison....

Putting an end to racial profiling

Although this decades-old problem cannot be solved overnight, it is time to launch an all-out frontal assault on DWB [Driving While Black]. The ACLU calls on the U.S. Justice Department, law enforcement officials and state and federal legislators to join us in a comprehensive, five-part battle plan against the scourge of racial profiling:

1. End the use of pretext stops

Virtually all of the thousands of complaints received by the ACLU about DWB—and every recent case and scandal in this area—seem to involve the use of traffic stops for non-traffic purposes, usually drug interdiction.... All the evidence to date suggests that using traffic laws for non-traffic purposes has been a disaster for people of color and has deeply eroded public confidence in law enforcement. Using minor traffic violations to find drugs on the highways is like asking officers to find needles in a haystack....

For more details about the Traffic Stops Statistics Study Act go to www.aele.org/ HR1443.html.

2. Pass the Traffic Stops Statistics Study Act

At the beginning of the 105th Congress, Rep. John Conyers (D-MI) introduced H.R. 118, the Traffic Stops Statistics Act, requiring the collection of several categories of data on each traffic stop, including the race of the driver and whether a search was performed. The Attorney General would then conduct a study analyzing the data. This would be the first nationwide, statistically rigorous study of these practices.

The idea behind the bill was that if the study confirmed what people of color have experienced for years, it would put to rest the idea that African Americans and other people of color are exaggerating isolated anecdotes into a social problem. Congress and other bodies might then begin to take concrete steps to channel police discretion more appropriately. The Act passed the House of Representatives in March of 1998 by a unanimous vote and was then referred to the Senate Judiciary Committee, but the Committee never voted on the measure or held any hearings.

Read more about the progress of the Traffic Stops Statistics Study Act at www.csun.edu/~ hcpas003/ PAS300nomw4.html.

In April 1999, Congressman Conyers reintroduced he Traffic Stops Statistics Study Act (HR 1443), sponsored in the Senate (S.821) by Frank Lautenberg (D-NJ) and Russell Feingold (D-WI). Passage of the Act should be viewed as a first step toward addressing a difficult problem.

3. Pass legislation on traffic stops in every state

Even if the Traffic Stop Statistics Study Act does not become federal law, it has already inspired action at the state and local level. The ACLU calls upon legislators in every state to pass laws that will allow the practice of traffic enforcement to be statistically monitored on an ongoing basis.

In North Carolina, a bill requiring data collection on all traffic stops was passed by overwhelming majorities in both houses of the state legislature and signed into law by the governor on April 21, 1999. This became the first law anywhere in the nation to require the kind of effort that will yield a full, detailed statistical portrait of the use of traffic stops. Similar bills have been introduced in Pennsylvania, Illinois, Virginia, Massachusetts, New Jersey, Maryland, Arkansas, Texas, Connecticut, Rhode Island, Florida, and California....

The American Civil Liberties Union Freedom Network, for example, has begun a net-based campaign to collect data about racial profiling. Visit the site at www.aclu.org/profiling/background.

4. The justice department must take steps to ensure that racial profiling is not used in federally funded drug interdiction programs

...Attorney General Reno has stated it is "very important to pursue legislation" on data collection. But to date, the Justice Department has not taken a position on the pending federal bills. The Justice Department should actively support the passage of the federal Traffic Stops Statistics Study Act....

5. The 50 largest U.S. cities should voluntarily collect traffic stop data

Jerry Sanders, San Diego's Chief of Police, announced in February of this year that his department would begin to collect race data on traffic stops without any federal or state requirement or any threat of litigation. In March, Chief William Lansdowne of the San Jose Police Department announced that his department would follow suit, and in April, Portland Police Chief Charles Moose spearheaded an anti-profiling resolution signed by 23 Oregon police agencies—including the State Police—that included a commitment to gather traffic stop data. These efforts should be replicated in all 50 of the largest cities in the U.S....

If some police departments are willing to voluntarily collect data on traffic stops, might this not suggest that they feel they have nothing to hide?

Conclusion

Although some police officials are still in denial, we have presented strong and compelling evidence, of both an anecdotal and statistical nature, that racial profiling on our nation's roads and highways is indeed a nationwide problem. As such, it demands a nationwide solution. The steps towards a solution are clear....

Is one anecdotal incident and one set of statistics enough to be considered "strong and compelling" evidence?

THE MYTH OF RACIAL PROFILING
Heather MacDonald

NO

The anti-"racial profiling" juggernaut must be stopped, before it obliterates the crime-fighting gains of the last decade, especially in inner cities. The anti-profiling crusade thrives on an ignorance of policing and a willful blindness to the demographics of crime. Yet politicians are swarming on board. In February, President George W. Bush joined the rush, declaring portentously: "Racial profiling is wrong, and we will end it in America."

...Two meanings of "racial profiling" intermingle in the activists' rhetoric ... "hard" profiling uses race as the only factor in assessing criminal suspiciousness: an officer sees a black person and, without more to go on, pulls him over for a pat-down on the chance that he may be carrying drugs or weapons. "Soft" racial profiling is using race as one factor among others ... the highway police, for example, have intelligence that Jamaican drug posses with a fondness for Nissan Pathfinders are transporting marijuana along the northeast corridor. A New Jersey trooper sees a black motorist speeding in a Pathfinder and pulls him over....

Widening the debate

The racial profiling debate focuses primarily on highway stops. The police are pulling over a disproportionate number of minority drivers for traffic offenses, goes the argument, in order to look for drugs. Sure, the driver committed an infraction, but the reason the trooper chose to stop him, rather than the speeder next to him, was his race.

But the profiling critics also fault both the searches that sometimes follow a highway stop and the tactics of urban policing. Any evaluation of the evidence for, and the appropriateness of, the use of race in policing must keep these contexts distinct. Highway stops should almost always be color-blind, I'll argue, but in other policing environments (including highway searches), where an officer has many clues to go on, race may be among them. Ironically, effective urban policing shows that the more additional factors an officer has in his criminal profile, the more valid race becomes....

In New York, the mayhem eventually led to the development of the Giuliani administration's assertive policing that strives, quite successfully, to prevent crime from happening. Outside of New York, the widespread pleas to stop drug violence led the Drug Enforcement Administration to enlist state highway police in their anti-drug efforts. The DEA and the Customs Service had been using intelligence about drug routes and the typical itineraries of couriers to interdict drugs at airports; now the interdiction war would expand to the nation's highways, the major artery of the cocaine trade.

Telltale signs

The DEA taught state troopers some common identifying signs of drug couriers: nervousness; conflicting information about origin and destination cities among vehicle occupants; no luggage for a long trip; lots of cash; lack of a driver's license or insurance; the spare tire in the back seat; rental license plates or plates from key source states like Arizona and New Mexico; loose screws or scratches near a vehicle's hollow spaces, which can be converted to hiding places for drugs and guns. The agency also shared intelligence about the types of cars that couriers favored on certain routes, as well as about the ethnic makeup of drug-trafficking organizations.

A typical DEA report from the early 1990s noted that "large-scale interstate trafficking networks controlled by Jamaicans, Haitians, and black street gangs dominate the manufacture and distribution of crack." The 1999 "Heroin Trends" report out of Newark declared that "predominant wholesale traffickers are Colombian, followed by Dominicans, Chinese, West African/Nigerian, Pakistani, Hispanic and Indian...."

According to the racial profiling crowd, the war on drugs immediately became a war on minorities, on the highways and off. Their alleged evidence for racial profiling comes in two varieties: anecdotal, which is of limited value, and statistical, which on examination proves entirely worthless....

> *Anecdotal evidence is based on the experiences of a few people. It would require the statistical evidence of many people to establish whether these experiences represented an overall trend.*

Race as a monitor

Despite the hue and cry, there is nothing illegal about using race as one factor among others in assessing criminal suspiciousness. Nevertheless, the initial decision to pull a car over should be based almost always on seriousness of traffic violation alone—unless, of course, evidence of other law-breaking, such as drug use, is visible....

But compared with most other policing environments, highways are relatively cueless places. In assessing the potential criminality of a driver speeding along with the pack on an eight-lane highway, an officer normally has much less to work with than on a city street or sidewalk. His locational cues

> *Even though the author supports racial profiling, she agrees with the main gist of the first article—that drivers should not be stopped purely because of their skin color.*

—traveling on an interstate pointed toward a drug market, say —are crude, compared with those in a city, where an officer can ask if this particular block is a drug bazaar. His ability to observe the behavior of a suspect over time is limited by the speed of travel. In such an environment, blacks traveling 78 mph should not face a greater chance of getting pulled over than white speeders just because they are black and happen to be driving a car said to be favored by drug mules....

Fact or fiction?

On April 20, 1999, New Jersey's then-attorney general Peter Verniero issued his "Interim Report of the State Police Review Team Regarding Allegations of Racial Profiling." It was a bombshell, whose repercussions haven't stopped yet.

For a transcript of Verniero's interim report go to www.state.nj.us/lps/intm_419.pdf.

"The problem of disparate treatment [of blacks] is real, not imagined," the report famously declared. Governor Christine Todd Whitman chimed in: "There is no question that racial profiling exists at some level." The media triumphantly broadcast the findings as conclusive proof.... the *New York Times* started regularly referring to New Jersey's "racial bias" on the highways as incontrovertible fact. Defense attorneys and their clients celebrated as well. "Whenever I have a state police case, I file a suppression motion ... alleging that the stop was based on color of skin and therefore illegal," a Trenton criminal defense attorney told the *New York Times*. "And now guess what? The state agrees with me!"

Here MacDonald highlights a common media tendency: To jump on a single report and sensationalize it as if it were undisputed fact.

Yet the report's influential analysis is shoddy beyond belief.... Between 1994 and 1998, claims the report, 53 percent of consent searches on the southern end of the New Jersey Turnpike involved a black person ... and overall, 77 percent involved minorities. But these figures are meaningless, because Verniero does not include racial information about search requests that were denied, and his report mixes stops, searches, and arrests from different time periods.

Do these factors really make the overall figure meaningless?

But most important: Verniero finds culpable racial imbalance in the search figures without suggesting a proper benchmark. He simply assumes that 53 percent black consent searches is too high. Compared with what? If blacks in fact carry drugs at a higher rate than do whites, then this search rate merely reflects good law enforcement. If the police are now to be accused of racism every time that they go where the crime is, that's the end of public safety....

However much the racial profilers try to divert attention away from the facts of crime, those facts remain obdurate. Arlington has a 10 percent black population, but robbery victims identify nearly 70 percent of their assailants as black.

In 1998, blacks in New York City were 13 times more likely than whites to commit a violent assault, according to victim reports. As long as those numbers remain unchanged, police statistics will also look disproportionate….

How relevant are figures for robbery and assault in urban areas to the issue of highway searches for drugs?

Irrational effects

But the politics of racial profiling has taken over everything else. Here again, New Jersey is a model of profiling pandering, and it foreshadows the irrationality that will beset the rest of the country. In February 1999, New Jersey governor Christine Todd Whitman peremptorily fired the head of the state police, Colonel Carl Williams, whose reputation for honesty had earned him the nickname "The Truth." It was the truth that got him fired. The day before his dismissal, Williams had had the temerity to tell a newspaper reporter that minority groups dominate the cocaine and marijuana trade.

Note the choice of words here. Might they say something about the author's mindset? She seems to be implying that this is an accepted fact. Do you agree?

Of course, this information had constituted the heart of DEA reports for years. No matter. Stating it publicly violated some collective fairy tale that all groups commit drug crimes at equal rates…. One way to make sure that nasty confrontations with the facts … don't happen again is to stop publishing those facts. And so the New Jersey state police no longer distribute a typical felony-offender profile to their officers, because such profiles may contribute, in the attorney general's words, to "inappropriate stereotypes" about criminals. Never mind that in law enforcement, with its deadly risk, more information is always better than less….

Paying the price

The political classes are telling police officers that if they have "too many" enforcement interactions with minorities, it is because they are racists. Officers are responding by cutting back enforcement. Drug arrests dropped 55 percent on the Garden State Parkway in New Jersey in 2000, and 25 percent on the turnpike and parkway combined. When the mayor and the police chief of Minneapolis accused Minneapolis officers of racial profiling, traffic stops dropped 63 percent….

The Harlem residents who so angrily demanded more drug busts from Mayor Giuliani … didn't care about the race of the criminals who were destroying their neighborhood. They didn't see "black" or "white." They only saw dealers— and they wanted them out. That is precisely the perspective of most police officers…. If the racial profiling crusade shatters this commonality between law-abiding inner-city residents and the police, it will be just those law-abiding minorities who will pay the heaviest price.

A state trooper tells of his discontent with the political system in a letter at members.tripod.com/~Prince_Etrigan/rant.html.

Summary

Racial profiling is a controversial issue. The preceding two articles look at opposing aspects of the debate. In "Driving While Black: Racial Profiling on Our Nation's Highways" David A. Harris claims that racial profiling has been used as a racist pretext for stopping and searching African American and Hispanic drivers, leading to a breakdown of trust between the police and ethnic minorities. He suggests racial profiling is based on a circular argument: Police stereotypes of ethnic minority criminality make it more likely that ethnic minorities will be stopped, searched, and arrested. The crime statistics thus reinforce the original stereotype. Harris concludes that pretext stops must not be used for law enforcement, and that accurate data should be gathered to demonstrate how ethnicity affects police action.

In "The Myth of Racial Profiling" Heather MacDonald argues that statistics show ethnic minorities are more likely than whites to be involved in drug-related crime. She argues that this means the racial aspect of a criminal profile is as relevant as any other. She denies that the police are institutionally racist and argues that attacks on racial profiling have reduced the effectiveness of policing in inner cities. Given public demands for more assertive policing, she says, racial profiling is a necessary tool of law enforcement that enables police officers to act quickly against drug-related crime.

FURTHER INFORMATION:

 Books:

Davis, Kelvin R., *Driving While Black: Coverup.* Interstate International Publishing of Cincinnati, 2001.

Fredrickson, Darren D., and Raymond P. Siljander, *Racial Profiling: Eliminating the Confusion between Racial and Criminal Profiling and Clarifying What Constitutes Unfair Discrimination and Persecution.* Springfield IL.: Charles C. Thomas Publishing Ltd., 2002.

Meeks, Kenneth, *Driving While Black: What to Do If You Are a Victim of Racial Profiling.* New York: Broadway Books, 2000.

O'Reilly, James T., *Police Traffic Stops and Racial Profiling: Resolving Management, Labor, and Civil Rights Conflicts.* Springfield, IL: Charles C. Thomas Publishing Ltd., 2002.

Useful websites:

www.libertocracy.com/Webessays/police/drugwar/drugwar_racist.htm
Discussion on "The War on Drugs Is a Racist War."
www.nida.nih.gov/
National Institute on Drug Abuse site.

www.zmag.org/sustainers/content/2001-08/23wise.htm
Tim Wise, "Drugs, Race, and Reality in the 'Burbs."

The following debates in the Pro/Con series may also be of interest:

In this volume:
 Topic 1 Is the criminal justice system racist?

 Topic 7 Does community policing help reduce crime?

 Abner Louima, pages 86–87.

In *Government*:
 Topic 2 Are all human beings created equal?

IS RACIAL PROFILING WRONG?

YES: It is merely one of many tools necessary for effective law enforcement

YES: Racial profiles assume that ethnic minorities are more likely to commit crimes than whites

CONSTITUTION
Is racial profiling constitutional?

RACISM
Is racial profiling racist?

NO: It infringes the rights of citizens under the Fourth Amendment to be protected from "unreasonable searches," and under the Fourteenth Amendment to "due process" and "equal treatment under law"

NO: Statistics gathered by law-enforcement officers indicates that some racial groups are more heavily involved in criminal activity than others. Racial profiles reflect this trend.

IS RACIAL PROFILING WRONG?
KEY POINTS

YES: It is the nonwhite inhabitants of poor, urban districts who are calling for more vigorous policing. Racial profiling helps police officers respond to their needs.

YES: Racial profiling helps law-enforcement officers act quickly and efficiently against suspected criminals

LAW ENFORCEMENT
Is racial profiling an effective tool for law enforcement?

NO: Ethnic minorities feel they can be stopped for no reason other than that they are non-white. This destroys their trust in the police.

NO: Racial profiling encourages the police to make unnecessary and unjustified searches of ethnic minorities, wasting time and resources

Topic 11
SHOULD SOFT DRUGS BE DECRIMINALIZED?

YES
FROM "MARIJUANA SPECIAL REPORT: VRAAG EEN POLITIEAGENT"
NEW SCIENTIST, FEBRUARY 21, 1998
DEBORA MACKENZIE

NO
FROM "HOLLAND'S HALF-BAKED DRUG EXPERIMENT"
FOREIGN AFFAIRS, VOL. 78, NO. 3, MAY/JUNE 1999
LARRY COLLINS

INTRODUCTION

A drug is defined as a "substance used in or as a medicine" or a "substance that can cause addiction, psychological dependency, or a marked change in mental status." This topic deals with drugs that fall into the second category —drugs that governments throughout the world have sought to restrict or make illegal because of the harmful effects they can have on those who use them. For example, although the medical profession has long used morphine (an opium derivative) as a painkiller, its use is restricted in the United States and various other countries because of its high potential for abuse and the subsequent physical dependence that could result.

In much pro- and antidrug literature different drugs are categorized as either "hard" or "soft." Loosely speaking, these terms refer to how dangerous a drug is and whether or not it causes physical dependency—heroin and crack cocaine generally being designated as hard

drugs, and cannabis and LSD as soft. When people discuss the legalization or decriminalization (reducing the criminal status while maintaining some form of regulation) of certain drugs, they are normally talking about soft drugs—but these terms have no legal or pharmacological validity.

The government classifies drugs more rigidly according to their physical and psychological addictiveness, their potential for abuse, whether or not they have an accepted medical use, and how safely they can be used under medical supervision. For example, Schedule I drugs such as heroin are considered to have a high potential for abuse, no accepted medical use, and to be unsafe for medically supervised use. A Schedule II rating means a drug has an accepted medical use but is considered easily abused and likely to result in either physical or psychological dependency. It is strictly illegal for citizens to possess a Schedule I drug, while Schedule II drugs such as morphine can only be legally supplied or used if a DEA permit is secured.

The illegal status of even hard drugs is a relatively recent phenomenon in the United States, however. Prior to 1914 recreational drug use was tolerated—and cocaine was a common ingredient in wines and sodas, notably Coca Cola. It was only after Congress passed the Harrison Act that opiates and cocaine were banned and the use of marijuana outlawed—although it remained on the list of drugs that doctors could prescribe. Its illegal status was consolidated in the Marijuana Tax Act of 1941, which banned the drug's use even in medicine.

"[Members of the Commission] simply state that smoking marijuana in the privacy of your home should be perfectly legal—as long as no one gave it to you [or] sold it to you and you didn't grow it yourself."

—W. WALTER MENNINGER ON A PRESIDENT'S COMMISSION REPORT ON DRUG ABUSE, 1972

Cannabis, or marijuana, is the flowers, seeds, and dried leaves of the Indian hemp plant, *Cannabis sativa*. Resin extracted from this plant is known as hashish, or hash. Marijuana and hash contain an active substance known as THC (delta 9 tetrahydrocannabinol), which modifies certain mental and

physical functions and causes the well-known "high" sought by recreational users. Users normally smoke marijuana, with or without tobacco, or eat it.

In 1970 marijuana was classified as a Schedule I drug under federal law, giving it the same rating as heroin and LSD. Since then people have continued to debate whether or not this status is justified. Discussion has become particularly heated in recent years, partly as a result of research that points to the drug's beneficial medicinal properties. Historically marijuana was used to relieve pain, and it has also been found to help alleviate some of the symptoms of multiple sclerosis (MS).

There is also a growing perception that prohibition has done little to contain the use of marijuana. Many people feel that police and judicial resources would be better directed at combatting the use and sale of more harmful substances such as crack cocaine. And others suggest that decriminalizing marijuana would stop users from visiting illegal drug dealers and being exposed to harder drugs.

Those who wish to maintain prohibition contend that marijuana is psychologically addictive and that it can cause harmful side effects such as cell death in certain areas of the brain. They believe decriminalization would lead to an increase in its use, especially among the young. This, in turn, could lead to more young people graduating to harder drugs. Surely the state is justified in legislating to protect people from harming themselves in this way?

In the following articles arguments for and against the decriminalization of soft drugs are discussed with reference to the situation in Holland, where the possession of small amounts of marijuana has been legal since 1976.

MARIJUANA SPECIAL REPORT:
VRAAG EEN POLITIEAGENT
Debora Mackenzie

YES

Go ahead, ask a cop for dope. The Dutch don't mind. It is a weird experience. You walk up to a Dutch policeman, and ask where to get some marijuana. You are smilingly directed to the nearest "coffee shop," where the menu offers everything cannabinoid from something called Space Cake to Northern Lights, a local weed.

Holland's so-called "coffee shops" are places where customers can buy and smoke cannabis legally.

Dutch legalization of cannabis

In much of the world, this could never happen: the penalties for using cannabis are severe. But in 1976, the Dutch legalised the possession of small amounts. What has happened since? Some say that crime has soared, schoolchildren drop out, and heroin addiction is rife. Others insist the Netherlands is a stoned paradise of peace and love.

In 1976 Holland legalized the possession of 1 oz (30g) of cannabis per person. This amount has since been reduced to 0.2 oz (5g).

"I've visited their parks. Their children walk around like zombies," says Lee Brown, head of the US Office for National Drug Control Policy. "Hard drug use—heroin and cocaine—has declined substantially," says Paul Hager of the Indiana Civil Liberties Union.

Most comments seem to depend on the speaker's politics. So what is the truth about the great Dutch cannabis experiment? "There was no immediate increase in cannabis use after 1976," says Arjan Sas of the Centre for Drug Research at the University of Amsterdam. "Trends in use have generally been the same as in other countries." The percentage who regularly use either cannabis or hard drugs is lower in the Netherlands than in many European countries, including Britain. And the number of hard drug addicts in the Netherlands has not increased for a decade, while their average age is rising.

Many people believe that cannabis is a "gateway drug" that can lead to hard-drug use; but according to a report from the U.S. Institute of Medicine, "There is no conclusive evidence that the drug effects of marijuana are causally linked to the subsequent abuse of other illicit drugs."

First national drug use survey

Dutch statistics, however, are far from conclusive. The first national survey of drug use in the Netherlands is only just being done. There have been smaller-scale studies of particular towns or age groups but comparing them is fraught with statistical problems.

Nonetheless, Dirk Korf of the Institute of Criminology at the University of Amsterdam has used the smaller studies to estimate that 3 per cent of Dutch people had used cannabis at least once in 1970, rising to 12 per cent in 1991. The best guess for 1998 is 14 per cent.

Most of that increase, says Korf, is because "lifetime use" figures are cumulative: people who had used it in 1970 are still around, and are joined by younger users over time. More to the point, he says, is to compare the number of teenagers who start using cannabis. In 1970, he estimates that 20 per cent of all Dutch 18-year-olds surveyed had used it at least once; in 1980, that had fallen to 15 per cent. By 1987, it was 18 per cent, an increase, Korf says, that mirrors the increase in the number of coffee shops in the mid-1980s. Now, about 30 per cent of Dutch 18-year-olds are said to have tried cannabis, though some researchers think that is an overestimate based on studies of Amsterdam where coffee shops abound.

What conclusions, if any, can you draw from these statistics about the use of soft drugs?

Cannabis use before and after legalization

But did more people try cannabis after it was legalised? It seems so. At the Centre for Drug Research, Sas and Peter Cohen divided Amsterdamers surveyed in 1987, 1990 and 1994 into two groups—those that were born before 1958, who were 18 or older in 1976, and those that were born after 1976, for whom cannabis has always been legal. Only 19 per cent of the oldies had tried cannabis, compared with 38 per cent of the younger group.

Do you think legalizing soft drugs is likely to encourage more young people to start using them?

That difference could be partly misleading. Dutch surveys show that the vast majority of people who use cannabis do so almost exclusively in their 20s. The drug became common in the Netherlands in the mid-1960s, so for the older group members who were already more than 30, it was too late. Nonetheless, the data suggest that more people did try cannabis after decriminalisation.

But what counts, though, says Sas, is how many continue to use it. In Amsterdam, 55 per cent of people who say they have tried cannabis only end up using it a couple of dozen times or less. The rest may have used it more often, but more than half have not used it in the past month. The data show, says Sas, that legalising cannabis may make you more likely to try it, but it does not make it more likely that you will continue to use it.

Do you agree with Sas's conclusion about the effect of legalizing cannabis?

But it is by no means certain that the first half of that conclusion is correct. Korf finds that surveys of the number of Germans who use cannabis "virtually parallels" the peaks and troughs in Dutch surveys between 1970 and 1990, even though Germany has prohibited cannabis throughout the period. Surveys of young Americans in the 1970s and 1980s found "substantially higher prevalence rates" than in Holland, peaking at 50 per cent of high-school seniors in 1980, although the US was strongly prohibitionist.

Since then, says Korf, there have been no discernible differences in use between US states that have decriminalised, and those that have not, while cannabis use has increased in the US and Western Europe since 1990, regardless of the legal framework. "There is no appreciable causal connection between the Dutch decriminalisation of cannabis and the rate at which cannabis use has evolved," Korf concludes.

Four countries in the European Union (Portugal, Italy, Luxembourg, and Spain) do not penalize the possession of cannabis for personal use.

COMMENTARY: The Beat Generation

"The use of psychedelics for spiritual purposes was started in the 50s by Allen Ginsberg and William Burroughs."
—TIMOTHY LEARY (1920–1996), HARVARD PSYCHOLOGIST

The Beat poets were a group of writers who challenged American society in the materialistic, conformist postwar decade of the 1950s. The group, which had its beginnings in New York City in the late 1940s, grew to have a lasting influence on American politics and literature.

Massachusetts-born school dropout Jack Kerouac (1922–1969) met the rebellious young Allen Ginsberg (1926–1997) from New Jersey while both were attending Columbia University in New York City. They shared a love of literature and started experimenting with marijuana and other drugs to aid their creativity. This was the start of what was to become the Beat group.

The Beats were one of the first American groups to experiment with drugs, both soft and hard. Kerouac's famous novel *On the Road* (1957) is a collection of stories that celebrate the lifestyle epitomized by the "Beat Generation," in which recreational drug use and casual sex play an important part. Another important Beat writer, William Burroughs (1914–1997), was arrested for possession of heroin and marijuana in 1949.

Hand in hand with drug experimentation went experiments with sexuality. Poet Allen Ginsberg, a homosexual at a time when homosexuality was not accepted, wrote an autobiographical poem about his sexuality entitled *Howl* (1955). It was published by a fellow writer and publisher, Lawrence Ferlinghetti, who was arrested and charged with publishing obscene literature. The case was overruled and brought the poem and the Beats much publicity. Burroughs' most famous novel, *Naked Lunch* (1959), was also tried for obscenity. Today Beat poems and novels are widely recognized and studied by literature students in college.

Comparing trends in cannabis use

Last year, Robert MacCoun of the University of California at Berkeley and Peter Reuter of the University of Maryland, compared trends in cannabis use in the US, Norway (which bans it) and the Netherlands. They also concluded that "reductions in criminal penalties have little effect on drug use, at least for marijuana." While the 1976 legislation may have had little effect on cannabis use, how effective has it been in its main goal of keeping people off harder drugs? The Netherlands has fewer addicts per capita than Italy, Spain, Switzerland, France or Britain, and far fewer than the US. Frits Knaak of the Trimbos Institute in Utrecht, the Dutch national institute for mental health and addiction, says the number of hard drug addicts in the country has been the same for a decade because fewer young people are joining their ranks. The average Dutch junkie is now 44 years old and only 0.3 per cent of Dutch teenagers had tried cocaine in 1994, compared with 1.7 per cent in the US. In the Netherlands, virtually everyone who uses drugs tries cannabis first, and many seem content to go no further.

Holland's policy of tolerance—often referred to as the "harm reduction" approach—is based on the theory that by separating legal soft-drug users from illegal hard-drug sellers, the potential harm to soft-drug users will be reduced.

Cannabis-related problems

Cannabis addiction and other problems are uncommon. "The number of cannabis users treated in drugs outpatient facilities is low," says Knaak. "In 1996, there were only 2000 [patients] in the whole country—just 0.3 per cent of all Dutch cannabis users."

Statistics can be misleading—in this case the number of cannabis users being treated might not reflect the number of cannabis users who actually need treatment.

Of those, 42 per cent "are also having trouble with alcohol or other drugs—the rest usually just need counselling to help change their lifestyle," says Sas. Most people who find cannabis causing trouble with concentration or memory at work or school, he says, apply rules, like no smoking on week nights, or they limit their intake.

This self-policing seems to work. Dutch teenagers get among the highest scores in the world on international science and mathematics tests. If there are serious problems caused by legalising marijuana, then twenty-plus years of the Dutch experiment has not revealed what they are.

HOLLAND'S HALF-BAKED DRUG EXPERIMENT
Larry Collins

NO

X "Look at the Dutch example!" That phrase has become a kind of mantra, chanted whenever the advocates of liberalizing drug laws in Europe or the United States gather. The Dutch, liberalization proponents argue, got it right by legalizing the public sale ... of cannabis....

But did they? It has been almost a quarter-century since the Dutch Parliament set Holland's drug policy on a course of its own, one markedly different from that of the rest of Europe. Surely 23 years is enough time to examine the consequences of that policy. How has it affected drug use and addiction in the Netherlands? ...

The author uses rhetorical questions to challenge the opposition in his argument against decriminalizing soft drugs.

The revised Dutch drug policy was based on Parliament's 1976 acceptance of the recommendation of a commission headed by Pieter A. H. Baan, a psychiatrist and expert in rehabilitating drug addicts who was serving at the time in the Dutch Office of Mental Health. The Baan Commission's report proposed distinguishing between so-called List One drugs— those that present "an unacceptable risk (heroin, cocaine and LSD)"—and List Two drugs—cannabis products, such as hashish and marijuana—seen as less dangerous and "softer." Essentially, Parliament depenalized the possession of 30 grams of marijuana.... At the same time, the parliamentarians vowed to continue the fight against both domestic and international trafficking in the more dangerous List One drugs.

Coffee shops authorized to sell cannabis

Holland's coffee shops are subject to legal restrictions; they are not allowed to advertise, to sell to minors, or to operate in close proximity to schools.

Shortly after accepting the commission's primary recommendation, Parliament went a step further by authorizing the commercialization of cannabis products through their open sale in a network of licensed coffee shops.... Out of respect for Holland's international treaty obligations, the import, export, production, or sale of cannabis products outside the coffee shops remained illegal.

At the time the Baan Commission report was adopted, Holland had what was considered a serious heroin addiction problem, albeit one roughly comparable to that of its European neighbors. The nation was relatively untroubled by major international drug traffickers, with the exception of a number of Chinese "triads" (gangs) whose trafficking was pretty much confined to the Dutch marketplace. How has that situation changed today? First and most revealing, Holland (in the words of senior customs and police officers in the United Kingdom, France, and Belgium) has become "the drugs capital of western Europe"—and not just of those soft drugs depenalized by the Dutch Parliament but also of hard drugs such as heroin, cocaine, and now ecstasy.

How accurate does the description of Holland as "the drugs capital" seem? Are there concrete facts to back it up, or does it sound more like hearsay?

Holland's liberal drug policy a failure

But what about the policy's consequences for the Dutch themselves? "Our liberal drug policy has been a failure, but its advocates are so rooted to their convictions they can't bring themselves to admit it," says Dr. Franz Koopman, director of De Hoop (The Hope) drug rehabilitation center in Dordecht and an open opponent of the Dutch policy. "First, we banalized cannabis. We have left our kids with the idea that it's perfectly all right to smoke it, and from there it was an easy step for them to move to the notion that it's also okay to use mind-altering substances like ecstasy. It is that mentality that is behind the explosion in the use of these synthetics we've seen in the last three years...."

A good point to begin evaluating the Dutch policy is with the very drug that, in a sense, inspired it: cannabis. Legalizing the sale of cannabis products through licensed coffee shops at the end of the 1970s confronted the prospective owners of those shops with a problem. Where were they going to get their drugs from? After all, importing them into Holland was still illegal under the nation's international treaty obligations.

Dutch produce homegrown cannabis

The answer they came up with was simple: grow it. Today, thanks to Dutch agricultural skills and the know-how of a coterie of American hash-lovers, Dutch cannabis growers produce their own homegrown cannabis, Nederwiet.... It is ... enormously potent. In 1976, the joints smoked in Holland, like those elsewhere in Europe, were the joints of the 1960s protest generation. They contained three to five percent THC (delta-nine-tetrahydro-cannabinol), the element that gives a joint-smoker a high. The THC content of today's joints can rise as high as 35 percent—10 times what it was when the Baan Commission decided to label cannabis a "soft" drug....

During the 1960s a counterculture emerged that attacked the establishment and demanded greater freedom. Soft drugs played an important part in this movement.

Insoluble in water, THC is absorbed by the fatty tissues of the body and brain and retained for longer than either alcohol or nicotine. Hence its debilitating effects—short-term memory loss, diminished learning capacity, and lessened motor skills—remain with heavy smokers for much longer than they may realize....

Probably 70 percent of the cannabis now puffed in Holland's coffee shops is Nederwiet.... "We see more and more people getting into trouble with cannabis," acknowledges Dr. J. A. Wallenberg, the director of the Jellinek Clinic, Holland's best-known drug abuse rehabilitation center...."

Soaring use of marijuana among Dutch youth

How useful is the comparison between the increase in the number of cannabis users and cases of alcohol abuse?

As the coffee shops boomed between 1984 and 1996, marijuana use among Dutch youths aged 18 to 25 leapt by well over 200 percent. In 1997, there was a 25 percent increase in the number of registered cannabis addicts receiving treatment for their habit, as compared to a mere 3 percent rise in cases of alcohol abuse. In 1995, public Ministry of Justice studies estimated that 700,000 to 750,000 of Holland's 15 million people—about 5 percent of the population—were regular cannabis users. A much more recent study just completed by Professor Pieter Cohen of the University of Amsterdam disputes those figures, claiming that only 325,000 to 350,000 Dutch men and women are regular cannabis users. Unfortunately, however, his survey discovered that those smokers are particularly concentrated among the young in densely populated areas of Amsterdam, Utrecht, and Rotterdam. In the last three to four years, these same areas have witnessed a skyrocketing growth in juvenile crime and the number of youths involved in acts of violence associated by many Dutch law-enforcement officers with the abuse of "soft" drugs....

Words such as "skyrocketing" are usually considered too sensational for debate. Do they strengthen or detract from an argument?

To what extent can that rise be attributed to the impact of Dutch youth's grass of choice, Nederwiet? The question cannot be easily answered. What is striking, however, is the boom in Nederwiet's production....

Nederwiet production boom

Today, according to Holland's "grass guru," Professor Adrian Jansen of the Economics Faculty of the University of Amsterdam, the annual Nederwiet harvest is a staggering 100 tons a year, almost all grown illegally. And it does not stay in the Netherlands. Perhaps as much as 65 tons of pot is exported—equally illegally—to Holland's neighbors. Holland now rivals Morocco as the principal source of European marijuana. By the Dutch Ministry of Justice's own estimates, the Nederwiet industry employs 20,000 people. The overall commercial value of the industry, including not only the growth and sale of the plant itself but the export of high-potency Nederwiet seeds to the rest of Europe and the United States, is 20 billion Dutch guilders, or about $10 billion—virtually all of it illegal ...

Jansen estimates that this pot crop—a direct outgrowth of Holland's drug policy—comes from some 25,000 to 30,000 small- to medium-scale producers, most of them growing their grass indoors, in a garage, a basement, or a back room. Under Dutch law, anyone may possess five plants for personal use. Virtually all those growers are raising far more ...

Booming "home grow" cannabis industry

One area left untouched by Dutch law enforcement is the booming "home grow" industry—shops whose sole function is to help their customers set themselves up as cannabis growers. That's because they are legal—provided ... they do not sell to foreigners, which ... virtually all of them do....

In the 1970s, advocates of Holland's coffee-shop policy argued that providing soft-drug users with a shopping outlet in which to buy their drugs would keep them from falling prey to drug-peddling criminals.... Petty criminality would fall, and hard-drug consumption would be cut by offering young people an attractive alternative.

That was the theory. Unfortunately, it did not work. A 1997 report on hard-drug use in the Netherlands by the government-financed Trimbos Institute acknowledged that "drug use is considered to be the primary motivation behind crimes against property"—23 years after the Dutch policy was supposed to put the brake on that. Furthermore, the Trimbos report put the number of heroin addicts in Holland at 25,000, a figure so low that critics of the government say it "Promotes a policy, not a reality." That statistic is based, the skeptics note, on the number of heroin addicts who actually come into contact, one way or another, with the nation's social or justice departments. The real figure, they maintain, is far closer to 35,000.

What is this "real figure" based on? It is far higher than the one given in the Trimbos report. Do you think it comes from a reliable source?

But even if one accepts the Trimbos figures as correct, they represent almost a tripling of the number of Dutch addicts since the country liberalized its drug policies. They also mean that Holland has twice as many heroin addicts per capita as Britain, which is known for having one of the most serious heroin problems in Europe. Furthermore, the number of heroin addicts being treated in the methadone-maintenance programs run by the Ministry of Public Health went from 6,511 in 1988 to 9,838 in 1997, an increase of just over 50 percent...

Does this last sentence tell us simply that there are more heroin addicts, or that more addicts are getting treatment?

Summary

Both authors use the Dutch example to illustrate their arguments for and against the decriminalization of soft drugs.

Debora Mackenzie notes that the statistics on drug use since the possession and sale of small amounts of cannabis were legalized in 1976 are far from conclusive. Attempting to give a balanced view, she shows that while the legalization of cannabis has possibly made Dutch adolescents more likely to try the drug, this does not mean they are more likely to continue to use it. Indeed, in the United States youngsters are far more likely to smoke marijuana than they are in Holland. More importantly, the Netherlands seems to have been successful in its main goal of separating cannabis use from that of harder drugs. Mackenzie quotes statistics that show Holland to have far fewer young people turning to hard drugs, and fewer addicts per capita, than in the United States and other parts of Europe.

Larry Collins calls into question many of the arguments that give support to Dutch liberalization of drug laws. He contends that Holland has become the "drugs capital of western Europe" since 1976, both for soft and hard drugs. Cannabis legalization has not only encouraged Dutch youngsters to experiment with more dangerous, mind-altering substances such as ecstasy, but has resulted in dangerous, highly potent strains of marijuana being grown locally for sale in coffee shops. This, Collins maintains, has led to more people becoming dependent on the drug and to many young people turning to crime to support their habit. In direct contradiction to the first article, he also argues that hard-drug use is now higher in the Netherlands than elsewhere.

FURTHER INFORMATION:

Books:

Baum, Dan, *Smoke and Mirrors: The War on Drugs and the Politics of Failure*. Boston, MA: Little Brown & Co., 1997.

Himmelstein, Jerome L., *The Strange Career of Marihuana. Politics and Ideology of Drug Control in America*. Westport, CT: Greenwood Press, 1983.

Miller, Richard Lawrence, *The Case for Legalizing Drugs*. Westport, CT: Praeger Pub Text, 1991.

Articles:

De Kort, Marcel, "The Dutch Cannabis Debate, 1968–1976." *The Journal of Drug Issues*, 1994, 24 (3).

Useful websites:

mir.drugtext.org/
Links to sites about drug use, policy, and other issues.

www.druglibrary.org/
Online library of articles, reports, and other material on drugs and drugs-related issues.

www.drugpolicy.org/
Site for Drug Policy Alliance, an organization dedicated to broadening the public debate on drug policy.

The following debates in the Pro/Con series may also be of interest:

In *Health*:
Topic 5 Should cannabis be legalized for medical treatment?

SHOULD SOFT DRUGS BE DECRIMINALIZED?

YES: *Marijuana has been used in medicine for more than 5,000 years; many sick people could benefit from its legal availability*

YES: *Using marijuana can only harm the user. The state has no right to dictate what individuals can or cannot do, provided they are not harming others.*

MEDICAL USE
If marijuana can help alleviate suffering, surely it should be legally available?

INDIVIDUAL RIGHTS
Shouldn't it be up to the individual whether or not they use cannabis?

NO: *Research has usually found that the harmful side effects of cannabis, particularly when smoked with tobacco, outweigh any benefits*

NO: *The state is justified in legislating to prevent people from harming themselves. Moreover, cannabis use can lead to socially harmful effects such as higher crime rates.*

SHOULD SOFT DRUGS BE DECRIMINALIZED?
KEY POINTS

YES: *If users can buy soft drugs legally, they will not need to come into contact with illegal drug dealers. This will reduce their chances of trying hard drugs.*

YES: *Legalizing soft drugs will free police and judicial resources to concentrate on combatting the sale and use of hard drugs*

SEPARATING DRUG USE
Will decriminalization of soft drugs keep people away from hard drugs?

NO: *Decriminalizing soft drugs will increase availability and hence use. Increased use of soft drugs will lead to an increased use of hard drugs.*

NO: *"Zero tolerance" of small-time criminals such as soft-drug dealers and users has been found to succeed in tackling more serious crime*

Topic 12
SHOULD TRIALS BE TELEVISED?

YES
"LET PEOPLE SEE THE ACTION"
FROM *SUNDAY HERALD*, APRIL 30, 2000
VAL ATKINSON

NO
"CAMERAS ON TRIAL: THE 'O.J. SHOW' TURNS THE TIDE"
JOURNAL OF BROADCASTING AND ELECTRONIC MEDIA, FALL, 1995
GEORGE GERBNER

INTRODUCTION

In January 2002 District Judge Leonie Brinkema refused to let Court TV televise the trial of Zacarias Moussaoui, the alleged twentieth terrorist in the September 11, 2001, attacks on New York City. Moussaoui himself supported restricted television coverage, yet Brinkema said her decision did not "violate the constitutional rights of either the public or the broadcast media" and that "any societal benefits from photographing and broadcasting these proceedings are heavily outweighed by the significant dangers worldwide broadcasting of this trial would pose to the orderly and secure administration of justice...."

Brinkema's decision drew a mixed response. Here was a judge supporting the integrity of the justice system, but was her decision in fact constitutional?

Court TV's lawyer Lee Levine thought otherwise. He argued that television was a "normal part of the courtroom procedure." It is true that 37 states allow cameras in state criminal proceedings and that all 50 states allow some type

of TV coverage in their courts, although often with restrictions. Yet other countries still refuse to allow cameras into the courtroom, fearful of the influence the media could have on the working of their justice systems.

Allowing cameras into the courtroom remains a contentious issue in the United States since it raises many questions. Is it constitutional? Does it in practice impede the path of justice, or does it actually serve to deter others from committing similar misdemeanors? Does it give the public the opportunity to see justice being done, or does it merely reduce trials to some form of entertainment not unsimilar to a TV drama or soap opera?

Historically the public has always been interested in the courtroom. People used to attend public trials, avidly watching as the courtroom drama unfolded. If they could not attend, they followed the court's daily proceedings through newspaper coverage.

The first-ever live radio broadcast of a trial was made in 1925 by the Chicago-based radio station WGN. It covered the sensational "monkey trial" of John Scopes, a young biology teacher accused of illegally teaching evolution. The trial attracted so many listeners that it prompted WGN to carry on covering other cases. But while audiences grew, so did criticism of the sensationalist tactics often employed by journalists to attract listeners.

> "The televising of trials would cause the public to equate the trial process with the forms of entertainment regularly seen on television."
>
> —FORMER CHIEF JUSTICE EARL WARREN

Matters came to a head during the 1935 trial of Bruno Hauptmann, the kidnapper of Charles Lindbergh's baby. The case attracted so much media attention that the conduct of the press was called into question when journalists fought to photograph the Lindberghs. Critics argued that there was little or no educational value to be gained in broadcasting such trials and that people were following them because of prurient interest.

Following the Lindbergh case, the American Bar Association (ABA) banned camera coverage altogether. Many states and the federal courts endorsed that decision, despite questions about its legality and constitutional viability.

With the introduction of television, however, matters became even more complicated. Texas, one of the few states that still allowed cameras in court, televised the trial of Billy Sol Estes, a former associate of Lyndon B. Johnson. Following his conviction, Estes argued that the televising of his trial had deprived him of his right to due process of law under the Fourteenth Amendment. The Supreme Court agreed and reversed his conviction. Since then the Estes argument has been seized on by several human rights groups to show that television diminishes the rights of the accused to a fair trial. A series of high-profile televised trials, such as that of former actor and athlete O. J. Simpson, have served to underline that argument.

First Amendment attorney Douglas Mirell, a member of the ACLU of Southern California's board of directors, argues, however, that "the press and public have a right to observe the judicial process." But many critics argue that allowing the media into the courtroom is not a constitutional right but a privilege. Then again, the state of New York, which had a 50-year-old statute making it a misdemeanor to photograph or televise a courtroom procedure, reversed that decision in February 2002, when Justice Nicholas Colabella ruled that the statute was unconstitutional.

The United States may have a fairly liberal attitude toward televising trials, yet many other countries have differing views on the issue.

The first of the following articles looks at the Scottish Lockerbie trials, when the media was refused access to the court. The second article examines the legality of televising trials with respect to the O. J. Simpson case.

LET PEOPLE SEE THE ACTION
Val Atkinson

For a report on the background to Lockerbie, the trial, and after the verdict, go to www. thelockerbietrial. com.

YES

On April 20, the BBC's application to broadcast the Lockerbie trial was refused by the High Court in Edinburgh. Here, Val Atkinson, BBC Scotland Deputy Head of News and Current Affairs, explains why she believes this was the wrong decision.

The trial of the two Libyan nationals accused of bombing PanAm flight 103 will attract enormous interest throughout the world. It is the international trial of the decade. Newspapers in every country will cover the proceedings, some with extensive verbatim reports of critical parts of the evidence. But television, the most popular medium of the 21st century, will only be able to offer its viewers a few headlines from reporters outside the court. "Pieces to camera", lasting just a few minutes, are totally inadequate to cover complex evidence.

Television may be popular, but does that mean it is the best medium for all types of communication?

No cameras in court

Justice may be done at Camp Zeist, but it will not be seen to be done. Nothing new there, you may say. In England and Wales, it is a criminal offence to take photographs in court. In Scotland, there is no such legal bar. However, except for a few documentaries and news reports of trials and appeals, allowed on an experimental and tightly-regulated basis, cameras are not allowed in courts and certainly never for a live broadcast. But in Scottish legal history the Lockerbie trial is unique. And it was on the grounds of its uniqueness, as well as its importance, that the BBC, supported by eight other broadcasters, applied to the Scottish courts for permission to televise and transmit the trial in full.

Camp Zeist is located about eight miles from Utrecht in central Holland. Until 1994 it was part of a U.S. military base, but was chosen in 2002 to be the site of the Lockerbie trial.

For the first time a Scottish criminal trial will sit abroad, thereby, in practice, denying access to the ordinary citizen who will pay for this long and expensive trial. Again uniquely, this trial is to be heard by a panel of Scottish judges. There will be no jury to be influenced by television reports. Witnesses who fear intimidation will be physically screened from press and public view, their voices distorted. There is no question of protecting the anonymity of the accused, their images have already been beamed around the world many times by newspapers and television stations.

What effects might the televising of trials have on potential witnesses? Do you think it might affect their evidence?

COMMENTARY: The Lockerbie trial

On December 21, 1988, Pan American Flight 103 was heading for New York from Frankfurt after a stop at London's Heathrow airport. Just a few minutes before reaching the Atlantic, a bomb blew the jet apart over the Scottish town of Lockerbie, killing the 259 passengers and crew, as well as 11 people on the ground. Experts were able to gather evidence from the tons of debris they collected on the ground.

A massive international inquiry followed, thought to be the biggest criminal investigation in history. Because the jet blew up over Britain, and most of its passengers were U.S. citizens, the United States and the United Kingdom operated a joint investigative operation. At first Iran and Syria were suspected of carrying out the bombing, but by 1991 the Libyans had emerged as the prime suspects. However, because of conflicting and sometimes confusing evidence, some people believe that it was political expediency to use Libya as a scapegoat.

A case was prepared against two Libyan men, Abdel Basset Ali Mohmed Al Megrahi and Al Ami Khalifa Fhimah, and the trial was set to take place, under Scottish law, in a specially built court at Camp Zeist in the Netherlands. The trial judge agreed to allow the proceedings to be broadcast to the families of the victims who were watching in London, Washington, New York, and Dumfries, Scotland. Because this was in effect a mass-murder trial, and there was huge worldwide interest, BBC Scotland launched an appeal in the High Court in Edinburgh seeking permission to televise the trial. The BBC bid, which was supported by eight other broadcasters, was rejected by Lord MacFadyen of the High Court in Edinburgh on the grounds that the Libyans' right to a fair trial was of more importance than the rights of the media.

Appeal televised

The trial began on the May 3, 2000, and ended in January 2001. One defendant was found guilty, and the other was acquitted. A year later the lawyer acting for the man convicted of the Lockerbie bombing asked an appeal court to consider fresh evidence. The appeal began on January 23, 2002, and ended on March 14, 2002, when the bomber lost his appeal. The BBC was granted permission to televise the proceedings of the appeal, a decision acclaimed as a milestone. The judges reserved the right to veto the filming of witnesses if they felt that the cameras would influence what the witnesses said or would affect the result of the appeal. After high-profile trials, such as the O.J. Simpson and Louise Woodward cases, which resulted in many members of the legal profession questioning the advisability of televising trials, the Lockerbie appeal may be a genuine breakthrough—if the circumstances are deemed to be favorable to the courtroom and do not compromise the evidence.

There was huge media interest in the Lockerbie trial, shown here outside the specially built Scottish court at Camp Zeist, Netherlands.

> Do you think cameras are appropriate in court? For opposing viewpoints see http://news.bbc. co.uk/hi/english/uk/ newsid_652000/ 652173.stm.

Issues around the disruption, or the effect on nervous witnesses, of cameras in court do not apply in this case. Cameras have already been installed in court to relay pictures to the press centre. These pictures will also be sent to sites in New York, Washington, London and Dumfries by means of a secure cable feed so the relatives of the victims can follow the trial.

The BBC wanted to enable the interested observer, anywhere in the world, the same access to the evidence as he or she would have from the public gallery in the Netherlands through its News OnLine service.

There would be no editing, no sound bites, no trivialisation, no possibility of biased or selective reporting. We believed that these were convincing arguments that, in the particular circumstances of the Lockerbie trial, this extension of freedom of expression would not interfere with the administration of justice and the Libyans' right to a fair trial.

On April 20, the BBC's second petition to televise the trial was turned down by the High Court in Edinburgh. The court was not satisfied that the broadcasters had proved that there was no risk to the administration of justice, in particular the court recognised the fears expressed by the Crown and the defence that witnesses, who are appearing voluntarily, would refuse to come if they knew they would be seen on public television. This condition is impossible for the broadcasters to satisfy as journalists have not been given a list of witnesses and cannot ascertain their views.

> *"A long line of cases shows that it is not merely of some importance, but is of fundamental importance that justice should not only be done, but should manifestly and undoubtedly be seen to be done."*
>
> —*REX V. SUSSEX JUSTICES,*
>
> NOVEMBER 9, 1923

The objections of the two accused men to appearing on public television were also cited. The importance the Court itself gave to considerations of the sensitivities of the accused or the witnesses can be judged by the fact that permission was given for limited television coverage to the Office for the Victims of Crime, an agency of the United States Justice Department, without the prior consent of either the witnesses or the accused. The failure of the courts to grant permission for the live public televising of the Lockerbie trial is a lost opportunity to show Scottish justice in action and to allay any suspicions of politicians or press in unfriendly countries that Abdel Basset Ali al-Megrahi and Lamen Khalifa Fhimah will not get a fair trial in the West....

Despite sanctions, it has taken nine years, the intervention of the UN ... and the signing of an international treaty, before Libya agreed to surrender its nationals for trial. What better way to have demonstrated the fairness of that trial than to broadcast, via the internet, the unvarnished evidence to the interested citizen in Washington?

Should people accused of a crime have a say in whether or not their trial is televised?

Compare the Lockerbie case with another famous case that was televised. For information go to www.cnn.com/US/OJI.

CAMERAS ON TRIAL: THE "O.J. SHOW" TURNS THE TIDE
George Gerbner

NO

X   … It began with the low-speed chase of the white Ford Bronco followed by seven helicopters, displaying TV news air power not to be seen again until the helicopters followed another white car with O.J. Simpson a free (if marked) man. Between June 17, 1994 and October 3, 1995, the world has been treated to the most mesmerizing, polarizing, and precedent-shattering television show in history.

For further detail about the O.J. Simpson trial see pages 162–163.

An opening-day audience 95 million in the U.S. alone (I watched in a hotel room in Paris where I had been attending a conference) witnessed, In the words of the *New York Times* headline (June 22, 1994, p.A12), the "Struggle … for the Minds of Potential Jurors." Once the jury selection was completed, the struggle went on for the minds not only of jurors but of the communities into which jurors, judge, witnesses, attorneys, and all other participants must return. That struggle raged in and out of court but in sight of television cameras, through 266 days, 126 witnesses, 20 attorneys, 1105 pieces of evidence, and 45,000 pages of transcript, plus many more episodes kept from the jury as potentially prejudicial, irrelevant, or inflammatory, but all seen by the television audience.

Do you think televising the O.J. Simpson trial influenced the outcome of the trial?

The end of the explosive trial, but by no means of its far-reaching fallout, came at 1 p.m. in the afternoon of the day when 150 million viewers at home and another estimated 50 million outside of home held its collective breath for 10 minutes. New York viewers had suddenly turned on 750,000 television sets, boosting Con Edison's load by 93 million watts. Long-distance phone calls dropped 58 percent, lightening AT&T's load. Trading on the New York stock exchange plunged by 30 million shares. Airlines delayed departures, legislatures delayed votes, presidents, prime ministers, and cabinet members suspended state business until the verdict was announced. Then, again on television, instant history was frozen into memories of racial conflict, gender division, general consternation about what had happened and why, and heated table conversations in 65

Gerbner uses a list of statistics to prove the impact of the trial verdict.

Does TV make for instant history?

million homes. As the post-mortems replaced the coverage, the toughest decisions the participants faced was whether and how to cash in on the market for their notoriety, how to vindicate their roles, how to reveal what the cameras had concealed or distorted, and how to settle scores. The *New York Times* published "An O. J. Bibliography" on October 1, reporting that "Thirty O. J.-related books have gushed forth so far…. And … there will be more." If there ever was a need to demonstrate that cameras can transform, prolong, and make a travesty of a trial, we had it in the O. J. Simpson Show's spectacular run for over a year. It has begun to turn the tide that threatened to make high-profile justice a captive of show business.

Do you think "travesty of a trial" is a harsh judgment on the trial? Was justice compromised in the O.J. Simpson trial? What was the effect on views on racism and the justice system?

Cameras make the difference

The combustible mixture that went into the trial—sex, violence, celebrity, and the ostentatious display of all the legal talent that money can buy—would have produced fireworks in any medium. But the O. J. Show exploded more like a nuclear chain reaction. The reason can be found in the difference cameras make in the total cultural environment.

The claim that a television trial is not much different from the usual publicity surrounding sensational cases is in the wrong ballpark. It confuses the retail dissemination of news to a relatively selective readerships with the universal wholesaler discharging massive streams of images and messages into the mainstream of the common cultural environment….

On September 17, 1995, even before the verdict was announced, the *New York Times* headline observed that "Simpson Case Backlash Keeps Cameras Out of Other Courtrooms." News media lawyers, jurists, and other experts, some of who favored cameras before, were cited as blaming cameras for turning "the search for justice into a spectator sport," for intimidating some and emboldening other participants, and for the interminable length of the trial. The issue I pose is not one of guilt or innocence, or even just the length of the trial, but the total quantitative and qualitative difference that real-time television saturation makes to the conduct, outcome, and aftermath of a high-profile criminal trial. The chief legal and social policy question is whether that difference is compatible with the mission of the courts, as distinct, for example, from televising legislatures dealing with public policy matters rather than with private lives and the search for convincing evidence. As any student of communication (or any performer) knows,

Do the media have a responsibility to help justice be served? Do you think O.J. Simpson was treated differently from other defendants because of his celebrity?

Is allowing viewers to witness "real history in the making" a valid reason for allowing trials to be televised?

if you change the audience you change the performance. ... Transporting the trial scene into a public arena, as political tribunals and long-discredited show trials tended to do, makes hundreds of millions of viewers feel that they are actually witnessing real history in the making. Their reaction affects trial participants, influences the outcome, and alters the subsequent course of the now irreversibly modified sequence of events far beyond any previous feats of publicity....

Legal issues

In general, the courts have focused on three issues: (a) whether a ban on coverage of trials violated the broadcast media's First Amendment right of free speech; (b) whether such a ban undermines the defendant's Sixth Amendment right to a public trial; and (c) whether camera coverage deprives the defendant in a criminal trial of his Fourteenth Amendment right of due process.

For a discussion on the First Amendment argument go to http://writ.news.findlaw.com/hilden/20020122.html.

On January 26, 1981, the Court held in *Chandler v. Florida* (449 U.S. 560), that a ban on television coverage of trials did not violate the broadcast media's First Amendment right of free speech. It held that camera coverage (as distinct from reporting) is not protected by the First Amendment....

Chief Justice Warren Burger observed in *Chandler* that "the requirement of a public trial is satisfied by the opportunity of members of the public and the press to attend the trial and to report what they have observed." On the other hand, *Chandler* also held that television coverage is not a per se denial of defendants' constitutional right to a fair trial. The reason is the lack of scientifically acceptable evidence bearing on the issue. Thus *Chandler* posed the key challenge: States are free to experiment in order to demonstrate whether or not the addition of cameras makes a difference that affects the ability of the courts to conduct a fair trial.

But as a 1983 decision, *United States v. Hastings* (695 F.2d 1278, 11th Cir.) observed in upholding the federal court ban, it is very difficult to detect the adverse impact of television coverage. In an unpublished 1989 review of experiments undertaken by the court, my students and I at the Annenberg School for Communication at the University of Pennsylvania found that they were conducted by interested parties, employed no controls, had specified no criteria for "success," and did not test effects on participants in scientifically acceptable ways. Predictably, they came to the foregone conclusion that television coverage did not disturb the proceedings, a rationale that had become irrelevant to the issues that had emerged since the Hauptmann trial. In contrast, a 1986 survey of participants and observers by a New Orleans researcher, William M. Henican, asked about a broader range of impacts, and concluded that "the risks of allowing cameras into the trial courts of this country are very high" and that "when prejudice does occur it will be very difficult to demonstrate." Paul Thaler's 1994 book offers mixed but equally troubling evidence. The key question posed in *Chandler* remained unanswered—until now....

Now we know

When lead defense attorney Johnny Cochran was asked on national television if he would favor cameras in the future, he hesitated a bit and said, "Well, in this case, it turned out to help us. I believe that because of the presence of the cameras, Judge Ito made some decisions that were favorable to our side. Without cameras he might have been much tougher...."

On September 30, 1993, the Federal Judicial Center released a little-publicized study by an independent research organization, designed to assess the Federal courts' experiment with admitting cameras into civil trials. They found little or no evidence that the use of courtroom footage provides additional information to viewers about either the facts of the case being covered or the legal process involved....The pictures frequently seemed to dramatize and personalize the story, rather than adding any factual material to it.... Within the confines of our investigative procedures, we could not confirm that the use of cameras in the courtroom served any educative function.

Shortly thereafter, the Federal Courts terminated the experiment. The study provides an at least partial answer [to] the questions posed in *Chandler* about the legal, informational, or educational value of the addition of cameras to the reporting of trials. It is now only a question of time until the reversal of another major verdict on grounds of television contamination, as in *Estes*, leads to the renewal of the long-standing safeguards protecting the integrity of the judicial process. In the meantime, the state courts are expected to review their policies and Courts of Appeal to take a careful and critical view before dismissing appeals on grounds of prejudicial camera coverage.

It is high time to join other democratic countries in refusing to deliver our courts, juries, and defendants to television exploitation and experimentation whose consequences for lives and justice we may never know.

This implies that the presence of cameras in the courtroom may have altered the judge's decision. Go to www.cnn.com/2002/LAW/01/18/inv.moussaoui.tv.trial/ for details of the case of a suspected terrorist for which the judge has denied a request to televise the proceedings.

For more detail on the trial of Billy Sol Estes, see page 151.

Do you think that televising trials in a controled environment would help show that justice has been served properly?

Summary

The issue of whether trials should be televised is interesting because it raises all kinds of ethical, legal, and constitutional issues. In the two preceding articles the main points in the debate are examined.

In "Let People See the Action" Val Atkinson, BBC Scotland deputy head of news and current affairs, examines the refusal of the High Court in Edinburgh, Scotland, to grant the BBC's application to broadcast the Lockerbie trial. Atkinson argues that "justice may be done at Camp Zeist, but it will not be seen to be done." The author feels that this is unfair since newspapers and journals around the world will report the case, sometimes verbatim, while television will have to rely on quotes. Atkinson asserts that this is a major injustice, not least because the taxpayer will be footing the bill for the case while not actually seeing firsthand what it is all about, but also because any fears of an unfair trial in the West will not be dispelled.

George Gerbner, on the other hand, looks at the sensational trial of media star O.J. Simpson. Gerbner claims that he is not looking at the issue of guilt or innocence, but rather at the "quantitive and qualitative difference that real-time television saturation makes to conduct, outcome, and aftermath of a high-profile criminal trial."

Gerbner argues that media pressure and public visibility have persuaded 47 states to admit cameras into the courtroom, but that it is high time that the United States join other democratic countries in "refusing to deliver our courts, juries, and defendants to television exploitation and experimentation whose consequences for lives and justice we may never know."

FURTHER INFORMATION:

Books:

Goldfarb, Ronald L., *TV or Not TV: Television, Justice, and the Courts.* New York: New York University Press, 1998.

Thaler, P., *The Watchful Eye: American Justice in the Age of the Television Trial.* Westport, CN: Praeger, 1994.

Useful websites:

http://crime.about.com/library/weekly/aa20thHijacker.htm
Links to articles on the trial of Zacarias Moussaoui.
http://www.nysda.org/Hot_Topics/Cameras_in_the_Court/cameras_in_the_court.html
Examines the televising of trials in New York's courts.
http://www.townhall.com/columnists/davidlimbaugh/dl20020112.shtml

David Limbaugh, "Say No to Televised Trial."
http://writ.news.findlaw.com/hilden/20020122.html
Julie Hilden, "Why the Zacarias Moussaoui Trial Should Be Televised."

The following debates in the Pro/Con series may also be of interest:

In this volume:
 O.J. Simpson: The trial of the century, pages 162–163.

In *Media*:
 Topic 3 Do people watch too much television?

SHOULD TRIALS BE TELEVISED?

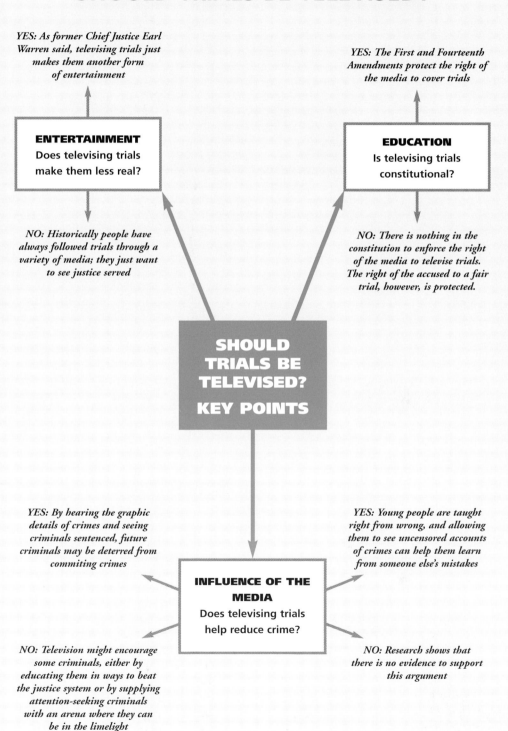

YES: As former Chief Justice Earl Warren said, televising trials just makes them another form of entertainment

YES: The First and Fourteenth Amendments protect the right of the media to cover trials

ENTERTAINMENT
Does televising trials make them less real?

EDUCATION
Is televising trials constitutional?

NO: Historically people have always followed trials through a variety of media; they just want to see justice served

NO: There is nothing in the constitution to enforce the right of the media to televise trials. The right of the accused to a fair trial, however, is protected.

SHOULD TRIALS BE TELEVISED? KEY POINTS

YES: By hearing the graphic details of crimes and seeing criminals sentenced, future criminals may be deterred from commiting crimes

YES: Young people are taught right from wrong, and allowing them to see uncensored accounts of crimes can help them learn from someone else's mistakes

INFLUENCE OF THE MEDIA
Does televising trials help reduce crime?

NO: Television might encourage some criminals, either by educating them in ways to beat the justice system or by supplying attention-seeking criminals with an arena where they can be in the limelight

NO: Research shows that there is no evidence to support this argument

O.J. SIMPSON: THE TRIAL OF THE CENTURY

"If we had God booked and O.J. was available,
we'd move God."

—LARRY KING, CNN TALKSHOW HOST

In 1994 former professional football player and sometime actor Orenthal James (O.J.) Simpson became possibly the most famous criminal defendant in U.S. legal history when he was tried for the double-murder of his second wife Nicole Brown and waiter Ronald Goldman. The nine-month trial was the longest ever held in California and cost over $20,000,000 to fight and defend. It attracted enormous media attention and was watched by millions around the world. The trial and Simpson's subsequent acquittal brought all kinds of questions to the fore, such as: Is the justice system racist? Was Simpson's trial a fair one? Did the media sway public opinion? Should trials be televised?

Background

On Sunday, June 12, 1994, the body of 35-year-old Nicole Brown was discovered in the driveway of her home in Brentwood, Los Angeles. A few feet away lay 25-year-old Ronald Lyle Goldman. Both of them had been viciously stabbed to death. Nicole was the estranged wife of the media star O.J. Simpson.

The murders attracted a lot of media attention from the start. O.J. Simpson had been a famous sports star, although at the time of the murder he was largely unknown to most of the U.S. public; but more than that, he was news—a black man who had possibly murdered his white wife and another white man. But what was his motive? Had Brown been having an affair with Goldman? Had Simpson's jealousy driven him to murder? Was Simpson a wife-beater, unable to control his temper? Many tabloid headlines linked the two victims romantically, but in the end it was established that Goldman was merely returning a pair of glasses that Brown's mother had left behind in the restaurant where he worked.

It quickly became apparent that the police suspected Simpson; police interviews with him were leaked to the press. The media frenzy grew, especially after serological tests on blood drops collected at the crime scene placed Simpson at the crime scene. On the strength of this evidence an arrest warrant was prepared, and O.J.'s attorney was informed that the police planned to arrest him on June 17 on two accounts of first-degree murder. However, O.J. fled with his friend A.C. Cowlings, leaving behind a "farewell note" in which he proclaimed his innocence and asked the media to leave his children alone.

The note was subsequently read and analyzed on every major network station. The highest-ranking LAPD public spokesman went on television to announce that O.J. was now a fugitive sought by all law-enforcement agencies.

At around seven o'clock in the evening Cowlings' vehicle was spotted, and a cellular phone call between Cowlings and the police was also intercepted. Cowlings told them that Simpson was sitting in the back of his vehicle with a gun to his head. L.A. radio stations broadcast several well-known sports commentators pleading with O.J. not to kill himself. All regular television programming was dropped. The skies above southern California were filled with media helicopters filming dozens of police cars slowly following Cowlings' vehicle as crowds of people cheered from overpasses. Cowlings' Ford Bronco eventually stopped at Simpson's Rockingham estate, where after an hour of filmed negotiation, O.J. Simpson was arrested.

The "trial of the century"

The trial began on January 24, 1995. It quickly became obvious that O.J. Simpson's trial was more than just a battle to find out who had killed Nicole Brown and Ron Goldman—in fact, that almost seemed a secondary issue.

For many people the trial was all about race. Could a black person accused of murder find justice in a legal system designed and run mainly by white people? As the trial went on, evidence emerged to suggest that certainly in Simpson's case he could not. A 1995 interview revealed homicide detective Mark Fuhrman to be sexist and abusive to offenders; he referred to black people as "niggers." Although Fuhrman denied using that word, he was quickly labeled a bad cop by the media, who also made much of the fact that he was accused of planting evidence—a bloody glove—in order to bring Simpson to trial.

The makeup of the jury led many critics to question whether a predominantly minority-led jury would ever convict a black celebrity regardless of the evidence before them—certainly critics have argued that discrediting an LAPD policeman as a possible racist played a big part in their decision to find Simpson innocent. The fact that Simpson's lead counsel, Jonnie Cochrane, compared Fuhrman to Hitler in his closing statement cannot have helped. After the trial CNN conducted a poll that found that many Americans thought the trial had set race relations back by about 30 years. To other critics the trial fueled the debate over the influence of the media on public opinion.

The nine-month trial was televised around the world, and around 2,000 reporters were present throughout. Many of the witnesses and lawyers became celebrities almost overnight. One poll showed that 74 percent of Americans could identify Simpson's lodger Kato Kaelin, but only 25 percent recognized Al Gore—the vice president at the time. In the end around 142 million people listened to the radio or watched on television as O.J. Simpson was acquitted of the crime on October 3, 1995. A civil suit was subsequently brought against him. The Goldmans and Browns split the amount earned from the auctioning of Simpson's estate. Although Simpson still denies the murder, his trial raised all kinds of questions about the working of the U.S. justice system.

PART 3
THE PENAL SYSTEM

INTRODUCTION

"It isn't true that convicts live like animals: Animals have more room to move around." The Peruvian novelist Mario Vargas Llosa may have been being ironic about conditions in prison, but his observation reflects an important concern about conditions in the penal system. This in turn is connected to an even more fundamental question: What are prisons for?

The incarceration of criminals is as old as civilization itself. Throughout history societies have locked away lawbreakers or even people who have spoken out against the social system of the time. Part of the reason for imprisonment is simple: to protect society by putting criminals in a position where they cannot reoffend. Therefore prisons need to be secure and prisoners guarded in order to prevent escape.

Another basic purpose of prisons is to punish wrongdoers and to deter others from committing similar crimes. Detention would clearly not function as a punishment or deterrent, critics argue, if it were possible to live as comfortably in prison as in the outside world. In recent centuries another purpose for prisons has emerged: rehabilitation. Prisons have come to be seen as institutions where criminals can be reformed through education and counseling, so that they can be released as better members of society who will be unlikely to offend again.

The situation today

There are currently more than two million people in prison in the United States, a higher proportion of the population than in virtually any other country in the world. At the same time, crime figures show little sign of falling. Critics argue that this proves that the penal system is not working as a protection, a deterrent, or a means of rehabilitation. Supporters of the prison system, on the other hand, believe that the increase in the prison population and rises in crime figures are both the result of changes in society. They argue that the penal system is coping admirably with the problems it faces.

Conditions within prison are also the subject of heated debate. Supporters of the system argue that common sense alone would suggest that the harshness of some prison regimes acts as a deterrent to other potential criminals, particularly juveniles. Critics argue that although prisoners have broken the law, society has a duty to care for their well-being. They are concerned that conditions that are too cramped and brutal are unconstitutional and violate prisoners' human rights. In addition, they argue that creating harsh conditions in prisons reflects only the role of incarceration as a punishment. They believe that deterrence does not work—that few people who are about to commit a crime stop to consider the consequences of their action—and that a more positive approach is needed to achieve rehabilitation.

Other people believe once a criminal, always a criminal, and that there is little point in trying to reform people who cannot be reformed. The main purpose of prisons in such a view is simply to take as many lawbreakers out of society for as long as possible.

The final section in this book examines four issues to do with the penal system and punishment.

Topic 14 looks at the issue of prisoners' rights. Both articles look at Camp X-Ray in Cuba where suspected Al Qaeda and Taliban fighters are detained. Peter Beaumont, in the first article of Topic 14, argues that these men are being abused and that normally people would object to such a breach of human rights. However, Michael Hoes claims that the prisoners are well treated. He argues that they do not have the rights of prisoners of war.

> *"To assert in any case that a man must be absolutely cut off from society because he is absolutely evil amounts to saying that society is absolutely good, and no one in his right mind will believe this today."*
> — ALBERT CAMUS, 20TH-CENTURY FRENCH NOVELIST

Do prisons work?
The current prison system has come under increasing attack.

In the first article of Topic 13 Robert Worth argues that prisons can work. He looks at McKean, a federal correction center in Bradford, Pennsylvania" that seems to have extremely good results. Prisoners attend classes, tend gardens, and live in a clean and orderly environment; thus Worth believes that McKean is an example of how prisons should work if operated in an efficient and civil manner. But is McKean a rare example?

However, the second article argues that prisons are overcrowded, inhumane, and too expensive. It claims that prisons have two functions— to keep dangerous criminals off the streets and to act as a deterrent. The system fails on both accounts.

Privatization vs. the state
Topic 15 looks at the issue of private prisons. Today there are almost 160 private prisons in America.

The National Center for Policy Analysis in the first article of Topic 15 argues that private prisons are less expensive and more efficient. The American Federation of State, County, and Municipal Employees, however, argues that it is a myth that private prisons are better operations or that they save money.

Castration
The final topic deals with the controversial issue of whether sex offenders should be chemically castrated. Kevin Giordano argues that it helps stop reoffending, but Eric Lotke claims that it is not the most effective approach.

Topic 13
DO PRISONS WORK?

YES
"A MODEL PRISON"
THE ATLANTIC MONTHLY, NOVEMBER 1995
ROBERT WORTH

NO
"PRISONS DO NOT WORK"
HTTP://WWW.CWRL.UTEXAS.EDU/~TONYA/FINAL_PROJECTS/
PRISONS_DON'T_WORK-FINAL.HTML
HUGH MAHONEY

INTRODUCTION

There are various reasons for sending someone to prison. The most common are to punish the offender, to protect the public from dangerous people, to rehabilitate and reform the prisoner before releasing him or her into society, to reduce crime rates, and to serve as a deterrent for others intending to commit crime. Yet there is much debate as to the primary purpose of prisons. Should prisons punish offenders or rehabilitate them to keep them from reoffending? Are prisons a deterrent to those intending to commit crime or only holding houses to keep criminals off the street and the public safe?

Many people believe that the only way to teach someone not to commit crime is to incarcerate them for a period befitting their crime: The harsher the crime, the harsher the sentence. Prisons are to punish, they claim, and are not meant to give offenders an easy ride or to serve as educational facilities.

However, an increasing crime rate has led to a corresponding growth in the prison population—in 2002 there were almost 2 million people in state prisons—along with accusations of overcrowding, poor conditions, and mistreatment in prisons. In 1995 the UN Human Rights Commission stated that conditions in certain maximum-security prisons were incompatible with international standards. Human rights organizations, such as Amnesty International, argue that an emphasis on punishment in prisons leaves the door open to human rights violations of inmates. According to their report, these violations include the use of high-tech tools of repression and torture, assaults by guards, the use of pepper spray and Mace, chain gangs, deficiencies in medical treatment, unsanitary conditions, sexual abuse by staff and other inmates, and the use of restraints, such as chains and leg irons.

Yet those who believe that the primary purpose of prisons is to punish criminals think it is necessary to treat prisoners harshly. Otherwise, they say, most state prisons serve merely as criminal universities, where minor offenders can learn the "tricks of the trade" from more hardened criminals.

But are criminals not entitled to basic rights and reasonable treatment? Some recent cases have suggested that certain authorities and institutions do not think so. In 1998, for example, a case came to court of ex-prisoners of Holmesburg Prison in Pennsylvania who were used as guinea pigs for chemical skin tests. Some prisoners were infected with viruses (including hepatitis), syphilis, malaria, and tularemia; some suffered injection of cancer cells and irradiation of the testicles. The case caused human and civil rights organizations to protest.

> *"There is no such thing as justice—in or out of court."*
> —CLARENCE DARROW (1857–1938),
> CRIMINAL LAWYER

Human rights groups are also concerned about the large number of prisoners who come from minority groups. They question whether this reflects the high incidence of crime among those groups or shows how racist the U.S. criminal justice system is (see Topic 1, pages 10–21).

Some people think that the primary purpose of prisons is to rehabilitate offenders rather than to punish them. They argue that if prisoners are treated harshly in prison, they are more likely to think that they are worthless human beings and will probably commit similar or worse crimes when they are freed.

But do violent criminals or murderers deserve the chance to be rehabilitated? How would that make the victim or the victim's family feel? What message does that send to anyone contemplating a similar crime? Some people also worry that rehabilitation leads to a "revolving door" syndrome—that if a person leaves prison as a hardened offender, he or she may commit another, similar crime just so that they can go back to jail. They argue that this is more likely to occur if prisoners are treated well. If offenders know that they can commit a crime and live in nice conditions in prison, gain an education, and receive opportunities that may not be available to them in the outside world, prison will not serve as a deterrent to committing further crimes. They believe that only punishment can serve as an essential threat to deter further deviant behavior, and that if punishments did not vary according to the severity of the offense, there would be no incentive to commit a lesser offense rather than a more serious one. Yet if prison life was harsh, people might think twice before offending, and recidivism might be lessened at the prospect of another term in jail.

However, people are now questioning whether the prison system really works. But what are the alternatives? Some suggestions for minor offenders have included fines, electronic monitoring, community service, or correctional supervision (punishing offenders by restricting their lifestyles but offering them a chance to develop within the communities they live in and curb their bad behavior through participation in programs such as anger management or alcohol or drug rehabilitation).

The following articles discuss in greater detail the pros and cons of the prison system at present.

A MODEL PRISON
Robert Worth

YES

Setting a scene or giving a sense of place is a useful way to start an argument.

Approaching McKean, the federal correctional institution in Bradford, Pennsylvania, one is not likely to think of a prison. The buildings, low and modern, display a pseudo-Navajo motif in soft gray and salmon colors. In the air-conditioned entryway there are carpets over an immaculate tile floor, the glimmer of polished glass, the green tint of tropical plants. Tasteful couches sit in the corners. Well-dressed employees walk up and down the stairs, speaking in hushed, respectful tones. Beyond, on the prison grounds, are a broad expanse of well-tended lawn and distant athletic fields. Inmates walk alone or in pairs along the concrete pathways, offering greetings as they pass. Across the compound inmates sit quietly in classrooms, learning everything from basic reading skills to masonry, carpentry, horticulture, barbering, cooking, and catering....

Effective prison or resort?

This prison and others like it are the targets of a fierce campaign that is changing the shape of the U.S. criminal-justice system. For several years journalists and politicians all over the country have spoken and written angrily about such prisons as "resorts" or "country clubs." They have railed against a philosophy of rehabilitation that "coddles" inmates with too many amenities. Punishment is in vogue, along with hard labor and "no frills" prisons, stripped of weight rooms, TVs, and computers. Republicans in Congress have added a no-frills-prison section to the Contract With America's "Take Back Our Streets Act," and they have passed it as an amendment to the 1994 crime bill. Massachusetts Governor William F. Weld has argued that prisons should be "a tour through the circles of hell," where inmates should learn only "the joys of busting rocks."

Go to www.google.com, and find out more about the Take Back Our Streets Act.

Alabama has already reinstituted the chain gang, forcing inmates to do hard labor in leg irons for up to ten hours a day. State administrators and sheriffs, sniffing the political wind, have begun to crack down, cutting educational and treatment programs, making prison life as harsh as possible.

Go to www.amnestyusa.org/rightsforall/prison.html for an Amnesty International article on the use of restraints.

Yet McKean, by several measures, may well be the most successful medium-security prison in the country. Badly overcrowded, housing a growing number of violent criminals, it costs taxpayers approximately $15,370 a year for each inmate. That is below the average for prisons of its type, and far below the overall federal average of $21,350. It is about two thirds of what many state prisons cost. And the incident record since McKean opened, in 1989, reads like a blank slate: No escapes. No homicides. No sexual assaults. No suicides. In six years there have been three serious assaults on staff members and six recorded assaults on inmates. State prisons of comparable size often see that many assaults in a single week. The American Correctional Society has given McKean one of its highest possible ratings. No recidivism studies have been conducted on its former inmates, but senior staff members claim that McKean parolees return to prison far less often than those from other institutions, and a local parole officer agrees. According to the Princeton University criminologist John DiIulio, "McKean is probably the best-managed prison in the country. And that has everything to do with a warden named Dennis Luther...."

> The author argues that there have been no escapes, homicides, assaults, or suicides and that therefore McKean's record is good. Is that a valid way to judge a prison?

The root of Luther's approach is an unconditional respect for the inmates as people. "If you want people to behave responsibly, and treat you with respect, then you treat other people that way," Luther says. McKean is literally decorated with this conviction. Plaques all over the prison remind staff members and inmates alike of their responsibilities; one of these plaques is titled "Beliefs About the Treatment of Inmates." There are twenty-eight beliefs, the product of Luther's many years as a warden, and they begin like this:

"Beliefs about the treatment of inmates"

1. Inmates are sent to prison *as* punishment and not *for* punishment.
2. Correctional workers have a *responsibility* to ensure that inmates are returned to the community no more angry or hostile than when they were committed.
3. Inmates are *entitled* to a safe and humane environment while in prison.
4. You must believe in man's *capacity* to change his behavior.
5. Normalize the environment to the extent possible by providing programs, amenities, and services. The denial of such must be related to maintaining order and security rather than punishment.
6. Most inmates will respond favorably to a clean and aesthetically pleasing physical environment and will not vandalize or destroy it.

> What do you think the warden's distinction means?

The Oscar-nominated Midnight Express *is based on a true-life story about a young man's grueling experiences in a Turkish jail following his arrest for drug smuggling. The film resulted in a lot of debate about prisoners' rights and human rights abuses.*

Clean and orderly

To a visitor, McKean's "clean and aesthetically pleasing" environment is its most striking feature. Impressions gleaned from *Midnight Express*, *Judge Dredd*, or an ordinary state prison are out of place here. Luther insists that these physical details help to maintain order, just as the programs do. During my visit, as he led me past the special housing unit that is known in most prisons as "the hole" to the recreation area, a group of inmates appeared in the distance, jogging on a circular track around an athletic field. "Some of the staff think there's too much recreation here," he told me. "Most think it's important. On a summer evening you've got three to five hundred men in this rec yard, with three staff. If you had less recreation, you'd need more staff … Many inmates earn licenses that help them to get jobs when they are released. They also have opportunities to teach one another—a mentors' group, for instance, and the "I Care" group, which holds discussions about issues of prison life. Many inmates teach Adult Continuing Education as well. These programs are not mere frills, Luther claims, because they help to keep the prison running smoothly.

A stricter prison

The author recounts how Luther reversed a punishment once the prisoners showed that they could behave. Do you think trust is an important factor in rehabilitation?

In some respects McKean is stricter than other prisons, because inmates are held to higher standards. Three years ago, after a few minor incidents, Luther imposed a condition known as "closed" movement, restricting inmates' activity during evening hours. The condition was meant to be permanent. A group of inmates asked him if he would restore "open" movement if the prison was incident-free for a period of ninety days. He agreed, and the prison has run on open movement ever since. Many McKean inmates will also say that they do not carry "shanks"—homemade knives or blades —because they don't need them.

The McKean staff takes weapons very seriously, and inmates found with them will be prosecuted and put in isolation…. Nonetheless, Dennis Luther achieved his successes against the will of Bureau of Prisons senior management. The bureau declined to comment, but Luther claims that officials there saw him as "a maverick, as someone who violates bureau policy flagrantly." Some of the more successful programs at McKean—the Inmate Benefit Fund, for instance (which raised $50,000 a year, much of it for local charities)—have been cut by the bureau, whose director serves at the discretion of the Attorney General. Inmates' access to computers and other amenities has been reduced in the past year, and now, with Luther retired, the trend may continue. Education also suffered at McKean—and at all other prisons—when the 1994 crime bill denied prisoners the right to apply for Pell grants. Grants to prisoners, according to congressional logic, were unfair to those hardworking citizens who cannot afford to pay for a college education. In fact, no eligible applicant for a Pell grant ever lost out to an inmate, because the grants are awarded on a merit basis, with any costs above the yearly appropriation coming out of the next year's budget….

Intelligent prison policy

Within a decade a baby boomlet will add another million boys in the fourteen-to-seventeen-year-old range to our population. According to James Q. Wilson, of the University of California at Los Angeles, at least six percent of those will commit violent crimes. That means 30,000 more young killers, rapists, and thieves. Some of them will be what DiIulio calls "super-predators"—a new variety of young criminal who has no adults in his life and no apparent capacity for remorse…. Intelligent prison policy is necessary now more than ever before. Yet politicians have been unwilling to forsake the popular fixation with "getting tough on crime" by getting tough on prisoners. The 1994 crime bill authorized $7.9 billion for prison construction, and House Republicans have added another $2.3 billion to that. Some of the new prisons are necessary, but they will be counterproductive if they are run on the no-frills principle, with no vocational programs, no drug treatment, no education…. Some politicians appear to recognize the gravity of the problem. New Jersey Governor Christine Todd Whitman now pays lip service to the idea that more prison educational programs could reduce recidivism. But she will not fund them….

Dennis Luther is still convinced that his methods would work in any prison, even those most plagued with violence, overcrowding, and gangs…. But he has no illusions about the future of crime policy.

"If the trend continues, prisons are going to become very different places to work in," he told me. "It's hard enough now to recruit a qualified staff for a prison. And I don't think we've seen anything yet." McKean staff members who worked under Luther feel the same way … they consider McKean a shining example of the difference good management can make. They don't expect it to last. Nor do the inmates…

A Pell grant is a federal grant that, unlike a loan, does not have to repaid. Generally, these grants are awarded to undergraduate students who have not earned a bachelor's or professional degree. They were an important factor in helping prisoners get degrees.

If you want to read more about super predators or juvenile psychopaths, look up a discussion with John DiIulio, professor of Politics and Public Affairs at Princeton University, on www.screwschool.com/term/psy1.htm.

Using quotations to back up your arguments is a good tool in debates. It can also help make your argument more accessible.

PRISONS DO NOT WORK
Hugh Mahoney

NO

Right now in the United States of America murderers, rapists, and child molesters are being set free. Prisoners are watching T.V., eating a meal, and using exercise equipment while law abiding citizens are starving and living in the gutters. Prisoners even have their own periodical. Dangerous criminals are walking the streets and crime is a way of life to many Americans. In America, crime does pay because our nation's prison system is not working.

The nation's prison system must be changed because of major problems with the system such as overcrowding and the fact that early release programs do not work. Building more jails is expensive and does not solve anything. These problems can be solved by giving prisoners no chance for parole and imprisoning only violent offenders. The non-violent offenders should enter a work program for the duration of their sentence.

Read a discussion about California's Corcoran State Prison, a system under pressure, at www.csmonitor. com/durable/1998/ 08/06/p1s2.htm.

Growth industry

Since 1980, jail and prison populations have grown by 172 percent. Overcrowding is both inhumane to the prisoner and dangerous to the prison staff. When you put a lot of people, especially criminals, in close quarters tensions rise and the chance of a riot increases. If a riot occurs both prisoners and guards are put in danger.

Under the governorship of George W. Bush Texas had the largest and fastest growing prison population in the United States. See www.salon.com/ politics/feature/ 2000/08/29/texas/ print.html.

In Texas the jails are full. There is an estimated backlog of 29,000 state prisoners who are incarcerated in county jails awaiting new cells. Texas is not the only state with overcrowding problems. For example, Ohio's prison system is operating at 180 percent of capacity. Also, the federal prison system is 37 percent over-capacity. Statistics like this are found across the country.

Prisons should have two results:

Are there any other aims prisoners might have?

1) keep dangerous criminals off the streets and
2) create a deterrent for committing a crime.
Our system has failed to do either.

Early release programs let prisoners out of jail before their sentence is complete. This promotes good behavior in prison and keeps the prison population lower. However, many released prisoners just commit another crime and are returned to jail. In 1992, one in three state prison admissions was a probation or parole violator....

Statistics from a United States Bureau of Justice Statistics report:

* State courts in 32 counties across 17 states sentenced 79,000 felons to probation in 1986.
* Within 3 years of sentencing, while still on probation, 43% of these felons were rearrested for a felony.
* Half of the arrests were for a violent crime (murder, rape, robbery, or aggravated assault) or a drug offense (drug trafficking or drug possession).

> Bullet points can help clarify your argument.

This proves that the current system puts dangerous criminals back on the streets without being rehabilitated and that imprisonment is not a successful deterrent. The three times you're out strategy attempts to solve this problem. Although it is a step in the right direction, criminals should not be allowed to break the law three times before they are punished. It would be a much greater deterrent if they were not offered parole at all....

Work programs

Violent offenders are the prisoners convicted of crimes in which a victim was emotionally or physically harmed, for example; murder, rape, or child abuse. They are dangerous and need to be incarcerated. Non-violent offenders are the criminals convicted of crimes such as embezzlement, drug possession, or petty theft. These non-violent criminals should be put into work programs. There is plenty of work to do on both the national and state levels. Road crews could be used to build and repair roads. National and state parks always need manpower to build and improve on their lands. The possibilities are endless. Where would these criminals be housed? Since they will only be working in an area until the work is done, they could build their own temporary shelters or stay in tents. Texas is currently implementing this by putting hundreds of inmates to work on land owned by Texas Parks and Wildlife. It could be argued that this would take jobs away from the public. Actually work programs would create jobs. The prisoners would not be skilled at building roads, buildings, or whatever so they would need almost constant supervision by experienced workers and the final work would have to be done by skilled workers. Extra security would also be needed to preserve the guard to prisoner ratio, therefore creating even more jobs.

> The author suggests making prisoners work and that this in turn would create more jobs. Do you think this is a valid suggestion?

COMMENTARY: Prisoners and voting

Most states have laws that disenfranchise convicted felons and ex-felons. Increasingly, these laws are affecting the political voice in many communities. Only two states, Maine and Vermont, allow prison inmates to vote. Some states, 32 of them, do not allow felons to vote while they are on parole, while 28 of these states exclude felony probationers as well. Where states do have a process for restoring voting rights, it can be so lengthy and difficult that few offenders can gain satisfaction. In Alabama ex-offenders must provide a DNA sample before they can regain their voting rights. While disenfranchisement laws have been around since the founding of the country, there is now concern on the part of human rights campaigners that the laws are unfairly targeting certain sectors of society. Challenges to the disenfranchisement laws are being mounted under the 14th Amendment's equal protection clause. Any disenfranchisement law that had a racially discriminatory intent would violate the clause.

Some statistics on disenfranchisement
* There are about 4 million felons and ex-felons who currently or permanently have had their voting rights taken away.
* Almost 73 percent of those who are disenfranchised are only on probation or on parole, or have completed their sentences.
* A large proportion of the disenfranchised are African American men, and 1.4 million, about 13 percent of this group, have had their right to vote taken away. This rate of disenfranchisement among African Americans is almost seven times greater than the national average.
* More than 2 million white Americans (Hispanic and non-Hispanic) are also disenfranchised.
* In Florida one in three African American men has lost the right to vote.
* In Iowa, Mississipi, New Mexico, Virginia, and Wyoming one in four black men, about 24 to 28 percent, has lost the right to vote.

The rest of the world
Many countries in the developed world allow those in prison to vote. They include France, Germany, Sweden, Norway, and Poland. The reason behind allowing felons to vote is that since most of them will be released at some stage or another and return to their own community, their sense of social responsibility and engagement should be kept active. Voting rights are a large part of this process.

Many critics of the U.S. system also argue that prison is punishment enough, and taking away such a basic right dehumanizes the felon. Legal actions are taking place to challenge state laws that disenfranchise prisoners and ex-prisoners; it may take a while to change the system, but reformers hope it will eventually take place.

What would the violent offenders be doing…? They would be working towards self-support as well by farming their own food, doing prison maintenance, and getting psychological help for their rehabilitation. However, they would be allowed no extracurricular activities, no television, and limited contact with the outside world. Having prisoners farm their own food will not only save money, but also teach prisoners that they can have productive lives. Prisoners already do prison maintenance such as laundry and food preparation. This should be continued and increased to keep the prison costs down and keep the inmates busy. Both violent and non-violent offenders would receive the psychological attention necessary for rehabilitation. This will help ex-convicts to become productive members of society and increase their chances of staying out of jail.

Do you think a culture in which prisoners are made to work hard but receive no benefits from that work would lead to resentment?

Economic advantages

This proposal is also economically beneficial. On average, it costs over $20,000 to incarcerate someone for a year and it costs at least $50,000 to construct one prison bed. With work programs these numbers would be significantly reduced. Prisoners could construct their own housing and supply their own food. If they refuse to work, then they do not eat.

Prisoners are human beings too, and refusing them food if they refuse to work could be construed as a human rights abuse. Does the Constitution protect the basic rights of prisoners?

Many people believe that building new jails will solve the problems. New prisons would temporarily relieve the overcrowding problem. However, the new prisons would soon fill up as the courts convict more criminals to fill the empty beds and then we are right back where we started. As mentioned earlier, building jails is also expensive. It costs at least $50,000 to construct one prison bed.

Work programs would immediately relieve prison overcrowding as the non-violent criminals move to their work areas and if new prisons are absolutely necessary in the future then the convicts can help build them and therefore greatly decrease the cost.

Change the system

How will new prisons help deter crime and rehabilitate prisoners? The simple answer is they will not. New prisons will only cater to the serious problems that exist in the system and make room for new criminals. This proposal will stop overcrowding, help to deter crime, and help to rehabilitate criminals. The only way to make the prison system work is to change it. Many polls show crime is the No. 1 concern of voters so now is the time for action.

Summary

The issue of whether prisons work is a contentious one. Robert Worth believes that prisons do work, but he is looking at a model prison, which is the exception rather than the rule. He extols the achievements of McKean prison: It costs two-thirds of what most state prisons cost, yet its incident record is far superior; there have only been three serious incidents in six years, no escapes, no homicides, no suicides, and no sexual assaults. The level of recidivism is, as far as former staff members can tell, much lower than that in other institutions. The former warden, Dennis Luther, operated prison policies that emphasized education, vocational programs, and rehabilitation and got good results. Worth argues that Luther proved that good management brought rewards for all concerned.

In the second article Hugh Mahoney argues that prisons do not work. The author feels that because of overcrowding and early release programs, prisons are not effective. The system is open to abuse in that prisoners are on their best behavior to get early release, then commit another offense and return to jail. The author's solution is to imprison only violent offenders, who have committed murder, rape or child abuse, and give them no chance of parole. Nonviolent offenders, who are convicted of crimes of embezzlement, drug possession, or petty theft, could be made to work in the interest of society in work programs that would help improve the community at the same time. Mahoney claims that building new prisons to combat overcrowding is self-defeating; that will just make room for new criminals. Thus a rethink of the whole system is needed.

FURTHER INFORMATION:

Books:

Bosworth, Mary, *The U.S. Federal Prison System*. Thousand Oaks, CA: Sage Publications, Inc., 2002. Burton-Rose, Daniel (ed.), *The Celling of America: An Inside Look at the U.S. Prison Industry*. Boston, MA: South End Press, 1996.

Articles:

Lee, Jennifer, "Putting Parolees on a Tighter Leash." *The New York Times*, January 31, 2002.

Useful websites:

www.guardian.co.uk/notesandqueries/query/ 0,5753,-18814,00.html For a discussion on the question "Does imprisonment really protect or otherwise benefit society?" www.salon.com/politics

Site of current affairs journal, with articles on prisons. www.thirdworldtraveler.com/Prison_System/ ForJustice_AgainstPrison.html For the article "For Justice and Against Prison."

The following debates in the Pro/Con series may also be of interest:

In this volume:

Topic 1 Is the criminal justice system racist?

Topic 14 Do prisoners have rights?

DO PRISONS WORK?

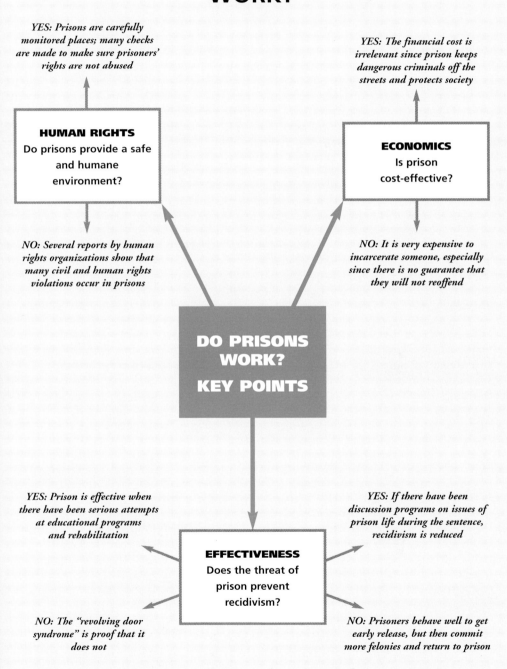

YES: Prisons are carefully monitored places; many checks are made to make sure prisoners' rights are not abused

HUMAN RIGHTS
Do prisons provide a safe and humane environment?

NO: Several reports by human rights organizations show that many civil and human rights violations occur in prisons

YES: The financial cost is irrelevant since prison keeps dangerous criminals off the streets and protects society

ECONOMICS
Is prison cost-effective?

NO: It is very expensive to incarcerate someone, especially since there is no guarantee that they will not reoffend

DO PRISONS WORK?
KEY POINTS

YES: Prison is effective when there have been serious attempts at educational programs and rehabilitation

YES: If there have been discussion programs on issues of prison life during the sentence, recidivism is reduced

EFFECTIVENESS
Does the threat of prison prevent recidivism?

NO: The "revolving door syndrome" is proof that it does not

NO: Prisoners behave well to get early release, but then commit more felonies and return to prison

Topic 14
DO PRISONERS HAVE RIGHTS?

YES
"WITHOUT PREJUDICE: AMERICAN CANT"
THE OBSERVER, JANUARY 13, 2002
PETER BEAUMONT

NO
"PRISONERS OF WAR: NO X-RAY NEEDED TO EVALUATE CONTROVERSIAL CAMP"
HTTP://WWW.NORTHWESTERNCHRONICLE.ORG/TOOLS, JANUARY 31, 2002
MICHAEL HOES

INTRODUCTION

Prisoners have long been treated cruelly by their captors. The Romans, for example, used to throw them to the lions or used them as entertainment, watching them fight to the death in specially built arenas. The Aztecs slaughtered thousands of prisoners at a time in festivals honoring their gods. In the United States the first prisoners were subject to a harsh British penal system that carried the death penalty for numerous, often quite minor, offenses.

While many people over the centuries have argued for more humane treatment of prisoners, it was only really in the 20th century that the idea that prisoners were entitled to rights was recognized. However, many people question whether those members of society who have committed crimes against society should enjoy the same rights that society gives to law-abiding citizens. In the United States today prisoners do not have the same constitutional rights as other people. That situation is

epecially emphasized at times of war or terrorist action, such as the events that took place on September 11, 2001.

It was really only after World War II that the treatment of prisoners became a global issue. The 1948 Universal Declaration of Human Rights set out standards for the humane treatment of prisoners. As a result, anyone imprisoned has rights that are recognized by international law. But that fact is sometimes hard to endorse; and several countries around the world, including Nigeria, Chile, and the United States, have been accused of failing to respect prisoners' rights.

However, while prisoners do not enjoy complete constitutional rights in the United States, they are protected by the Eighth Amendment, for example, which prohibits "cruel and unusual" punishment, and the Equal Protection Clause of the Fourteenth Amendment, which protects them from unequal treatment on the basis of sex, race, and creed. But constitutional protection does not guarantee that prisoners are treated fairly and humanely while they are incarcerated. A recent Amnesty International report on police brutality, for example, claimed that many prisoners were shot, beaten, dangerously restrained, sprayed with dangerous chemicals, and verbally abused while in custody. It further stated that thousands of individual complaints about police abuse are reported each year. In 1997 there were around 8,235 reported complaints, but by 1996 that figure had increased to around 40,000.

> *"When you see one prisoner, you see all ... ill fed and innocent."*
> —ALEXANDRE DUMAS,
> *THE COUNT OF MONTE CRISTO*

In 1995 Congress introduced the Prison Litigation Reform Act. The provision within the act that limits the federal courts' ability to impose court orders on state prisons has generated a lot of opposition from civil rights groups, who see it as an attack on the role of the federal courts as protectors of constitutional rights. Without the federal courts to defend them, civil rights groups claim that prisoners have less chance of mounting successful legal protests against alleged unacceptable conditions or practices in jails.

However, many people argue that prisoners have forfeited their entitlement to any rights, including the right to vote—seen by most citizens as a basic civil right.

Opponents of prisoners' rights also argue that the death penalty should be imposed in cases in which felons have committed murder or serious or violent crime. While around 111 countries have abolished the death penalty in law or in practice, the United States remains one of those with an active policy in place. Civil rights activists argue that the death penalty is unconstitutional, since it is a "cruel and unusual" punishment and thus against the Eighth Amendment; but it still continues to exist. The morality of the death penalty has resulted in heated debate on prisoners' rights, particularly in cases in which the accused has subsequently been found to be innocent and in juvenile offender cases.

The issue of whether prisoners should have rights has become even more heated since the terrorist action of September 11, 2001. A series of laws has been introduced, among them the Patriot Act, which extends the powers of the Immigration and Naturalization Service (INS) to arrest and detain immigrants, and the Military Order, which allows military tribunals to try noncitizens charged with terrorism. Civil rights groups assert that these laws are being used to circumvent treaties protecting prisoners, especially since they have led to thousands of immigrants being detained and hundreds of suspected Taliban and Al Qaeda fighters being held on a naval base at Guantanamo Bay, Cuba. The Pentagon argues that these men are not prisoners of war, since they were not part of a regular army. The United States has also withdrawn its support for an international tribunal to try people accused of war crimes. These issues are discussed further in the following articles.

WITHOUT PREJUDICE: AMERICAN CANT
Peter Beaumont

The author immediately draws the reader in by asking him or her to imagine a cinematic scene. He then states that the episode in fact happened.

Imagine the scene. A group of alleged Irish terrorists is seized and handed over to the British Government by a third country. They are held without access to any lawyers. Some are threatened by interrogating intelligence officers. They are told that if they don't tell them what they want to know then they might simply 'disappear'. Some of the men are tortured while being held in prison and forced into confessing that they are members of a terrorist organisation.

These men are drugged and bound and then flown out of the country to an island camp, where lawyers are appointed for them but where the normal guarantees of defendants' rights do not apply. Those lawyers cannot appeal for their release—no mechanism exists—nor can they challenge their extradition or the criteria for it. In that island camp, they will face an emergency military tribunal that has the right to kill them. Confronted with these gross violations, the international media and human rights organisations would rightly be up in arms in protest.

The article appeared in the British Sunday newspaper The Observer. By highlighting the fact that a Briton was among those arrested, he personalizes the experience for his immediate audience. Using examples that your audience can relate to is a very useful skill in debating.

Yesterday, a group of unidentified men, including a Briton, completed a journey identical in almost every detail to the one described above. Manacled, with some sedated, they were chained to their seats in the aircraft that delivered them. The difference is that this group of 20 men were alleged terrorists with the Taliban and Al Qaeda and their destination was the US base at Guantanamo Bay in Cuba. The difference, too, is that what complaint there has been about their treatment has been curiously muted.

A "scandal of international proportions"

The reality of what is happening to the prisoners of Afghanistan is a scandal of international proportions. Brutalised, often tortured, these are men who have been stripped of their most basic rights under international and US law, rights guaranteed at the International Tribunal in the Hague…. In a few deft strokes, the administration of President George W. Bush has dropped a 'daisycutter' not only on the Geneva Conventions, designed to protect the rights of prisoners of war, but also America's own constitutional guarantees for defendants.

It is possible, even likely, that many of these people committed terrible crimes—some may even have had foreknowledge of the attacks of 11 September—but their special treatment presupposes a special guilt.

They are the kind of people, we are assured, after all, by General Richard B. Myers, US Chief of the Joint Staffs, who are so 'dangerous that they would gnaw through the hydraulic cables' on their transport plane to bring it down.

It is a description appropriate to an animal, not to a man.

The situation in Afghanistan

A few weeks ago, I was in Afghanistan looking for some of these almost mythically self-destructive creatures. The first man we tried to see was an elderly Taliban official our fixer had come across at an anti-Taliban base in the suburbs of the former Taliban stronghold of Kandahar. When our fixer saw him, he was being beaten … to death by a local warlord. We reached the camp too late. When we arrived, the man who had been doing the beating told us that he no longer had any Taliban prisoners. They had buried some Al Qaeda fighters that day whom they had killed in the liberation of the city, he told us. We asked again about the prisoner. He clarified the situation: 'There are no prisoners any longer.'

It was not an isolated incident. Ten days later, I found myself with a group of Western journalists in the office of the governor of the Third Directorate prison in Kabul. Abdul Qayum, a lean and hard-faced man in his fifties, had been promising for a week to let reporters see his prisoners and check on their conditions. He told us he was both jailer and the man who leads the interrogations. He told us, too, that he regarded the Taliban and Al Qaeda as indistinguishable. So how, we asked, does he persuade them to confess? 'We ask them in a friendly and Islamic way to confess their crimes,' he explained to us. 'If they do not confess, then we use force.'

If one cannot condone this sort of behaviour, perhaps one can understand it in a virtual state, stripped of its institutions and atomised by two decades of war. But the role of America and its allies in the maltreatment of the Taliban and Al Qaeda prisoners defies comprehension.

The consequences of forced confessions

What is most alarming are the potential consequences of those beaten and forced confessions in the context of the legal process that has been constructed for the Al Qaeda prisoners. For the torture, threats and humiliation of the Taliban and Al Qaeda prisoners in Afghanistan's jails pale

> Should everyone be innocent until proven guilty? Are there any exceptions to that rule?

> The Taliban is made up of Afghans trained in religious schools in Pakistan, along with former Islamic fighters or members of the mujahedin. They were in power in Afghanistan from 1997 to 2002.

> Al Qaeda ("the base") was formed by Osama Bin Laden in 1988. It is a multinational terrorist organization whose senior leaders are also members of other terrorist groups. It was formed to bring together Arabs who fought in Afghanistan against the Soviet Union, but its current goal is to establish a pan-Islamic caliphate around the world by working with Islamic extremist groups. Al Qaeda was behind the terrorist action in New York on September 11, 2001.

Two U.S. soldiers accompany a prisoner into Camp X-Ray, Guantanamo Bay, Cuba.

into insignificance before the cynical acrobatics that George Bush's administration has gone through to strip these prisoners of their most basic rights to a fair legal process.

A fair legal process

Let's start with the Geneva Conventions. Not the obvious stuff like the proscriptions on summary executions … or torture … or the humiliating and degrading treatment … but the niggly details of legal process. Details like the proscription on the handing-over of prisoners of war to a third party that is not a party to the war, which America insists implausibly to the International Committee for the Red Cross that it is not; in other words, the US claims that it is merely assisting the anti-Taliban forces rather than prosecuting a war. Or the little detail that insists that those prisoners must be tried by regularly constituted courts, not military tribunals constituted under emergency powers. If they are combatants—and prisoners of war—acting under orders, then, as the US Supreme Court's *ex parte Quirin* ruling declared in 1942 in the case of a group of German saboteurs seized in America in the Second World War, they 'are subject [only] to capture and detention as prisoners of war by opposing military forces'.

But then, say Mr Bush's advisers … these aren't prisoners of war. These are men who fought without uniforms.… They are criminals, they argue, 'unlawful combatants', and therefore not covered by the protections of the Geneva Conventions. And there lies the source of the Bush administration's greatest contortions. For if the prisoners of Guantanamo Bay are not covered by the 'laws of war', then they are ordinary criminals. And the rights of ordinary— and even extraordinary—criminals are guaranteed by the US Constitution. The Sixth Amendment, in case Mr Bush has forgotten, insists that in 'all criminal prosecutions' in the United States inalienable rights apply. Those rights include the right to a jury trial, a right underlined by case law in the US Supreme Court that insists that if the civilian courts are open and functioning then the armed forces cannot convene a military tribunal to try offences that fall within the jurisdiction of civilian courts.

So if the prisoners of Guantanamo Bay are not criminals or combatants, what are they? They are the examples that America feels it needs to make before the world, condemned before the fact by their alleged membership of a criminal association. They are triply damned, one suspects, by their nationality, religion and the colour of their skins.

For further information on the Geneva Conventions see the box on page 186.

Ex parte Quirin refers to the 1942 decision of the Supreme Court to uphold the military trials of eight German saboteurs caught planning to blow up various U.S. factories, bridges, and department stores.

The author argues that the Bush administration's argument is contradictory. If the people held in Cuba are not prisoners of war, then they are ordinary criminals whose rights are protected by the Constitution. Do you think his argument is valid?

PRISONERS OF WAR: NO X-RAY NEEDED TO EVALUATE CONTROVERSIAL CAMP
Michael Hoes

NO

Hoes states that many of the critics of Camp X-Ray are "domestic leftists." Do you think that is a fair comment? Go to www.google.com, and search for articles on the detention center.

Camp X-Ray, the U.S. military detention center for Al Qaeda and Taliban fighters captured in Afghanistan, has been a public relations disaster for the United States. Foreign media and domestic leftists have made much of the camp's supposed violations of the Geneva Conventions.

In an editorial for the *Nation*, Charles Glass, formerly ABC News' chief Middle East correspondent, compared the detention of the Guantánamo Bay prisoners to his own kidnapping by the Hezbollah. The BBC wrote pieces with headlines like "Grim Life at Guantánamo."

The activist group Human Rights Watch warned in the *Philadelphia Inquirer* of the imminent demise of the Geneva Conventions, stating the United States must prove "that nations can bring terrorists to justice without sinking to their level."

But what do the Geneva Conventions actually say about the present controversy? Let's read the text from Article 4:

Article 4: Geneva Conventions

The Geneva Conventions were established about 50 years ago. Do you think they need updating?

Prisoners of war, in the sense of the present Convention, are persons belonging to one of the following categories, who have fallen into the power of the enemy:

(1) Members of the armed forces of a Party to the conflict, as well as members of militias or volunteer corps forming part of such armed forces.

(2) Members of other militias and members of other volunteer corps, including those of organized resistance movements, belonging to a Party to the conflict and operating in or outside their own territory, even if this territory is occupied, provided that such militias or volunteer corps, including such organized resistance movements, fulfil the following conditions:

(a) that of being commanded by a person responsible for his subordinates;

(b) that of having a fixed distinctive sign recognizable at a distance;

(c) that of carrying arms openly;

(d) that of conducting their operations in accordance with the laws and customs of war.

(3) Members of regular armed forces who profess allegiance to a government or an authority not recognized by the Detaining Power.

(4) Persons who accompany the armed forces without actually being members thereof, such as civilian members of military aircraft crews, war correspondents, supply contractors, members of labour units or of services responsible for the welfare of the armed forces, provided that they have received authorization, from the armed forces which they accompany, who shall provide them for that purpose with an identity card similar to the annexed model.

(5) Members of crews, including masters, pilots and apprentices, of the merchant marine and the crews of civil aircraft of the Parties to the conflict, who do not benefit by more favourable treatment under any other provisions of international law.

(6) Inhabitants of a non-occupied territory, who on the approach of the enemy spontaneously take up arms to resist the invading forces, without having had time to form themselves into regular armed units, provided they carry arms openly and respect the laws and customs of war.

Discrediting the evidence supplied in an official document or a recognized source is a good method by which to strengthen your own case.

Interpreting the convention

By any interpretation of the above, Al Qaeda members do not need to be treated as prisoners of war. They are not members of a nation's armed forces, do not carry arms openly, and do not respect the "laws and customs of war." Members of the Taliban do not qualify as POWs under section 1 since the Afghanistan "army" had no functioning command structure, uniforms, or any of the other characteristics that regular armies possess. Taliban militias and gangs might qualify as POWs by section 2. [H]owever, it seems probable that most— if not all—would not. The Taliban do not have uniforms or any other 'fixed distinctive sign recognizable at a distance' as required by (2) (b). Any Talib who actively assisted Al Qaeda has also violated (2) (d) by supporting terrorism.

The author claims that "by any interpretation" of Article 4 Al Qaeda members do not need to be treated as prisoners of war. If that is the case, how should they be tried?

Prisoners of war?

There is simply no reason to suppose that any of the captives at Camp X-Ray qualify as POWs, and even if they did, their treatment up to the present has hardly been a gross violation of the Geneva Conventions and certainly has not violated international standards for human rights. Although the press has expressed outrage over photos of hooded and bound

COMMENTARY: The laws of war

International humanitarian law, also known as the "laws of war," governs the treatment of men and women detained during armed conflict. The four Geneva Conventions, passed in 1949 and added to in 1977, set the framework protecting the rights and conduct of most detainees and are followed by most countries around the world—although the U.S. government refused to ratify the two additional 1977 protocols.

Prisoners' rights are also protected by Article 7 of the International Covenant on Civil and Political Rights, which the United States ratified in 1992, which states that "No one shall be subjected to torture or to cruel, inhuman, or degrading treatment or punishment."

Similarly the Convention against Torture and other Cruel, Inhuman, or Degrading Treatment or Punishment and the UN Standard Minimum Rules on the Treatment of Prisoners, which the United States agreed to in 1994, also govern treatment.

Types of prisoners under International Humanitarian Law

Men and women who are captured while serving in an armed force during an international conflict are usually called Prisoners of War (POWs) and are subject to international laws unless the country in which they are being detained argues otherwise, as is the case with the United States and those people being kept at Guantanamo Bay in Cuba.

The prisoner of war status includes:
- members of armed forces
- members of militia forces fighting as part of those armed forces
- people in an unoccupied territory who take up arms openly to resist invading forces
- captured members of irregular forces under responsible command
- those who bear a uniform, symbol, or anything else that marks them as being part of a force
- people who conduct themselves according to the laws/customs of war

POWs receive protection under the third Geneva Convention and may not be prosecuted for bearing arms against other combatants, but can face trial for war crimes and crimes against humanity. POWs must be treated humanely and are protected by the conventions from acts of violence or intimidation and against insults or public degradation. The holding country may interrogate them, but may not torture them. "Unlawful combatants" or "nonprivileged combatants" are those people not deemed to be POWs; but they are, many people argue, still protected under the fourth Geneva Convention's Protection of Civilian Persons in Time of War. It also protects civilians affected by a conflict.

prisoners, these precautions are normal when transporting dangerous captives. Furthermore, there is no evidence that this treatment continued after transit.

Excellent treatment

Firsthand reports from Camp X-Ray reveal that prisoners are getting hot showers, speedy access to restrooms, excellent medical treatment by more than 100 U.S. doctors, three hot halal meals a day, freedom of worship, and even permission to write letters to loved ones. The commander of the base is afraid to even use the word 'interrogation,' and Red Cross observers are watching at all times. The chief substantial complaint of pundits is that the prisoners are exposed to the elements. That point is undeniably true, since their cells have roofs but not solid walls, but it might not be quite the cause for concern some imagine.

Hoes refers to firsthand reports of the prisoners being treated well. Is this an occasion when quoting from official sources would strengthen his argument?

As this column is being written, it is a sunny day in Guantánamo Bay. The temperature is 73 degrees, with a low of 68 degrees and a high of 84 degrees. The forecast: a sunny day followed by a sunny day, followed by a rainy day, followed by sun, sun, sun, sun, sun and more sun to the limit of the extended forecast. Whatever living exposed to such weather may be, it is surely not a violation of human rights.

Do you think linking the weather to whether people have had their human rights violated adds to or detracts from Hoes' argument?

Perhaps the most striking indication that the prisoners are being treated humanely is the failure of three detained British citizens to complain to their government about their treatment. If citizens of a Western democracy don't think they are being mistreated, it is hard to imagine that violations of fundamental human rights are occurring.

Media manipulation

At bottom, the Camp X-Ray controversy is just another media-generated crisis. Its chief origin is a couple of photos rather than any substantial reporting or research, and its chief effect is to sell newspapers and waste the time of government officials. Sounds like business as usual for the press.

What would the media have to gain by generating a crisis about Camp X-Ray?

Summary

The preceding two articles contain very different views on the issue of prisoners' rights. In the first Peter Beaumont examines the situation of the suspected Al Qaeda and Taliban prisoners held at the U.S. naval base in Cuba. He asks why their situation has caused little public outcry. Beaumont claims that President George W. Bush's administration has undercut both U.S. and international law in stripping these prisoners of their rights as prisoners of war. Beaumont argues that if they are not prisoners of war, the government should treat them like ordinary criminals who have certain rights protected by the Constitution. In the second article Michael Hoes argues that the prisoners at Guantanamo Bay are not prisoners of war as protected by Article 4 of the Geneva Conventions. Hoes claims that the media have created a story out of nothing to serve their own purpose, and that far from being mistreated, the prisoners are enjoying the benefits of being held in a camp in a beautiful climate and are being fed, bathed, and treated well. He argues that only left-wing papers are claiming otherwise, and that since the British prisoners there have not complained, they are obviously not being abused.

FURTHER INFORMATION:

Books:

Palmer, John W., and Stephen E. Palmer, *Constitutional Rights of Prisoners*. Cincinnati, OH: Anderson Publishing Co., 1999.
Power, Jonathan, *Like Water on Stone: The Story of Amnesty International*. Boston, MA: Northeastern University Press, 2001.

Useful websites:

http://www.aclu.org/
American Civil Liberties Union site, lists articles on prisoners rights in the United States and reports on recent legislation and cases.
http://web.amnesty.org/ai.nsf/Index
Site of international human rights organization Amnesty IInternational lists useful statistics, reports, and information on current alleged international prisoners' rights abuses.
http://www.hrw/org/backgrounder/usa/pwo-bck.htm
Huiman Rights Watch background paper on international law and prisoners' rights.
http://www.law.cornell.edu/topics/prisoners_rights.html
Cornell University's law site. Presents an overview of prisoners' rights under state and federal law, as well as links to judicial decisions on prisoners' rights.

The following debates in the Pro/Con series may also be of interest:

DO PRISONERS HAVE RIGHTS?

YES: The essential rights of prisoners, such as protection from "cruel and unusual" behavior, are protected

YES: Depriving people of their essential rights just enforces the belief that they have no chance in society

CONSTITUTION
Are prisoners' rights protected by the Constitution?

MORALITY
If someone has committed a crime, should they have any rights?

NO: In reality prisoners are not allowed all their constitutional rights and are often abused by the institutions that are meant to look after them

NO: If someone has committed a crime, however minor, they have forfeited their civil rights

DO PRISONERS HAVE RIGHTS? KEY POINTS

YES: The government represents the people, and as such it has the right to act as it sees fit in the interests of its citizens

YES: If the government believes that it will be able to help or save its citizens from harm or war, then it must act as it sees fit

GOVERNMENT
Does the government have the right to deprive prisoners of their rights if it believes it is in the interest of its citizens?

NO: Depriving prisoners of their rights is a step toward barbarity. As the Russian novelist Fyodor Dostoyevsky said, a society should be "judged not by how it treats its outstanding citzens, but by how it treats its criminals."

NO: After the atrocities of World War II various laws were passed and signed by countries around the world to protect the rights of prisoners, especially prisoners of war

Topic 15
SHOULD PRISONS BE PRIVATIZED?

YES

"PRIVATIZING THE PRISON SYSTEM"

HTTP://WWW.NCPA.ORG/~NCPA/STUDIES/S181/S181N.HTML

NATIONAL CENTER FOR POLICY ANALYSIS

NO

"SHOULD CRIME PAY? A REVIEW OF THE EVIDENCE"

HTTP://WWW.AFSCME.ORG/PRIVATE/CRIMEPTC.HTM

THE AMERICAN FEDERATION OF STATE, COUNTY, AND MUNICIPAL EMPLOYEES

INTRODUCTION

The United States is a world leader in jailing its own populace, with almost two million presently incarcerated. For the last quarter of a century tougher sentences, less generous parole conditions, and increased drug prosecutions have contributed to a steadily increasing prison population that incurs ever higher costs. The shift toward private prisons, which began under President Ronald Reagan in the 1980s, is in part a consequence of free-market policies and a response to the exorbitant costs of maintaining such a huge jail population. But the issue of whether responsibility for penal institutions should be turned over to private companies is the subject of much heated debate, with controversy focusing not only on practical and economic questions but also on ethical ones.

In 2001 there were 158 private prisons in the United States. The market is divided between several dozen companies contracting with state entities to provide or operate jails.

More than half the industry's operations are controlled by the top two companies—Wackenhut and Correction Corporation of America (CCA)—and the market is growing. The main argument of those who support private prisons is that they are more efficient and save taxpayers money. The National Center for Policy Analysis cites several studies that find savings of up to 20 percent in construction and 5 to 15 percent in the management of private prisons.

Opponents of private prisons, however, dispute figures claiming huge savings. Any savings that are made, they say, are the result of cutting corners and services such as drugs rehabilitation and literacy classes. They cite cases in which resources were diverted from such services: In 1995, for example, Wackenhut was investigated for diverting $700,000 intended for drug programs. In his book *Punishment for Profit: Private Prisons, Public Concerns* criminologist David Schichor pointed to the hidden costs to the government of supervising private jails.

The issue of the supervision of private prisons is cited by both supporters and opponents of private jails. Supporters say that contracting increases accountability because market mechanisms of control are added to the political process. In simpler terms, private jails are under stringent contractual obligations to perform well, and competition adds a new motive. Since the first modern private prison opened in 1985, very few contracts have been terminated because a prison is judged to have failed. Supporters say that contracting, along with government monitoring, adds a new layer of independent review of correctional decisions and actions.

"The new ownership structure of prisons rewards investors for imprisoning us and keeping us in prison.... This is a bad idea run amok."
—DAVID MORRIS, INSTITUTE FOR LOCAL SELF RELIANCE

Such arguments fail to allay critics' concerns about the accountability of private prisons. Opponents still ask: Who will watch the watchmen? The issue of using deadly force on inmates, for example, has ethical implications in the environment of a private prison.

The American Federation of State, County, and Municipal Employees warns of higher levels of violence in private jails where staff may be relatively inexperienced. In 1997 there were 13 stabbings, including two

homicides, at a single CCA correctional facility in Youngstown, Ohio, compared to 22 assaults with weapons at all 29 state prisons in Ohio. Managers had to call for help from state prison officials when a riot broke out at a private jail in Elizabeth, New Jersey. But Adrian Moore of the Reason Public Policy Institute, a public policy thinktank in Los Angeles, attributes such problems to teething troubles. The law now requires private prisons to have adequate staffing levels, and inmates of private prisons have more legal recourses in case of complaint.

At the heart of the arguments against private prisons lies the ethical question of whether the state should ever hand over responsibility for administering the penal system in any society and the implications for that society if it does. Supporters of private prisons say that the state remains responsible for putting criminals in jail and monitoring their care even in private prisons. They question whether the inmate cares whether he or she is guarded by a state or a public employee.

As the private prison industry has developed, so have concerns about the underlying profit motive of such enterprises. If private corporations increase revenues by maximizing the cell time of their prisoners, can they be trusted to act in the best interest of the inmates? Prisoners generated around $392 million in 1980 and $1.31 billion in 1994 from the sale of prison goods. Yet supporters of private prisons say that provided that they are paid the prevailing wage, private sector use of prison labor benefits everyone— prisoners, their families, and victims who are paid compensation. The following articles examine the issue.

PRIVATIZING THE PRISON SYSTEM
National Center for Policy Analysis

YES

Studies show that prisons can be built and maintained less expensively in the private sector. A number of studies find savings of 20 percent for private construction costs and 5 to 15 percent for private management of prison units. Further, independent observers who monitor, for example, the contracts of Corrections Corporation of America (CCA), a Nashville, Tenn., company, praise the quality of the company's operations. George Zoley of Wackenhut Corp. in Coral Gables, Fla., years ago predicted a gradual building process in which the private sector establishes a "good track record and proves it can do the job."...

It has come to pass:

The National Center for Policy Analysis begins this article with a simple assertion and then supports it with a list of statistical evidence.

• With 20,698 adult prisoners in private correctional facilities on June 30, 1993, the market share of private prisons has risen to 1.5 percent of the prison and jail population.
• The number of management firms with contracts for prison operations rose from 17 to 21 between 1992 and 1993.
• Private facilities under contract also rose from 62 to 71 (including 65 in the United States), a one-year increase of 14.5 percent.
• The Federal Bureau of Prisons awarded its first contract to design, construct and manage a 1,000-bed medium security prison (to be located in Eloy, Ariz.) to Concept, Inc., of Louisville, Ky.
• Texas leads the nation with 28 private adult correctional units, followed by California with seven.
• CRSS Constructors, Inc., has over $1 billion in corrections construction across 12 states under way.

Major companies in the industry include CCA, with a rated capacity of 9,045 including facilities under construction and planned expansions, Wackenhut Corrections Corporation with 6,109 and Concept, Inc. with 4,044. Profits, however, remain elusive. For example, CCA reports that it makes a small profit, but Pricor, Inc., of Murfreesboro, Tenn., an early leader in the industry, recently exited adult corrections after suffering a series of losses.

The evidence indicates that if there were a formal market to buy, sell, and rent prison cells, there would be much less of a problem in funding and efficiently allocating prison space for convicts. And there are numerous—but unexploited—opportunities to reduce the net costs of prisons by creating factories behind bars, having prisoners earn their keep and compensating victims.

The most promising ways to control taxpayer costs involve the privatization of prison construction and operation. Short of full privatization, government-operated correctional facilities could be corporatized and operated like private businesses.

Do you think it is ethical that prison labor should be used to reduce the costs of private companies?

Prison operation

There is no insurmountable legal obstacle to total privatization of prison operation. Unlike government agencies, private firms must know and account for all the costs of prison operation, including long-run costs. If they can do so and still operate prisons for less than the government —and all indications are that they can—then government should set punishments for felons and let the private sector efficiently supply prisons.

Although the law would allow total privatization, does that mean it is ethical or acceptable?

- CCA charges Harris County, Texas, and the Immigration and Naturalization Service only $35 per inmate per day to operate a 350-bed minimum security facility in Houston, a charge that includes recovery of the cost of building the facility.
- Operating costs for government-run prisons can run twice that amount, even without taking construction and land costs into account.

Employing prisoners

Prisons originally were intended to be self-supporting and during the 19th century many state prisons ran surpluses, returning excess funds to their state governments. In 1885 three-fourths of prison inmates were involved in productive labor, the majority working in contract and leasing systems. Fifty years later only 44 percent worked, and almost 90 percent worked in state rather than private work programs. Today, prison inmates are a huge drain on taxpayer wallets despite the millions of available hours of healthy, prime-age labor they represent....

Increasing productive work for prisoners requires the repeal of some federal and state statutes and clearing away bureaucratic obstacles. The federal Hawes-Cooper Act of 1935

The Hawes-Cooper Act was actually passed in 1929. It is important to double-check your facts when presenting an authoritative argument.

For a more comprehensive definition of the Walsh–Healy Act go to www.lectlaw. com/def2/ w030.htm.

authorized states to prohibit the entry of prison-made goods produced in other states. The Walsh–Healy Act of 1936 prohibited convict labor on government contracts exceeding $10,000. The Sumners–Ashurst Act of 1940 made it a federal offense to transport prison-made goods across state borders, regardless of state laws.

Throughout the nation, a score of exceptions to the federal restrictions on prison labor have been authorized, provided the inmates were paid a prevailing wage, labor union officials were consulted, other workers were not adversely affected, and the jobs were in an industry without local unemployment.

What kind of skills do you think prisoners might learn from the types of assembly work listed here? Would they be a benefit in the job market?

A survey commissioned by the National Institute of Justice identified more than 70 companies that employ inmates in 16 states in manufacturing, service and light assembly operations. Prisoners sew leisure wear, manufacture water-bed mattresses and assemble electronic components. PRIDE, a state-sponsored private corporation that runs Florida's 46 prison industries, from furniture making to optical glass grinding, made a $4 million profit in 1987.

Such work benefits everyone. It enables prisoners to earn wages and acquire marketable skills while learning individual responsibility and the value of productive labor. It also ensures that they are able to contribute to victim compensation and to their own and their families' support while they are in prison.

Do you think it is fair that prisoners should be able to make money while they are being punished for crimes they have committed?

South Carolina and Nevada have become leaders in private sector use of prison labor, yet nationally only 5,000 prisoners (far less than 1 percent) work for private companies because of the additional costs of doing business in prisons. By the end of 1992, South Carolina prisoners in the start-up phases of two private-sector programs had already earned $2.4 million in wages, of which nearly $500,000 went to taxes, $119,000 to victim compensation, $322,000 to room and board and $364,000 to family support. The prisoners retained $1.1 million in inmate savings accounts....

Examples of companies that use prisoners for labor
Fred Braun, Jr., president of Workman Fund in Leavenworth, Kan., has been a key promoter of Private Sector Prison Industries—PSPI. Organized as a nonprofit foundation, Workman lends venture capital to private enterprises interested in training and employing prisoners on-site in "real world" work. Workman reported promising results from an enterprise in which convicts worked along side nonconvict labor. Braun also is president of Creative Enterprises, the

umbrella company for two plants, Zephyr Products, Inc. (sheet metal products) and Heatron, Inc. (electric heating elements), which train and employ minimum-custody inmates at the Lansing East Unit in Leavenworth. Braun's original vision was an industrial park of three or four firms employing 200. Thirteen years after opening Zephyr, no more businesses had been added, but the two original plants were employing about 150 prisoners.

Bureaucratic inertia slows the transition to private work for prisoners. For example, the state corrections system in Texas traditionally was a leader in state-run prison industries, which probably has hindered the initiation of private-sector opportunities for prison employment and production there.

In what specific ways might a history of state-run prison industries hinder the introduction of private-sector employment for prisoners?

SHOULD CRIME PAY? A REVIEW OF THE EVIDENCE
American Federation of State, County, and Municipal Employees

The General Accounting Office (GAO) is the congressional watchdog agency that ensures the accountability of the federal government to the American people by helping it meet its constitutional responsibilities and improve its economy, efficiency, and effectiveness. Its primary tasks include examining the use of public funds, evaluating federal programs and activities, and providing Congress with analyses, recommendations, and any other relevant assistance.

For a definition, history, and other information about REITs go to www.nareit.com/aboutreits/thestorytext.cfm.

NO

Prison privatization does not save taxpayers money, nor does it improve prison operations. Recent studies and cases around the United States prove that privatizing not only fails to solve public problems, but also leads to new ones. Ultimately, communities pay the price for prisons built and run for profit.

The General Accounting Office recently stated that it "could not conclude whether privatization saves money." Other independent analyses show that in many cases, it costs more to incarcerate inmates in private facilities than in state prisons.

Hidden costs often inflate profits for private firms managing prisons. Understaffing, low wages, less-qualified staff, poorer benefits, and inferior working conditions are common business practices within private facilities. While costs appear to be lower, the public ultimately pays for this "savings." Documented escapes of rapists and murderers, rioting, and inmate abuse in prisons run by private companies have jeopardized the safety of communities and increased the bottom-line for taxpayers.

Despite these threats, citizens have less say in the building of new, privatized prisons. Traditionally, the public has had a voice in financing penitentiaries. Citizens can vote whether a government can issue bonds, or loans, to construct prisons. Tax revenues back these bonds. Privatization, however, removes the public from the decision-making process. A corporation can build a prison and lease it to the government. Companies can also raise capital through Real Estate Investment Trust, or REITs, in which stocks are sold to investors. In both cases, private firms and shareholders can benefit, while the government—and taxpayers—are liable for the prison's performance, and left holding the bag if it fails....

In addition, contracting increases opportunites for corruption. Politicians can exchange lucrative prison contracts or assistance with private prison financing schemes for campaign contributions. Firms offer highly paid jobs to former public officials who can help them obtain contracts.

Conflicts of interest and the rights and well-being of inmates are also at issue. When prisons exist in a quasi-judicial status with an emphasis upon savings and profits, due process may be undermined. A firm may benefit monetarily from extended sentences, and wardens who do not answer to the public may cast a blind eye toward excessive physical force against inmates.

Incarcerating criminals is and should remain a fundamental responsibility of government. The bottom line for sworn state and local correctional officers is to protect our communities from those behind prison bars. The bottom line for corporations is profits.

Private prisons do not save money

Proponents of prison privatization claim that private contractors can operate prisons less expensively than the government. Promises of savings in the range of 15 percent to 20 percent are commonly promoted—but fail to materialize. Despite the claims of private management firms, the big promise of double-digit savings simply do not exist.

This was the case during the recent legislative session in Tennessee, which featured a bill to turn over nearly the entire Tennessee correctional system to private profiteers. The prison privatization crusade failed because its proponents could not establish credibility in their contentions that privatization would save taxpayers' money. Initially, supporters claimed up to $100 million would be saved. Later, that was scaled down to $25 million, but even then a close examination of the evidence proved the claims were exaggerated and tenuous.

The United States General Accounting Office (GAO), a nonpartisan congressional agency, spent a full year examining comprehensive studies of private and public operational costs of several state prisons. The GAO detected "little difference," "mixed results," and ultimately "could not conclude whether privatization saved money...."

Private prison operators often promise decision-makers the world to get a contract. However, once a private firm sets up shop, its loyalty is to its shareholders and not to local residents. The following examples illustrate both of these points:...

In Youngstown, Ohio, CCA touted a new privately owned and operated prison as a way to bring jobs to the community. Town officials were so happy about the prospect they sold CCA the land to build the prison for a token payment of $1, and gave the company a five-year partial tax abatement and free utility hookups. However, Youngstown officials became outraged upon finding out that CCA sold the prison for a $13

Can you think of other situations in which the aims of a company are potentially incompatible with the aims of the public or the community in which it operates?

Backing up broad statements with detailed evidence is a well-established technique for building an argument.

million profit, accusing the company of alleged profit-making at the expense of local taxpayers. CCA argued, nonetheless, that selling its own prisons is "part of CCA's business strategy."

The Youngstown facility houses inmates from Washington, D.C. CCA opened the prison last May, and it has been a headache for Youngstown officials since opening its doors. CCA has acknowledged 13 stabbings, including two recent homicides, since the facility opened. To put the Youngstown violence in perspective, the 29 Ohio state prisons reported a total of 22 assaults with weapons in 1997.

In the wake of an inmate's murder on February 22, 1998, U.S. District Judge Sam H. Bell issued a preliminary injunction that prohibits the District of Columbia from transferring any more inmates to Youngstown. According to CCA Chief Executive Officer Doctor Crants, "what happened in Youngstown was unfortunate, but there we had a sophisticated inmate population mixed with a rookie staff." Inmates and the city of Youngstown are suing CCA....

> In the Youngstown v. CCA case CCA Prisoners Classification Chief Karen Young admitted falsifying records. Do you think this sort of fraud would be as likely to happen in a government-owned prison?

Private firms do not follow through with agreements. New Mexico contracted with CCA to operate a women's correctional facility in Grants. However, the deal led to a nearly $4 million "misunderstanding" about how much the state would pay the company to house female prisoners. "Frankly, it's absurd," Corrections Secretary Rob Perry said of the CCA rate. The cost is about double what the state pays to keep overflow New Mexico male prisoners in county jails, officials said. New Mexico, frustrated with CCA, has not renewed the contract and has tried to buy the facility from CCA. However, CCA filed a lawsuit in the district court to prevent the state from buying the women's prison.

Private firms conceal crimes from local officials. Although CCA employees were committing drug and weapons violations at the facility in Hardeman County, Tennessee in 1995, the manager of the facility refused to report the crack cocaine use and weapons smuggling to the local sheriff. CCA officials said they weren't aware of any arrangements in which they had to file reports....

Private prisons foster corruption

Contracting increases opportunities for corruption. With so many tax dollars at stake, there are great temptations for politicians to exchange lucrative prison contracts or subsidize private prison financing schemes for campaign contributions. In addition, private corrections firms reward former public officials with highly-paid jobs. For instance, as the commissioner for the Alaska Department of Corrections,

Frank Prewitt wrote memos stating that due to "public safety concerns" and the state's "demographics," building private prisons in Alaska was not a good idea. Now, two years later, he is the president of Allvest Inc., a private corrections firm, and has changed his tune....

Prison privatization raises conflicts of interest

Prison privatization also raises policy concerns about the routine quasi-judicial decisions that affect the legal status and well-being of inmates. To what extent, for example, should a private corporation's employee be allowed to use force, perhaps serious or deadly force, against a prisoner? Or, should the employee of a private company be entitled to make recommendations to parole boards, or to bring charges against a prisoner for an institutional violation, possibly resulting in the forfeiture of good time credits toward the inmate's release? Decisions in the parole and good-time areas can increase the inmate's period of confinement.

Do you think an employee of a private company is properly qualified to make decisions regarding the length of an inmate's term in prison? Isn't that the job of the criminal justice system?

This concern can be especially sensitive, raising a possible conflict of interest, if the private company is paid on a per diem basis, or if the company's employees are given stock options as a fringe benefit, both of which exist in many of the current contracts. In fact, a recent article noted that some CCA guards in Tennessee said privately that they were encouraged to write up prisoners for minor infractions and place them in segregation. Inmates in segregation not only lose their good time, but also have 30 days added to their sentence—a bonus of nearly $ 1,000 for the company at some prisons....

Conclusion

The case against prison privatization is clear. The profit motive does not improve prison operation, nor does it save the taxpayer money. In fact, prison privatization creates incentives to "grow" the prison population, pushing up long-term prison costs. Prison privatization decreases public accountability, while increasing opportunities for waste, fraud and corruption. Incarcerating criminals is one of government's most fundamental responsibilities. It is crucial that this responsibility stays in the hands of public citizens and elected officials. By their very nature, private incarceration companies are more interested in doing well than in doing good. They serve only the interests of their officers, directors and shareholders. The bottom line for a corporation is profit. The bottom line for sworn state and local correctional officers is to protect our communities from those who are behind prison bars.

The United States already has practically the largest prison population in the world. Is an incentive to increase the prison population cause for serious concern?

Summary

The National Center for Policy Analysis argues that the case for private prisons is proven, and that private companies will inevitably increase their share of the market. It says that the potential for reducing the net costs of prisons has yet to be tapped, and that private prisons are showing they can do the job. The article welcomes an increase in private prisons and says there is no insurmountable legal obstacle to the total privatization of prison operations. It says the "government should set punishments for felons and let the private sector efficiently supply prisons." It advocates reversing the drain on taxpayers' pockets by putting inmates to work and says steps have been taken to clear bureaucratic obstacles to private prison labor. It cites progressive initiatives to employ prisoners in "real world" work, which benefits everyone as well as making prisons profitable.

The American Federation of State, County, and Municipal Employees strongly opposes private prisons. It says the public ultimately pays the price for reduced costs: Poor training, understaffing, and inmate abuse contribute to a climate in which rioting and escapes occur more frequently. The public has no say in whether a private prison is constructed in the community, but must pay dearly for operational failures. The article is suspicious of private firms' motives, saying that the firms will promise anything to get a contract and then renege on the deal. Private prisons also create more opportunities for corruption: Politicians may be tempted to give away lucrative contracts in exchange for campaign funds. Conflicts of interest arise because of private firms' inherent advantage in keeping inmates behind bars. The bottom line for state correctional officers is to keep our communities safe, it says, while the bottom line for private prisons is profit.

FURTHER INFORMATION:

Books:

Harding, Richard, *Private Prisons and Public Accountability*. Somerset, NJ: Transaction Publishers, 1997.
Neufeld, Rodney, Allison Campbell, and Andrew Coyle (editors), *Capitalist Punishment: Prison Privatization and Human Rights*. Atlanta, GA: Clarity Press, 2002.

Useful websites:

http://www.mediafilter.org.caq/prison.html
"Private Prisons: Profits of Crime," an article from the Fall 1993 issue of *Covert Action Quarterly*.
http://www.rppi.org/prison
Frequently asked questions about private prisons.
http://www.ucc.uconn.edu/~logan
Prison privatization research site.

The following debates in the Pro/Con series may also be of interest:

In this volume:
Topic 14 Do prisoners have rights?

In *Economics*:
Topic 3 Does privatization always benefit consumers?

In *Environment*:
Topic 16 Should corporations be socially responsible?

SHOULD PRISONS BE PRIVATIZED?

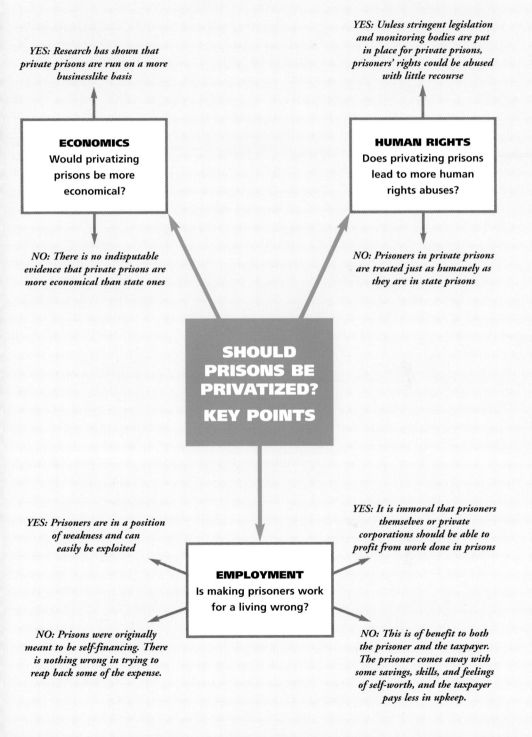

YES: Research has shown that private prisons are run on a more businesslike basis

YES: Unless stringent legislation and monitoring bodies are put in place for private prisons, prisoners' rights could be abused with little recourse

ECONOMICS
Would privatizing prisons be more economical?

HUMAN RIGHTS
Does privatizing prisons lead to more human rights abuses?

NO: There is no indisputable evidence that private prisons are more economical than state ones

NO: Prisoners in private prisons are treated just as humanely as they are in state prisons

**SHOULD PRISONS BE PRIVATIZED?
KEY POINTS**

YES: Prisoners are in a position of weakness and can easily be exploited

YES: It is immoral that prisoners themselves or private corporations should be able to profit from work done in prisons

EMPLOYMENT
Is making prisoners work for a living wrong?

NO: Prisons were originally meant to be self-financing. There is nothing wrong in trying to reap back some of the expense.

NO: This is of benefit to both the prisoner and the taxpayer. The prisoner comes away with some savings, skills, and feelings of self-worth, and the taxpayer pays less in upkeep.

Topic 16
SHOULD SEX OFFENDERS BE CHEMICALLY CASTRATED?

YES
FROM "THE CHEMICAL KNIFE"
SALON.COM, MARCH 1, 2000
KEVIN GIORDANO

NO
"SEX OFFENDERS: DOES TREATMENT WORK"?
NATIONAL CENTER ON INSTITUTIONS AND ALTERNATIVES
ERIC LOTKE

INTRODUCTION

On September 18, 1996, California passed AB 3339. The statute stated that in cases in which the victim was less than 13 years of age, first-time sexual offenders on parole were required to receive Medroxyprogesterone Acetate—better known as Depo-Provera. It also required all second-time offenders to receive the drug while on parole.

Depo-Provera is a derivative of the hormone progesterone. Women use it as a contraceptive device; in men it lowers the testosterone level and thus the male sex drive. Its administering by injection is called chemical castration.

While there is little argument that sexual crime is a problem in the United States, the use of chemical castration has caused much heated debate. Many advocates argue that it is a humane and sensible method of preventing further abuse; opponents assert that using Depo-Provera and similar drugs is not only inhumane, but unconstitutional—a reference to the Eighth Amendment,

which protects people from "cruel and unusual" punishment.

After AB 3339 was passed, the American Civil Liberties Union (ACLU) stated that "the complex reasons that impel people to assault children cannot be eliminated by giving people shots." But what is the alternative?

Surgical castration (removing a man's testes) has been performed around the world for centuries. In ancient China and Egypt castrated males or eunuchs —who posed no sexual threat—served as guards to the women's quarters. So it seems castration has long been seen as a way of controling the sexual impulse.

More recently Denmark, Finland, Norway, and Sweden have all required sex offenders to be surgically castrated, although Denmark now uses chemical castration instead. And some U.S. states, such as Texas and California, also offer a voluntary surgical castration option.

Surgical castration is for the most part disapproved of in the United States, but the issue received considerable attention during the 1990 case of convicted child molester Larry Don McQuay. Following his claim that he had molested more than 200 children, McQuay repeatedly requested surgical castration, stating that he was "doomed to eventually rape then murder my poor little victims." He argued that only surgical castration would save them.

Texas officials refused to pay for the surgery since it was elective rather than compulsory, and McQuay was later paroled. However, he was charged with indecency with a child shortly afterward.

> "The recidivism rate—repeat criminal activity—drops from 87 percent to 2 percent (with some sort of castration). That's pretty darn effective."
> —CALIFORNIA REPUBLICAN ASSEMBLYMAN BILL HOGE

The Association for the Treatment of Sexual Abusers (ATSA) is one of several bodies that opposes the use of surgical castration, suggesting that chemical castration is less intrusive and more effective in reducing reoffense rates.

According to research published in the *American Journal of Psychiatry*, Depo-Provera "may diminish sexual … urges, making self-control easier." But ATSA warns that a substantial number of chemical castrates continue to function sexually after treatment. ATSA also argues that sexual aggression often involves more than just the ability to have an erection or to ejaculate.

One of the most comprehensive studies on the subject was carried out by Meyer, Cole, and Emory in 1992. They compared the recidivism (habitual relapse into crime) rates of 40 convicted sex offenders who received both group and individual therapy as well as Depo-Provera with a group of peer offenders who received therapy but refused to take the drug. They found that only 18 percent of the Depo-Provera patients reoffended, but that this figure rose to 35 percent once the drugs were stopped.

A more recent study has found that drug treatment may be more effective in older men, whose testoterone levels take longer to return to normal.

Critics of chemical castration argue that administering drugs like Depo-Provera violates what experts call the right to "bodily integrity." They also question the state's right to adminster potentially dangerous drugs to sex offenders on parole and to prevent them from having children. They argue that drug-induced treatment fails to address the real issues behind sex-related crime and pedophilia, and assert that determined felons could find ways to reduce the drug's effects or just stop treatment altogether.

In an article on usatoday.com journalist DeWayne Wickham suggests that many "sex predators are opting for chemical castration to avoid or lessen a prison sentence." Wickham and other critics argue that chemical castration does not stop people from committing sexual crimes, and Florida prosecutor Jerry Buford agrees: "It's not their gonads that cause them to commit sexual battery. It's their heads."

The following articles look at some of the pros and cons of the debate on sexual castration.

THE CHEMICAL KNIFE
Kevin Giordano

By giving explicit examples to illustrate his argument, Giordano immediately gains the audience's attention and shows the seriousness of the issue.

On Jan. 8, Shannon Coleman, a convicted sex offender, circumvented a 21-year prison term by agreeing to be chemically castrated. A self-described sex addict, Coleman had used the Internet to strike up chats with two Florida girls. He managed to visit one, a 12-year-old, at her house, where he fondled her and then masturbated. The other, a 15-year-old, invited him over to her house, where they had sex.

For further information on Florida's 1997 sex offender law go to www.fdle.state.fl.us/ sexual_predators/ Documents/ SexPredLegalBrief. asp.

At his trial, Coleman, his lawyer and his psychiatrist, Fred Berlin, seized upon Florida's 1997 sex offender law, which gives the court discretion to sentence people convicted of sexual battery to undergo drug treatment to stop and/or reduce testosterone production. With help from Berlin, Coleman was able to trade prison time for a life under the chemical "knife."

Eighth Amendment

Go to aclu.org, and look at the archive to find recent reports on this issue.

…Once referred to as a form of mutilation by the American Civil Liberties Union, a reference to the Eighth Amendment to the Bill of Rights (which says, "Excessive bail shall not be required, nor excessive fines imposed, nor cruel and unusual punishments inflicted"), chemical castration is slowly gaining ground throughout the country as a means of sentencing and treating sex offenders.

The author wrote this article in March 2000, when such legislation was being discussed.

Tennessee is currently debating whether to adopt a bill that would make it the ninth state with a law governing the use of the drug medroxyprogesterone acetate (MPA), which acts as a sexual suppressant. "There's been a heightened recognition of sex offenses," says Berlin, referring to the "two strikes, you're out" Child Protection Act of 1999, which says repeat sex offenders get life in prison, and "Megan's Law," which requires that sex offenders be registered with local authorities and the FBI upon release from incarceration.

Says Berlin, founder of the sexual disorders clinic at Johns Hopkins University in Maryland: Such laws are "likely to progress to other states, after they establish committees to advise legislators."

State Sen. Tim Burchett, at 35 the youngest member of the Tennessee Senate, is sponsoring the bill that would make the use of drugs such as Depo-Provera and Depo-Lupron an optional part of a convicted person's sentence. "Part of the problem is just the name 'castration,'" Burchett says. "I hear the jokes and talk, it doesn't bother me. If you've ever talked to a mother whose daughter or son has been raped, you'd never question my reasons."

Burchett's steadfast efforts to bring up the bill began in earnest four years ago when he was in the state House. The committee considering the bill was undecided and deferred it, but assisted Burchett in drafting new versions. "Castration was something we needed to look at," Burchett says. "Everyone assumed it was some kind of mutilation, but it doesn't have anything to do with mutilation. It's just a form of treatment."

The word "castration" is more commonly used to refer to the surgical removal of a male's testicles, resulting in a reduction in the sex drive.

The situation in the United States

In 1996, California became the first state to pass a measure known as a chemical castration law, which requires chemical castration of any person found guilty a second time of specified sex offenses. Florida, Georgia, Louisiana, Montana, Oregon, Texas and Wisconsin followed shortly thereafter with similar laws. Dr. Mark Graff of the California Psychiatric Association is wary of this trend and says the California measure was intended to be harsh. The law "gives an illusion of protection because its punitive 'castrate 'em and hang-'em-up model' attracts legislators," Graff says. "This was no attempt to rehabilitate people."

Go to "Castrations and Drug Therapy with Sex Offenders" at http://members. tripod.com/~dazc/ sexdrugs.htm to find more information on this subject.

Burchett, in a cogent response to other states' laws, made an alternative suggestion. Under present Tennessee law, any person who commits or attempts to commit a sexual offense is to be sentenced to community supervision for life. Burchett's bill would add that as part of supervision, a qualifying offender would be required to submit to Depo-Provera treatment, a drug that contains MPA. (To qualify for testosterone-reducing drugs, an offender would first have to be determined to have uncontrollable sexual urges, that is, be labeled a child molester or a pedophile. If it was found that he was sexually abusive because of problems with authority or a desire to break rules, or because he was seeking power, he might be termed a sadist, and therefore might not qualify for testosterone-reducing drugs.)

Pedophilia is the condition of finding children sexually attractive. Most countries have legislation in place to protect children from sexual abuse. Go to www.usdoj. gov/kidspage, the Justice Department's Kids and Youth site, to find out more about recent laws and practices.

A deterrent?

...Despite the laws already in place in eight states, and cases documenting drug treatment's effectiveness, there remains a split in the legal and medical communities. Most feel the treatment can be helpful if a patient is amenable to it. "I don't know if it's a deterrent," says Burchett, "but if someone wants to get help, this is something that can help them."

The effects

The word "castration" evokes haunting images of men strapped to a table, heavily anesthetized and fearing for their life. Just the mention of the word makes men wince and women giggle. To be sure, physical castration and chemical castration both have the same goal: to stop the production of testosterone, which is considered by mental health experts to be one of the sources of sexually offensive or aggressive behavior. Surgical castration involves removal of the testes, after which it is possible but unlikely for a man to have an erection, and his sex drive is considerably lowered. Chemical castration—also called sexual suppression—entails taking a drug that inhibits or reduces the production of testosterone. Again, the patient can still "perform," but his drive is considerably lowered. (In the handful of women convicted as sex offenders, similar drugs would merely act as oral contraceptives.)

…Even if it hasn't been sufficiently thought through, the use of chemical castration on pedophiles in the United States dates as far back as the mid-'60s. Drugs such as Depo-Provera and Depo-Lupron have been and are being used in efforts to stop crimes before they happen. Explains Berlin, "In layman's terms, with chemical castration you are providing people with a sexual appetite suppressant."

European history

Europeans have employed surgical and chemical castration since before the time of Hitler. Berlin points to a well-known study conducted in Scandinavia over a 30-year period that demonstrated significant results. Among the more than 900 sex offenders in that country who underwent surgical castration, the recurrence of sexual offenses was less than 3 percent. This is a staggering figure when compared with some American studies showing that as many as 50 percent of sex offenders who are released commit similar crimes again. Yet statistics on the subject are few and far between….

Presenting the facts

Dr. Richard Krueger, medical director of the sexual behavior clinic at New York State Psychiatric Institute, has been treating sex offenders since the mid-'80s. He is currently preparing a symposium on treatment of sexual offenders to

Testosterone is a hormone produced by the testes and in smaller quantities by the adrenal glands of both sexes. In men it is responsible for sexual function and arousal, anabolism (tissue building), and secondary sexual characteristics such as facial hair.

Depo-Provera was developed as a form of contraception for women and has also been used to induce sex change in men. Depo-Lupron causes an "artificial menopause" in women and can be used to control heavy and irregular bleeding, to shrink fibroids prior to surgery, and to regulate the recipients of donor eggs. It is also used to treat prostate cancer in men.

Visit the New York State Psychiatric Institute at www.nyspi.cpmc.columbia.edul.

present before the American Academy of Psychiatry Law meeting in October in Vancouver, Canada. In the past, he has prescribed testosterone-reducing drugs to patients, but only after the patient's request....

Likely candidates?

Who should qualify for chemical castration in the United States is a hotly argued issue. In the first place, legal and medical professionals differ in their definitions of what a sexual offense is. According to the Family Research Council, sex crimes against children include rape, sodomy, intimate touching, exposing oneself, voyeurism, forcing a child to engage in prostitution, pornography and live sex performances. Crimes against women include many of the same behaviors.

The Family Research Council is an organization dedicated to defending "family faith and freedom." Find out more at www.frc.org.

Yet many sex crimes committed against children are labeled molestation instead of sexual offenses. There's also confusion over the difference between a child molester and a pedophile, not to mention a sadist. According to the American Psychiatric Association, a pedophile can be successfully treated with drugs like Depo-Provera, but a sadist (a person who acts out against written laws just to break them) is not a good candidate for chemical castration.

Visit the website of the American Psychiatric Association at www.psych.org.

Will the results merit the costs?

In May 1999 and in January of this year, the Tennessee bill was deferred by the judiciary committee. It is now under consideration once again. Burchett reports that funding is the main problem, not a lack of support. The fear of many in the Tennessee Senate and House is that administration of the drugs will be too costly to the state. "They think every offender who gets the drug each month will eventually hop on welfare, and then we pay for it," says Burchett. But there's an amendment in the bill, he says, that would make offenders pay for treatment themselves (at a cost of as much as $500 per monthly injection).

...In a 1992 interview with the *Los Angeles Times*, convicted offender Komarenski said the results of taking the testosterone-reducing drug Depo-Lupron were startling. "My sex drive is practically zero," he said. "It works. It really works."

After his release from a psychiatric hospital in 1999 convicted pedophile Robert Komarenski was turned down by the government-funded clinics he visited. Jobless, he wandered the streets, unable to afford expensive prescription drugs. It was only after repeated inquiries from the L.A. Times that officials pledged to continue his drug treatment.

SEX OFFENDERS: DOES TREATMENT WORK?
Eric Lotke

X If you ask the average citizen to describe a sex offender you will probably get a picture of a drooling violent predator, either retarded or scheming, who rapes and kills women and children for sexual pleasure. If you ask what can be done about these offenders, responses will likely range from castration to electrocution because it is believed nothing less will stop them from offending again in the future.

Do these stereotypes exist?

Such stereotypes do not reflect reality but they do drive criminal justice policy. Sex offenders have become the new bogeymen, used by politicians to intimidate and scare citizens concerned about public safety. Often the claims have more to do with scoring political points than creating a safer society.

This paper attempts to bring some clarity to the issue. Though more research is always helpful and needed, enough is now known to draw some broad conclusions: Treated or untreated, few sex offenders reoffend after being caught. Sex offenders actually reoffend less than other types of offenders, and treatment works to lower reoffense rates.

Who are the real sex offenders?

The most important thing to realize about sex offenders is that we do not know who most of them are. Sex crimes tend to be private. Often they involve possession of child pornography or soliciting for prostitution, so there is no "victim" in the traditional sense to register a complaint.

The most troubling sex crimes occur behind closed doors, with family members or friends, usually children, who are manipulated or intimidated into silence. Most of these crimes involve fondling or undressing; rarely do they rise to the level of sex acts or intercourse.

The perpetrators of most sex crimes are ordinary in most other respects. They are family members, hold jobs, play sports and maintain friendships. In addition, the majority of sex offenders were themselves victims of sexual molestation. This fact does not excuse their misconduct, but it helps to

In the UK, for example, the government has embarked on a controversial plan to identify sex offenders with "dangerous and severe personality disorders" (DSPD), a term coined by officials following outrage over the case of Michael Stone, who bludgeoned to death Lin Russell and her daughter, Megan in 1996. However, many psychiatrists believe that DSPD has no real medical basis.

A study of state prisoners serving time for violent crime in 1991 revealed that of those convicted for rape or sexual assault, two-thirds victimized children, and three out of four of those who victimized a child reported the crime took place in their own home or in the victim's home.

explain it. Addressing the psychological harm done to offenders in the past may help to reduce the harm they inflict on others in the future, thus preempting intergenerational cycles of abuse.

How many are there?

Because most sex crimes go unreported, it is difficult to determine exactly how many there are. A few observations help to clarify this crucial issue. First, reporting and recording of sex offenses has increased dramatically in recent years. Much of the apparent rise in sex offending is related to increased reporting rather than increased offending.

Second, enforcement is more aggressive and definitions of sex offenses are more expansive than ever before. Conduct that was once tolerated is now criminally prosecuted. This gives the appearance of increased criminal sexual activity when, in fact, the changes are in the official response. More than eight times more people were incarcerated for lower grades of sexual assault in 1992 than 1980.

Despite these increases, identified sex offenses are relatively rare. Arrests for rape and other sex offenses constituted 1% of all arrests in 1993. Perpetrators of such crimes constituted 9% of state and federal prison populations in 1992, compared to 22.4% for property offenses and 25.2% for drug offenses.

How are they punished?

People convicted of serious sex crimes are usually sentenced to prison. According to the 1992 National Corrections Reporting Program, average prison sentences in state courts were 12.8 years for rape (5 years average time served) and 9.5 years for other kinds of sexual assault (2.5 years average time served). Though this is the most recent official information on sentence lengths, it is over three years old and much is based on sentences imposed over eight years ago. Sentences have gotten longer since the information was collected.

Little or no psychological treatment is available for sex offenders sentenced to prison. Those sentenced to probation are rarely ordered to attend treatment sessions....

Do sex offenders reoffend?

Contrary to popular belief, convicted sex offenders have relatively low rates of recidivism compared to other offenders. On average, untreated sex offenders sentenced to prison have a recidivism rate of 18.5%. In comparison, recidivism rates range around 25% for drug offenses and

Since sweeping changes were made to the law in the 1970s and 1980s, sexual assault now includes incest, rape, unwanted sexual contact, sexual harassment, forced prostitution, exposure to pornography, and voyeurism. Activities such as sexual staring, "accidental" touching, verbal invitations to engage in sexual activity, reading sexually explicit material to children, and exposing others to inappropriate sexual activity are all included.

Are these figures convincing? Statistics often vary according to the source and how crimes are defined and measured. For example, a National Violence Against Women Survey found that 1 in 6 women and 1 in 33 men have experienced an attempted or completed rape. And the author has already told us that most sex crimes go unreported.

For more statistics on recidivism go to www.ojp.usdoj. gov/bjs/crimoff.htm #recidivism.

30% for violent offenses….The public trial, shame and humiliation of getting caught appears to deter most sex offenders from further misconduct….

Does treatment reduce recidivism?

A popular misconception is that nothing can cure a sex offender. This myth can be traced largely to a paper published by Lita Furby in 1989. Furby's paper, however, focused on the lack of sophisticated, reliable data with which to evaluate treatment regimes. It concluded only that evidence of the effectiveness of psychological treatment was inconclusive. Politicians and the mass media picked up this judgment, often converting it to the claim:"Nothing Works!"

For more information about treating sex offenders go to the site of the Association for the Treatment of Sexual Abusers at www.ATSA.com.

That conclusion, however, is against the general weight of the evidence. Most research shows that sex offenders do indeed respond positively to treatment. A comprehensive analysis by Margaret Alexander of the Oshkosh Correctional Institution found far more studies reporting positive results than otherwise.

Alexander found that recidivism rates after treatment drop to an average of 10.9%. Thus, a picture has begun to emerge in which treated sex offenders reoffend less than untreated sex offenders. Many sex offenders appreciate the wrongness of their conduct and intensely desire to reform themselves. Treatment helps them to achieve this end.

Moreover, treatment has become more effective as more attention has been devoted to the problem. When Alexander classified the studies by date, she found recidivism rates in recent surveys to be 8.4%.

Distinguishing types of sex offenders

The conclusion that treatment reduces recidivism can be refined further by distinguishing between different kinds of sex offenders. Treatment cuts the recidivism rate among exhibitionists and child molesters by more than half … among rapists by just a few percent. Juveniles respond very positively to treatment, indicating that treating sex offenders as soon as they are identified can prevent an escalation of their pathology. The state of Vermont reports offense rates after treatment as: 19% for rapists, 7% for pedophiles, 3% for incest, and 3% for "hands-off" crimes such as exhibitionism.

Is a 19 percent risk of recidivism among rapists an acceptable rate? Do distinctions need to be made between different sexual offenses when prescribing treatments for paroled offenders?

One word of caution is in order. Reoffense rates tend to increase over the years and, around the ten year mark, reoffense rates among treated offenders is nearly the same as among untreated offenders. This finding indicates the need for sex offenders to be in booster sessions and maintenance groups for many years. Additional research is needed to produce statistically rigorous and consistent measures of the long-term effects of treatment.

Can we afford treatment?

Psychological counseling is expensive, but not as expensive as prison. The average cost of building a new prison cell is about $55,000 and the average cost of operating it for a year is $22,000. A year of intensively supervised probation and treatment may cost between $5,000 and $15,000 per year, depending on the regimen. Thus, a full year of treatment costs far less than an additional year of prison.

Treated offenders can generally be integrated fully into society as normal productive citizens after a period of treatment. Offenders in prison, on the other hand, will continue to cost taxpayers $22,000 a year for as long as they are incarcerated.…Treatment is therefore an essential means of protecting the community at an affordable cost.

Does this section add to the argument? Keeping sex offenders in prison may be expensive, but the author does not compare the costs of supplying the drugs for chemical castration with the costs of providing counseling.

The community response

A concerned citizen once asked a criminologist what could be done about child molestation. "Don't molest your children," he replied. The truth behind this response is undeniable. Most sexual misconduct happens within families or among friends; the stalking predator is more a myth than a reality.

For this reason, community notification provisions like Megan's Law in New Jersey are deceptive. They focus attention on individuals who have been caught—not because of the threat they pose but because of other threats we are unable to solve. They also invite excoriation and vigilantism against individuals who have paid their debt to society and need to be peacefully reintegrated.

The best community response is to focus on recognized ways to keep the problems at a minimum. Punishment and incapacitation have a role to play, but they are inadequate by themselves. Psychological treatment while in prison and after release is vital; education and aftercare are proven to reduce the likelihood of reoffending in the future. Most importantly, the public must make an effort to remain sane and sober in the face of these serious crimes.

"Megan's Law" is named after Megan Kanka, who was raped and killed in 1993 by repeat offender Jesse Temendequas. Megan's Law requires authorities to tell communities the whereabouts of convicted sex offenders in their neighborhoods. There is now a version of Megan's Law on the books in all 50 states. Opponents argue that these laws simply drive sexual predators underground.

Summary

Although the National Crime Victimization Survey reported that the total number of rapes, attempted rapes, and sexual assaults in the United States declined from 383,000 in 1999 to 261,000 in 2000, sex-related crime remains a serious problem, especially since it is difficult to estimate the number of unreported cases. Many people advocate therapy and rehabilitation as a way of dealing with convicted offenders, but chemical castration is becoming an increasingly popular option, particularly for paroled sex felons.

In the first article, "The Chemical Knife," Kevin Giordano examines recent chemical castration legislation and considers how various European countries have used castration drugs successfully. He states how research shows that sexual offenders tend to repeat offend and cites examples demonstrating how chemical castration has helped prevent this.

In "Sex Offenders: Does Treatment Work?" on the other hand, Eric Lotke argues that convicted sex felons rarely tend to reoffend and suggests that therapy helps lower reoffense rates even further. He says it is a myth that sex offenders cannot be treated and suggests that most research shows they respond positively to treatment. Lotke also suggests that such treatment is less expensive than housing felons in prison: "Treatment is therefore an essential means of protecting the community at an affordable cost."

FURTHER INFORMATION:

Books:

Jenkins, Philip, *Moral Panic: Changing Concepts of the Child Molester in Modern America*. New Haven, CT: Yale University Press, 1998.

Kincaid, James R., *Erotic Innocence: The Culture of Child Molesting*. Durham, NC: Duke University Press, 1998.

Lundrigan, Paul Stephen, *Treating Youth Who Sexually Abuse: An Integrated Multi-Component Approach*. Binghamton NY: Haworth Press, 2001.

Russell, Diana E. H. and Rebecca M. Bolen, *The Epidemic of Rape and Child Abuse in the United States*. Thousand Oaks, CA: Sage Publications, 2000.

Wazir, Rekha, and Nico van Oudenhoven, *Child Sexual Abuse: What Can Governments Do? A Comparative Investigation into Policy Instruments Used*. Cambridge, MA: Kluwer Law International, 1998.

Useful websites:

www.aclu.org/
Site of the American Civil Liberties Union.

www.cnn.com/US/9608/29/castration/

Article about the California castration bill with related links.

www.csun.edu/~psy453/crimes_y.htm

For links to articles arguing that chemical castration is a suitable punishment for male sex offenders.

www.debatabase.org/details.asp?topicID=133

The International Debate Education Association's site contains pro and con views on the chemical castration of sex offenders.

www.house.gov/judiciary/sweeney_073101.htm

One mother's view of chemical castration.

www.ojp.usdoj.gov/

Statistics and research from the Department of Justice.

The following debate in the Pro/Con series may also be of interest:

In this volume:

 Topic 14 Do prisoners have rights?

SHOULD SEX OFFENDERS BE CHEMICALLY CASTRATED?

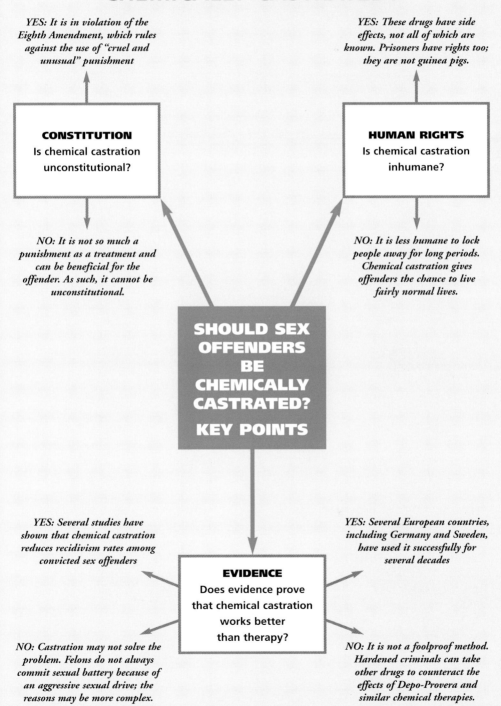

YES: It is in violation of the Eighth Amendment, which rules against the use of "cruel and unusual" punishment

YES: These drugs have side effects, not all of which are known. Prisoners have rights too; they are not guinea pigs.

CONSTITUTION
Is chemical castration unconstitutional?

HUMAN RIGHTS
Is chemical castration inhumane?

NO: It is not so much a punishment as a treatment and can be beneficial for the offender. As such, it cannot be unconstitutional.

NO: It is less humane to lock people away for long periods. Chemical castration gives offenders the chance to live fairly normal lives.

SHOULD SEX OFFENDERS BE CHEMICALLY CASTRATED?
KEY POINTS

YES: Several studies have shown that chemical castration reduces recidivism rates among convicted sex offenders

YES: Several European countries, including Germany and Sweden, have used it successfully for several decades

EVIDENCE
Does evidence prove that chemical castration works better than therapy?

NO: Castration may not solve the problem. Felons do not always commit sexual battery because of an aggressive sexual drive; the reasons may be more complex.

NO: It is not a foolproof method. Hardened criminals can take other drugs to counteract the effects of Depo-Provera and similar chemical therapies.

GLOSSARY

Al Qaeda an international terrorist group headed by Osama bin Laden, Al Qaeda is thought to be behind several major acts of terrorism, including the events of September 11, 2001. It was initially formed to unite Arabs fighting in Afghanistan against the Soviet Union.

attorney general the chief law officer of a state or nation and the principal legal adviser to the government.

Broken Windows an initiative to crack down on minor public-order offenses, instigated under the theory that an unrepaired broken window is a signal that no one in the community cares and that this in turn leads to further crime. *See also* Three Strikes.

Camp X-Ray the U.S. military detention center on a naval base at Guantanamo Bay, Cuba. The base holds Al Qaeda and Taliban fighters who were captured in Afghanistan. *See also* Al Qaeda, Taliban.

capital punishment the legal ending of a person's life as punishment for a serious, or "capital," offense.

castration the removal of the reproductive organs (surgical castration) or reduction of the sex drive through hormone-altering chemicals (chemical castration). Some countries require the castration of convicted sex offenders.

civil rights a group of advantages such as the right to vote and equal treatment of all that are guaranteed by law to all citizens.

community policing combines the efforts and resources of the police, local government, and community members to reduce crime in local neighborhoods.

constitution a written codification of the basic principles and laws under which a government operates.

corruption a decline in moral principles, especially in politicians, which leads to abusing power, lying, or taking bribes.

Drug Enforcement Administration (DEA) the leading federal agency for the enforcement of narcotics and controlled substance laws and regulations. The agency's mission is to end major drug-trafficking organizations.

Eighth Amendment bans "cruel and unusual punishment" and states that "excessive bail shall not be required, nor excessive fines imposed."

Fourteenth Amendment provides protection from unequal treatment on the basis of sex, race, and creed. The Equal Protection clause in the amendment prohibits discrimination during jury selection on the basis of race or religion.

General Accounting Office (GAO) an independent and nonpartisan agency that advises Congress and the heads of executive agencies about how to make government more effective and efficient.

Geneva Conventions there are four Geneva Conventions (dating to 1949 and 1977) that aim to protect the rights of men and women detained during armed conflict. The conventions are adhered to by most countries around the world.

habeas corpus under this safeguard of personal liberty a judge can require that a jailer or custodian bring a prisoner to court and explain why he or she is held captive.

harm reduction a policy practiced in Holland, based on the theory that less harm will come to legal soft-drug users if they are separated from illegal hard-drug sellers.

inequality a disparity in distribution of a specific resource or item, such as income, education, employment, or health care.

judicial branch one of the three branches of government (alongside the legislative and the executive). It consists of courts that decide arguments about the meaning of laws, how they are applied, and whether they are constitutional.

juvenile court a special court that deals with the problems of delinquent, abused, or neglected minors (usually under age 18). Unlike ordinary courts, juvenile courts favor rehabilitation rather than punishment for crimes.

Juvenile Justice and Delinquency Protection an act introduced in 1972 in an attempt to protect juvenile criminals in institutions. The act requires that juveniles be separated from adult criminals in group homes and halfway houses. *See also* juvenile court, parental responsibility.

morality standards of conduct or moral codes that establish the principles of right and wrong behavior.

parental responsibility in moral terms the notion that parents should provide for the welfare of their offspring and teach them the concepts of right and wrong behavior. In legal terms the liability of a parent if their child's behavior causes damage to another person or property.

pedophile someone with a sexual perversion that causes him or her to be sexually attracted to children. *See also* castration.

racism a belief that race determines human traits and capacities and that racial differences produce the inherent superiority of a particular race. *See also* racial profiling, zero-tolerance policing.

racial profiling the use of ethnic characteristics to decide if someone is a likely suspect for committing a crime.

recidivism the tendency to relapse into a previous mode of behavior, usually criminal.

Sixth Amendment states that in all criminal prosecutions the accused has the right to a speedy and public trial by an impartial jury.

social responsibility a set of behaviors and beliefs that includes a commitment to fostering the well-being of everyone in society, to resolve conflict peaceably, to foster cooperation and community, and to counter bias and prejudice.

Street Terrorism Prevention Act (1988) a law aimed at controlling gang crime. Under it parents found guilty of failing to exercise reasonable care, supervision, protection, and control over their children are liable to a maximum fine of $2,500 and a one-year prison sentence.

Supreme Court the final court of appeal and final interpreter of the Constitution.

Taliban a group composed of Afghans trained in religious schools in Pakistan, along with former Islamic fighters or mujahedin. *See also* Al Qaeda.

Three Strikes an initiative passed in 1994 in order to give felons longer sentences for second-time offences. If they commit a third serious or violent crime, they receive a sentence of 25 years to life. *See also* Broken Windows, community policing, racial profiling.

Universal Declaration of Human Rights a codification of basic human rights and freedoms drafted by an international committee after World War II and adopted by the United Nations in 1948.

USA PATRIOT Act (Uniting and Strengthening America through Providing Appropriate Tools Required to Intercept and Obstruct Terrorism) an act introduced after the terrorist action of September 11, 2001. It increases the powers of the Immigration and Naturalization Service, allowing it to arrest and detain immigrants. The act also extends the powers of the Military Order, which allows military tribunals to try noncitizens who have been charged with terrorism. *See also* Al Qaeda, Taliban.

zero-tolerance policing an approach to policing pioneered by the New York Police Department in which minor misdemeanors are pursued with the same vigor as more serious crimes. The theory behind the approach is that it is easier to prevent crime than to deal with its consequences.

Acknowledgments

Topic 1 Is the Criminal Justice System Racist?

Yes: From "Nothing Personal" by Barbara Smith, *Radcliffe Quarterly*, Fall/Winter 1997 (www.radcliffe.edu/quarterly/199703/page25a.html). Copyright © 1997 by Barbara Smith. Used by permission.

No: From "Lessons from Cincinnati: A Vivid Guide in How Not to Handle Riots" by Heather MacDonald, *Daily News*, July 22, 2001. Heather MacDonald is a contributing editor of *City Journal*, John M. Olin Fellow at the Manhattan Institute, and author of *The Burden of Bad Ideas: How Modern Intellectuals Misshape Our Society*. Copyright © 2001 by Heather MacDonald. Used by permission.

Topic 2 Should Juries Have Mandatory Representation of People of All Races?

Yes: "Tulia's Witch Trials" by Arianna Huffington, Salon.com, October 11, 2000. Copyright © 2000 by Salon.com. Used by permission.

No: From "The Second Circuit's Recent Reversal of Two Guilty Verdicts in the Yankel Rosenbaum Killing, and the Difficult Issue of Race-Conscious Jury Selection" by Sherry F. Colb. This column originally appeared on FindLaw.com, January 16, 2002. Reprinted with permission of FindLaw.com.

Topic 3 Is the Three-Strikes Law a Deterrent?

Yes: "Don't Believe the Experts: Three Strikes Reduces Crime" by Edward J. Erler and Brian P. Janiskee, The Claremont Institute. Reprinted with the permission of the authors.

No: From "Striking Out: The Failure of California's 'Three Strikes and You're Out' Law" by Mike Males and Dan Macallair, Justice Policy Institute. Reprinted with permission of the Justice Policy Institute.

Topic 4 Should Soldiers Be Prosecuted for Crimes Committed during War?

Yes: "Letter Written by Captain Aubrey M. Daniel to President Nixon" (www.law.umkc.edu/faculty/projects/ftrials/mylai/daniels_ltr.html). Public domain.

No: From "Summation of George Latimer for the Defense: The Court-martial of Lieutenant William Calley" (www.law.umkc.edu/faculty/ projects/ftrails/mylai/defence.html). Public domain.

Topic 5 Do Wartime Laws Violate Civil Liberties?

Yes: From "Free Speech R.I.P" by Hank Hoffman, *New Haven Valley Advocate*, November 20, 2001 (www.globalexchange.org/september11/valleyAdvocate112001.html). Copyright © 2001 by Hank Hoffman. Used by permission.

No: "Security Versus Civil Liberties" by Richard A. Posner, *The Atlantic Monthly*, December 2001 (www.theatlantic.com/issues/2001/12/posner.htm). Copyright © 2001 by Richard A. Posner. Used by permission.

Topic 6 Does the "Broken Windows" Policy Work?

Yes: "Study Praises Policing Strategy" by Tarek Tannous, Intercountynews.com, August 12, 2002. Reprinted with permission from the Daily Local News of West Chester, PA.

No: From "Brutal Verdict" by Bruce Shapiro, Salon.com February 26, 2000. Copyright © 2000 by Bruce Shapiro and the *Nation* magazine. Used by permission.

Topic 7 Does Community Policing Help Reduce Crime?

Yes: From "The False Trade-off" by Michael Crowley, Salon.com, April 27, 1999 (www.salon.com/news/feature/1999/04/27/boston). Copyright © 1999 by Mike Crowley. Used by permission.

No: "Cops in the 'Hood" by Debra Dickerson, Salon.com, June 14, 1999. Copyright © 1999 by Salon.com. Used by permission.

Topic 8 Should Juvenile Offenders Ever Be Tried as Adults?

Yes: "Juvenile Justice: Shawn" in *Frontline* (www.pbs.org/wgbh/pages/frontline/shows/juvenile/four/shawn.html). Reprinted with permission of *Frontline*.

No: "Testimony Submitted to the House Judiciary Subcommittee on Crime for the Hearing on Putting Consequences Back into Juvenile Justice at the Federal, State, and Local Levels," Child Welfare League of America Press Release, March 10–11, 1999.

Topic 9 Should Juveniles Be Sentenced to Death?

Yes: "Should Juvenile Offenders Get the Death Penalty"? by Josh Rubak (www.rubak.com/article.cfm?ID=5). Reprinted with permission of the author.

No: "Old Enough to Kill, Old Enough to Die" by Steven A. Drizin and Stephen K. Harper, *San Francisco Chronicle*, April 16, 2000. Copyright © 2000 by *San Francisco Chronicle*. Reproduced by permission of *San Francisco Chronicle* in the format Textbook via Copyright Clearance Center.

Topic 10 Is Racial Profiling Wrong?

Yes: From "Driving While Black: Racial Profiling on Our Nation's Highways" by David A. Harris, American Civil Liberties Union Special Report, June 1999. Copyright © 1999 by American Civil Liberties Union. Used by permission.

No: From "The Myth of Racial Profiling" by Heather MacDonald. Heather MacDonald is a contributing editor of *City Journal*, John M. Olin Fellow at the Manhattan Institute, and author of *The Burden of Bad Ideas: How Modern Intellectuals Misshape Our Society*. Copyright © 2001 by *City Journal*. Reprinted with permission from the Spring 2001 issue of the Manhattan Institute's *City Journal* (www.city-journal.org).

Topic 11 Should Soft Drugs Be Decriminalized?

Yes: From "Marijuana Special Report: Vraag Een Politieagent" by Debora Mackenzie, *New Scientist*, February 21, 1998. Copyright © 1998 by *New Scientist*. Used by permission.

No: From "Holland's Half-baked Drug Experiment" by Larry Collins, *Foreign Affairs*, Vol. 78, No. 3, May/June 1999. Copyright © 1999 by Larry Collins. Used by permission.

Topic 12 Should Trials Be Televised?

Yes: "Let People See the Action" by Val Atkinson, *The Sunday Herald*, April 30, 2000.

No: "Camera's on Trial: The 'O.J. Show' Turns the Tide" by George Gerbner. The reprint permission is granted to use this BEA publication (*The Journal of Broadcasting & Electronic Media*) from the Broadcast Education Association, www.beawb.org.

Topic 13 Do Prisons Work?

Yes: "A Model Prison" by Robert Worth, *The Atlantic Monthly*, November 1995. Copyright © 1995 by Robert Worth. Used by permission.

No: "Prisons Do Not Work" by Hugh Mahoney (www.cwrl.utexas.edu/~tonya/final_projects/Prisons_Don't_Work-final.htm). Reprinted with permission of the author.

Topic 14 Do Prisoners Have Rights?

Yes: "Without Prejudice: American Cant" by Peter Beaumont, *The Observer*, January 13, 2002. Copyright © 2002 by *The Observer*. Used by permission.

No: "Prisoners of War: No X-Ray Needed to Evaluate Controversial Camp" by Michael Hoes (www. northwesternchronicle.org/tools/viewart). Copyright © 2002 by Michael Hoes. Used by permission.

Topic 15 Should Prisons Be Privatized?

Yes: "Privatizing the Prison System" by National Center for Policy Analysis (www.ncpa.org/~ncpa/studies/s181/s181n.html). Reprinted with permission of the National Center for Policy Analysis.

No: "Should Crime Pay? A Review of the Evidence" by the American Federation of State, County, and Municipal Employees (www.afscme.org/private/crimeptc.htm).

Topic 16 Should Sex Offenders Be Castrated?

Yes: From "The Chemical Knife" by Kevin Giordano, Salon.com, March 1, 2000. Copyright © 2000 by Salon.com. Used by permission.

No: "Sex Offenders: Does Treatment Work"? by Eric Lotke (www.igc.org/ncia/sexo.html). Reprinted with permission of National Center on Institutions and Alternatives.

The Brown Reference Group plc has made every effort to contact and acknowledge the creators and copyright holders of all extracts reproduced in this volume. We apologize for any omissions. Any person who wishes to be credited in further volumes should contact The Brown Reference Group plc in writing: The Brown Reference Group plc, 8 Chapel Place, Rivington Street, London EC2A 3DQ, U.K.

Picture credits

Cover: Corbis: Ed Kashi; **Corbis:** Jerry Arcieri 78; **Bettmann:** 162/163; James Marshall 74/75; **PA Photos:** EPA 18, 154, 182; **Rex Features Ltd:** Cook 112/113; Richard Jenkins: 34/35; **Ronald Grant Archive:** 6/7, 25; **Topham Picturepoint:** Image Works 40; **US Customs Service:** James R Tourtellotti 70

SET INDEX

Page numbers in bold refer to volume numbers; those in *italics* refer to picture captions.